CONTRIBUTORS

Roger Rapoport, who wrote most of this book, is currently editor of the travel section of the *Oakland Tribune,* for which he writes regularly. He has written numerous guidebooks on California, Asia, and the Pacific Rim, including *22 Days in California.*

The *Introduction* is by **Robert Taylor,** the San Francisco–based entertainment editor for the *Oakland Tribune.*

The *Restaurants* chapter is by a Bay Area restaurant critic who, in the interest of professional objectivity, wishes to remain anonymous.

The *Cultural Timeline* and literary excerpts were researched by **Margot Lind.**

Wine tasting consultant is **Axel Schug** of Schug Cellars in the Napa Valley.

Color maps are by Jeffrey L. Ward. Black and white maps are by Mark Stein Studios.

We wish to thank Linda Cohen and Harriet Swift for their research assistance, Diana Katchum, Bill Mann, and Larry Kelp for their ideas and advice. We are particularly grateful to Sharon Rooney at the San Francisco Convention and Visitor's Bureau and the San Francisco Department of City Planning and their invaluable resources. Special thanks to Carolyn Hubbard for her contributions.

The New York editors for the book are Charlotte Savidge and Barbara J. Farmer. Project management by Madigan Editorial Services.

A BANTAM TRAVEL GUIDE

SAN FRANCISCO

1990

BANTAM

NEW YORK • TORONTO • LONDON • SYDNEY • AUCKLAND

SAN FRANCISCO 1990
A Bantam Book / May 1990

Grateful acknowledgment is made to the following for reprint permission:
From Mark Twain's San Francisco, *as edited by Bernard Taper, copyright*
© *1963. Excerpt from* Herb Caen's Guide to San Francisco *by Herb Caen,*
copyright © *1957 by Herb Caen. Used by permission of Doubleday, a*
division of Bantam, Doubleday, Dell Publishing Group, Inc. Excerpt from
One Man's San Francisco *by Herb Caen, copyright* © *1976 by Herb Caen.*
Used by permission of Doubleday, a division of Bantam, Doubleday, Dell
Publishing Group, Inc.

ISBN 0–553–34841–8

Published simultaneously in the United States and Canada

Bantam Books are published by Bantam Books, a division of Bantam Double-
day Dell Publishing Group, Inc. Its trademark, consisting of the words "Ban-
tam Books" and the portrayal of a rooster, is Registered in U.S. Patent and
Trademark Office and in other countries. Marca Registrada, Bantam Books,
666 Fifth Avenue, New York, New York 10103

PRINTED IN THE UNITED STATES OF AMERICA

0   9   8   7   6   5   4   3   2   1

CONTENTS

FOREWORD

Publishing travel guides is, under the best of circumstances, a complex art. In the wake of a devastating earthquake, producing a guidebook to what is undisputably America's most beautiful city taxes the limits of the guidebook publisher's craft. Just as San Franciscans were pushed to the limit by the October 1989 earthquake, the writers and editors of this volume have had their talents and resourcefulness stretched in their efforts to bring you an up-to-the-minute guide to this storybook city.

Yes, the scars are there. You can't miss them if you spend any time at all in San Francisco. Beautiful old buildings, the kind that give the city by the bay its distinctive character, are gone, leaving only roped-off heaps of rubble or vacant lots. Other structures are designated for demolition. Across the Bay in Oakland, the Nimitz Freeway (Interstate 880) simply no longer exists. The psyches of San Franciscans bear scars, too. Locals are more sensitive than ever to the clearly real possibility that it could happen again—at any time.

Yet while all of these reminders of the October 1989 earthquake are clearly in evidence, the city remains indomitable. Much of the city and the entire Bay Area, for that matter, were left relatively unscathed. San Francisco is still America's most beautiful city. A visitor, who for some unfathomable reason had heard no news of the earthquake, would probably not view the city as changed in any way. In short, while the city took some hard punches, it is back on its feet and in some ways more full of life than ever.

As the drama of the earthquake and its all-too-frequent aftershocks unfolded, people around the globe kept asking the same question: Why do people live in a place like that? Everyone knows it's earthquake prone. Anyone who's ever fallen in love with San Francisco, and there are millions, can easily answer that question.

San Francisco is like no other place in the world. You can't say enough good things about it. The weather is crisp and clear and silky dry (except for surrealistic periods of morning fog that only add to the city's mystique). Aesthetically, San Francisco can't be beat. Think of pastel buildings in Greece or Spain, of hillside towns on the Côte d'Azur, of glorious sweeping views of Rio in its embrace with the sea—all of these are conjured up by one's first glimpse of San Francisco across the Bay.

Or is it history that makes your blood flow faster? You need only visualize '49ers descending upon the rough-and-ready 19th-century town of San Francisco after a gold strike. If you're into culture, this city has that, too, with world famous museums, opera companies, and symphonies, not to mention more contemporary music than you can keep up with.

And food. Ah, this is an eater's paradise offering a huge selection of restaurants representing all the world's cuisines. Naturally there's seafood in abundance. So, too, will you find an infinite variety of Oriental foods. If you enjoy food, this is the place.

One could go on forever about the things that make San Francisco worth visiting. Certainly the delicately balanced combination of the relaxed and the sophisticated makes for a lifestyle rarely seen in other parts of the United States. Then there are the bridges that are the delight of photographers the world over. There's major league sports. There's Nob Hill, Fisherman's Wharf, Chinatown, neighboring Sausalito, and on and on. But most of all there are the DREAMS. People dream of going to San Francisco. They dream of living there. Even if they never expect to live there, this is the ideal for millions of people when they think of the perfect place to spend the rest of their lives. And, for all these reasons, San Francisco is an equally perfect place to visit.

How can this travel guidebook help you?

At a bare minimum it should 1. Help you plan your trip, and 2. Help you make choices during that trip. Of course, any good guidebook can be useful, but the guide you're holding, one of Bantam's growing new series of travel guides, does it better. And that's not just promotional hype. In our first year of publication, the critics raved about us. The public is reacting even better than we dared hope when we embarked on this bold new publishing venture in late 1987. That both the critics and public alike have judged us so favorably is gratifying for us and good news for you. Our efforts have been recognized, and that's nice. But there are good reasons for that, and you benefit by having chosen this guide.

Here are just a few of the solid reasons why, as one critic put it, "Bantam has themselves a winner!"

- Bantam guides are affordable. You get more information for your dollar than you do with most other guidebooks.

- The books are up-to-date. (The San Francisco guide was produced after the October 1989 earthquake.) Since they're revised annually, they'll always be more current than the vast majority of guidebooks.

- Each Bantam guide includes a full-color travel atlas with maps detailed enough for the most demanding travel needs. These are supplemented with black-and-white maps throughout the text.

- Upon close examination you'll see that your Bantam guidebook is organized geographically rather than alphabetically. What this means is that descriptions of what's available in a contiguous geographical area make it easier to get the most out of a city neighborhood or country region. For those who still need to locate a place alphabetically, we provide a detailed index.

- Restaurants, hotels, shops, museums, and other sites are keyed into the maps so that you can locate these places easily.

- Finally, we think you'll enjoy reading our guidebooks. We've tried hard to find not only informed writers, but good writers. The writing is literate and lively. It's honest. Most of all it's a good read.

Yet no matter how good a guidebook is it cannot cover everything. It can't include every good restaurant, and it can't do justice to everyone's favorite place—though we believe we come closer than anyone else. Bear in mind, too, that prices can change at any time, and today's well-managed restaurant or hotel can change owners or managers tomorrow. Today's great food or service can be tomorrow's disappointment. We've recommended places as they are now and as we expect them to be in the future, but there are no guarantees. We welcome your comments and suggestions. Our address is Bantam Travel Guides, 666 Fifth Avenue, New York, N.Y. 10103.

Richard T. Scott
Publisher
Bantam Travel Books

Tips On Getting the Most Out of This Guide

Bantam Travel Guides are designed to be extremely user friendly, but there are a few things you should know in order to get the maximum benefit from them.

1. You'll find a special **Travel Arrangements** section toward the back of the book. This section can be invaluable in planning your trip.
2. The **Priorities** chapter will insure that you see and do the most important things when you visit your destination. Whether you're spending two days or two weeks there, you'll want to make the most of your time and certainly not miss the musts.
3. Note that in addition to our main selection of important restaurants you'll also find described in the text informal places to stop for lunch, a snack, or a drink. To help you instantly identify these places as well as restaurant and hotel write-ups, whether they're in a list or mentioned in the text, we've designed the following two symbols which will appear at the beginning of restaurant and hotel lists and in the margin of the text whenever a restaurant or hotel is described there.

Hotels

Restaurants

INTRODUCTION

When San Francisco realized in the 1980s that tourism had become its leading industry, more than one person in the city did a double take. What about San Francisco's reputation as one of the West Coast's major ports, California's financial center, the Bay Area's transportation hub? What about the printing industry in all those blocks south of Market Street, or the produce distributors, and flower wholesalers? There was both pride and resignation when the city's major product became its image, and San Franciscans found themselves not only residents and workers, but attractions. What had they done to deserve such attention? Nothing more or less than live in a place blessed by nature with a spectacular setting, dazzling weather, and breathtaking views. The challenge now is to keep these attributes in perspective without turning a living city into a theme park, and at the same time to deal with problems common to other American cities: a shortage of affordable housing, an overburdened public transportation system, the flight of businesses and prospective homeowners to land beyond the suburbs, and the homeless people who have become a part of every urban landscape.

San Francisco's primary struggle in the 1990s may be between the past and the future, preserving an image and aura for visitors and the quality of life for permanent residents, without allowing the city to stagnate. Every move seems to stir various facets of San Francisco into conflict: international city vs. historical landmark vs. tourist attraction vs. a collection of residential neighborhoods. When plans are announced for a big new downtown hotel, for example, a flurry of questions will be raised. Will notable old buildings be demolished? Will a hotel provide a full range of jobs? Would an office building do more for the economy in the long run? Can workers afford to live in the city? Will they crowd into already overloaded buses and streetcars, or move to suburbs and add to traffic on the freeways? Will their employer provide childcare?

A downtown building boom since the 1960s has changed the city's skyline forever, and not without controversy. During one campaign to limit the size of downtown buildings, the specter of more high-rises was called "the Manhattanization of San Francisco." Recent controversy focused on the new 1,500-room Marriott hotel on Market Street with a glistening, rounded roofline that earned it the nickname "the Wurlitzer Building" for its resemblance to a gigantic juke box. Yet at night, with its towers lit, it looks like a glamorous Hollywood version of an earlier Manhattan, a glimmering Art Deco skyline of the 1930s. The Transamerica Pyramid, originally derided as a space-age gimmick in the financial district, quickly became a landmark that immediately identified the silhouette of San Francisco. The corrugated, dark stone facade of the Bank of America World Headquarters loomed ominously when it was completed, but it has also settled comfortably into the picture. There is historical precedent here. In the 1850s, when the Montgomery Block of shops and offices was built, on the site of the future Transamerica Pyramid, few people believed San Francisco was ready for a building four stories high. When the Hallidie Building, which still stands, went up on Sutter Street, the city's first building with a facade entirely of glass must have looked like a precarious gamble.

It's a wonder that San Francisco has developed any stability and stature—financial or otherwise—considering its adventurous, brawling background, its unconventional spirit, and tenuous connection to reality. Gambling dens and brothels were among the first permanent buildings at a time when most San Franciscans were living in tents. Thousands of men jumped ship when they arrived in port in the mid-19th century and headed for the gold fields in the Sierra Nevada. The city burned down six times in two years. There were no paved streets until 1854. Images of San Francisco that reached the rest of the world began with the '49ers seeking quick fortunes as gold miners, and they continued through the 1906 earthquake and fire, the low-life entertainment of the Barbary Coast, the artists' colony in North Beach, the "Beatniks" of the 1950s, hippies of the 1960s, homosexual activists testing new-found freedom in the 1970s.

In the decade that followed, San Francisco's fast-living, hard-drinking image began to fade and the city mellowed. Drunks went out of style, even for comedy routines. The "He and She Love Acts" of Broadway's strip joints ended up on videotape, available throughout the country. AIDS tamed the sexual adventurers, and the city actually became a model for the nation in dealing with prevention and treatment of the disease. The earthquake on October 17, 1989, was the most powerful in the area since 1906, and 12 people in San Francisco were among the 67 killed in Northern California. "It makes us realize we don't live in paradise without some price to pay," declared a newspaper publisher in a nationally televised interview. Although the residential Marina district was hit hard, 95 percent of San Francisco survived the earthquake intact; the city was remarkably spared the devastation of earlier disasters. Nearly as remarkable was the mobilization to aid quake victims in and out of the city. True to San Francisco tradition, it was not without eventual bleak humor. "Any spare change?" asked a panhandler in the Civic Center. "Twenty-five percent of my money goes to earthquake relief."

Visitors approach San Francisco as an adventure, a fantasy, which mirrors the attitude of many of its residents who have moved to the city from the East and Midwest. Maybe it was never meant to be a solid, upright community like the one they left behind. When the romantic ballad "I Left My Heart in San Francisco" was named the city's official song in 1969, one of its composers, Douglas Cross, recalled another favorite line about the city—and it had nothing to do with little cable cars climbing halfway to the stars. Instead, Cross quoted turn-of-the-century cynic Ambrose Bierce's description of San Francisco: "Careful now, we're dealing here with a myth. This city is a point upon a map of fog . . . Like us, it doesn't quite exist."

Because the city's history has been fragile, San Franciscans can be fiercely protective of historical landmarks, even fragments of landmarks. The city's most majestic survivors are the Old Mint on Fifth Street and the Main Post Office on Seventh Street, both of which endured the 1906 earthquake and fire, and the Palace of Fine Arts in the Marina district, a restored relic from the 1915 Panama Pacific International Exposition. Elsewhere, bits of history can be just around the corner. The offices and antique shops of Jackson Square, north of the financial district, were once the saloons and dance halls of the Barbary Coast when San Francisco was "the wickedest city in the world." Preserved at the entrance to a high-rise office tower at 350 California Street is a portion of the Alaska Commercial Building facade from 1908, with granite walruses and stylized fish. In a display of Western money and gold nuggets at the nearby Bank of California are the pair of elaborate pistols used in a notorious 1859 duel between a United States senator and the chief justice of the state supreme court. At Union Square, the elaborate 1898 rotunda from the demolished City of Paris department store offers gilded splendor from behind the checkerboard facade of Neiman Marcus.

Long-time San Francisco residents may complain that the city isn't what it used to be; what city is? On the other hand, many districts are better than ever, with commerce thriving around Castro and Market streets, along the upper stretch of Fillmore Street near the city's Japantown, and on the former "auto row" along Van Ness Avenue. Haight Street is one of the city's most diversified neighborhood shopping areas, after a struggle of more than twenty years to regain stability following the "summer of love."

The influx of visitors from the Bay Area and beyond has transformed many areas of the city—and not just for tourists. There are startling comebacks. The construction of Davies Symphony Hall in 1980 spurred development south and west of the Civic Center. The neighborhood, dreary for decades, brightened with antique and craft shops, art galleries, and restaurants ranging from soup-and-sandwich lunch spots to the city's trendiest grills. In the old industrial area south of Market Street are more new restaurants and galleries, along with extensive new apartment developments that provide moderately priced housing without ripping up older residential neighborhoods. Other comebacks: the cable cars, vintage streetcars on Market Street, Market Street itself with the spectacular San Francisco Center as a downtown retail anchor, and the Embarcadero with its convenient public access to the bay that has been cleaned up after years of decline and neglect. What may follow is a revitalization of Fisherman's Wharf as a real wharf for real fishermen, reversing its image as the city's tackiest tourist trap. San Franciscans, unlike some urban counterparts elsewhere in the United States, haven't given up on their city. In the 1980s they were rediscovering such traditions as going downtown, dressing for dinner, as well as the joys of seafood restaurants, neighborhood ice cream shops, and bakeries that were turning out three or four different kinds of sourdough bread. Why, they asked, would anyone live anywhere else?

When San Francisco celebrates, it's like no other festival in the nation. The San Francisco Fair and Exposition, the city's version of the old-time county fair, includes dramatic tests of urban survival skills. "The Incredible Parking Space Race" sends cars and drivers from a starting line at City Hall to the most congested areas in the city—Fisherman's Wharf, Chinatown, and Union Square—in a frenzied competition for a place to park. Art is combined with architecture in the "Freeway to Nowhere" contest, in which San Franciscans try to create uses for the stub ends of freeway ramps, suspended in mid-air, that are remnants of the halted construction of a highway that would otherwise have plowed through Pacific Heights and Golden Gate Park.

Entertainment? The only-in-San Francisco events include operatic lip-synching and a fog calling competition in which contestants try to imitate the moan of foghorns, often while dressed as seagulls, lighthouses, and fog banks. The "Seafood Triathlon" involves cracking a crab, cleaning a squid, and filleting a salmon. And instead of traditional America's blue ribbons for apple pies and pickles, San Francisco's Fair and Exposition rewards the ethnic diversity of sourdough French bread, Chinese dim sum, and Italian cappuccino. The fair is an effective microcosm of San Francisco's variety of cultures and lifestyles as well as its traditional eccentricity. It reminds visitors to the city as well as its residents, including the rare few who call themselves "born-and-bred" natives, that San Francisco is a unique place to live.

What makes the city unique and distinctive? Certainly not sheer numbers: San Francisco has one-tenth the population of New York City, and, in terms of size, it has recently been surpassed by sprawling, ambitious San Jose, now the largest city in Northern California. San Francisco, however, retains and enriches its diversity on a compact playing field, and it clings to the past at the same time high-rise apartments transform the old commercial boulevard of Van Ness Avenue and office buildings dramatically revise the skyline along San Francisco Bay. What makes the city appealing to visitors, who continually give it the honor of being "America's favorite city," also appeals to residents: San Francisco's beauty, its views, weather, and relative small scale. Yet the city is challenged by the conflicts between preservation and progress, between liberals and conservatives who don't fit the categories of the past. San Francisco also attempts to deal with radical solutions that might, eventually, be as thoroughly accepted as past schemes that were originally considered crackpot.

San Francisco's tolerance makes up a large part of its reputation, and although there have been sometimes violent confrontations over the years, the city has remarkably accepted a variety of people and ideas. Who knows whether this year's eccentrics will be history's heroes? The most splendid example is "Hallidie's Folly," which turned into the cable car system developed by Andrew S. Hallidie in the 1870s, an attraction that now carries 13 million passengers a year. Lillie Hitchcock Coit loved to chase fires around the city, and she was so dedicated that the city made her an honorary firefighter. Her legacy is Coit Tower on Telegraph Hill, one of San Francisco's prime vantage points. John McLaren was considered more of a fool than Andrew Hallidie when he set out to tame a thousand acres of sand dunes in the 1870s. The result, thanks to the original layers of topsoil imported from the Peninsula and horse manure recovered from city streets, is the vast greenery of Golden Gate Park. In a more modern era, a performer named Carol Doda slipped into a scanty Rudi Gernreich bathing suit in the 1960s and invented topless dancing. When she retired in the 1980s, she was virtually the grand dame of Broadway's nightlife. In the 1970s, some kids dressed as Christmas trees tap-danced on the sidewalk outside the North Beach cafés; before long, under the direction of a zany-but-canny showman named Steve Silver, they were transformed into the musical revue *Beach Blanket Babylon,* which became the city's longest-running entertainment. Who knows what the future will bring? When the San Francisco Museum of Modern Art selected Swiss architect Mario Botta to design the new museum south of Market Street, one member of the screening committee said, "There's an inherent character to San Francisco that allows people to do nutty things. I'm not saying Botta's going to do something nutty, but there is a traditional generosity of spirit here."

Civic benefactors and boosters have been trying to improve San Francisco's image since the first street was paved in the 1850s. But often the city resists; there have been campaigns to clean up Broadway's entertainment since the beginning of the twentieth century, when the street in North Beach was called Devil's Acre. San Franciscans are known for being particularly stubborn about colorful names. Maiden Lane, a chic little stretch of shops just off Union Square, was originally and ironically the name of the city's most notorious red light district. San Francisco's old exposition hall is the Cow Palace, named for livestock shows and unchanged even when it hosted national political conventions. The sports stadium is Candlestick Park, built on bayside land that once resembled the outline of a candelabra. It took a mayor's plea to force San Franciscans to use the official name of the exhibit hall underneath Civic Center Plaza. It's Brooks Hall, the mayor declared, not Mole Hall or— even more embarrassing—the Gopher Palace.

The life of this city, which was built on the tip of a windswept peninsula between the Pacific Ocean and San Francisco Bay, has always been dominated by its geography. It could not have been a less hospitable place to settle, with its hills and sand dunes marked only by a few scrub oak trees and stretches of thatchlike weeds, with sand and dust blowing in the continual wind from the ocean. Of course there are more shelters now, including $2,500-a-night hotel suites, for instance, but the city can be just as cold and windy today as it was two-hundred years ago, as shivering visitors discover as they brace themselves for a climb up Nob Hill in a season that would be summer anywhere else in the country. The Catholic Church's Jesuits knew what they were doing when they established Mission Dolores on the east side of the hills that divide the city. It was the warmest place around. Nowadays, some of the city's most exclusive residential areas—Sea Cliff, Diamond Heights, and Forest Hill—endure some of the foggiest, windiest weather.

San Francisco was a thriving port until the mid-twentieth century, when larger ships and containerized shipping methods shifted the base to Oakland across the bay. The waterfront languished until recent years, when it was transformed with pedestrian walkways, restaurants, retail shops, and apartment buildings. San Francisco may have lost a port but gained an accessible waterfront and spectacular new views across the bay. In the next development, vintage streetcars are expected to roll along the Embarcadero, and since it was damaged in the earthquake of 1989 there is a renewed campaign to demolish the Embarcadero Freeway, which divides a mile-long stretch of the city from its waterfront.

In addition to the weather and the waterfront, San Francisco's hills—44 by the city's official count—have been a dominant force in its development. Neighborhoods grew in a balkanized pattern, eventually connected by cable cars over the hills, streetcars through tunnels under them. But housing didn't extend all the way to the city's western edge along the Pacific Ocean until the 1940s. The outer lands, as they were called in the 19th century, remain sociologically isolated, often politically conservative. Living at 47th Avenue and Wawona Street is some people's way of getting out of town, turning their backs on the city. Still, developers find space to build in a city that is already the third most densely populated in the nation. On hills too steep to hike, they build houses and apartments, one room on top of another and, on the ground level, a precious parking space. More and more, San Francisco is a city where visitors' second most frequently asked question—after "How do I get to Fisherman's Wharf?"—is, "How do you find a place to park in this town?"

When San Franciscans see a thick line of visitors at the Powell Street cable car turnaround, or a busload stopping briefly at Civic Center for a photo opportunity, their most likely response is, "They'll never see the real San Francisco." What will they miss? The neighborhoods, the cafés, the bookstores, and for many tourists, almost everything west of Van Ness Avenue and south of Market Street. On the other hand, San Franciscans who take an afternoon to escort visitors around the city may be as delighted by their discoveries as their guests. Among the surprises: the venerable mellow mood of

City Lights bookstore in North Beach, the rest
grandeur of the Art Moderne interior of I. Magnin on
Union Square, the fresh viewpoints from the ferry ride
to Sausalito. Views of the city, from the city, are continually breathtaking: from Ghirardelli Square, from the Carnelian Room cocktail lounge atop the Bank of America
building, from the Palace of the Legion of Honor museum, looking toward the Golden Gate Bridge from outside the gate, and from Fort Point in the Presidio,
virtually underneath the bridge. An alternative newspaper has even discovered a great view from public transportation: a ride on the MUNI Metro's J-Church
streetcar through Dolores Park, along the backyards of
homes in Dolores Heights, and on to the shops and cafés
of the Noe Valley neighborhood.

There are rewards even in portions of the city that
most San Franciscans avoid. Fisherman's Wharf is
jammed with street vendors and racks of T-shirts printed with such slogans as "Alcatraz Swim Team" and "I
Got Crabs at Fisherman's Wharf." But the wharf is still
the best place in town to buy fresh crab. Nearby Pier
39, which claims to draw more visitors than any attraction in the city, offers surprises beyond the theme-park
clichés. From the end of the pier there is a surprisingly
close-up view of Alcatraz, and upstairs, the Eagle Café
is still serving beer at a mahogany bar and corned beef
hash for breakfast and lunch, as it has since the 1920s
on the Embarcadero.

The economic importance of tourism to the city—
where two million visitors spend $3.3 billion a year—has
led to the development of such contrived attractions as
the waterfront's wax museum, haunted gold mine, and
an "Enchanted World of San Francisco" miniature cable
car ride. But these entrepreneurs might argue that they
are only following the spirit of San Francisco's fantasy
life. In the 1880s, fake opium dens lured tourists into
Chinatown, courtesy of the Chinatown Guides Association. In the Barbary Coast there were discreetly
screened "slummer's balconies" for respectable visitors
to watch the action in the dance halls. In the 1950s, real
or imagined Beatniks were on view in North Beach at
the Co-existence Bagel Shop. In the 1960s, guides led
tours through the Haight-Ashbury as hippies waved
flowers and sticks and incense. More than twenty years
after the flower children cavorted on the streets, anoth-

EARTHQUAKE SITE

N

0   20

miles

RIN

US-101

Richmond–
San Rafael
Bridge

I-80

I-80

I-680

Golden
Gate
Bridge

Bay
Bridge

Oakland

**San
Francisco**

CONTRA
COSTA

*San
Francisco
Bay*

I-880

I-680

Burlingame

San Mateo
Bridge

I-580

Redwood City

Dumbarton
Bridge

ALAMEDA

I-680

SAN
MATEO

US-101

San Jose

I-5

17

US-101

EPICENTER

SANTA
CRUZ

SANTA
CLARA

**Santa
Cruz**

1

Watsonville

*Pacific
Ocean*

Hollister

1

US-101

MONTEREY

SAN

BENITO

I-5

er generation of guides leads tours to the same neighborhood—now, of course, considered a historical landmark.

Earthquake Update

Only a month after the earthquake rumbled through Northern California in October 1989, it was difficult to find evidence of its damage in San Francisco. The major freeways were open, along with all the city's major attractions, the important museums, and all but one of the theaters. In the Marina district, the hardest-hit neighborhood, ten buildings had been demolished. In the older commercial and industrial area south of Market Street, only 25 buildings were judged unsafe. Portions of connecting freeways were closed for repairs, but otherwise San Francisco looked virtually the same as it had before the earthquake.

By the end of November, the San Francisco–Oakland Bay Bridge reopened, and soon after, the collapsed Cypress Structure of Interstate highway 880 in downtown Oakland was demolished. Construction crews expected to replace it with a ground-level highway by the middle of 1990, and with a newly designed elevated freeway in 1992.

In San Francisco, completion was also expected in mid-1990 for the repairs to Interstate 280 between U.S. 101 and 6th and 3rd streets downtown, and for the U.S. 101 on-and-off ramps at Gough and Franklin streets near the Civic Center. The fate of the Embarcadero freeway, which runs north from the Bay Bridge to Chinatown and Broadway, remained uncertain. There was a renewed campaign to demolish the elevated, double-deck freeway and replace it with a six-lane, ground-level parkway.

On the cultural scene, the major damage was the collapse of a portion of the ceiling and a lighting grid at the Geary Theatre, home of the American Conservatory Theatre. The initial damage estimate was $10 million, and although federal funds will pay for the repairs, the theater might not reopen until far into 1990. Meanwhile, ACT was finding other performance space in the city. The art collections at the Museum of Modern Art, M.H. de Young Memorial Museum, and Palace of the Legion

Earthquake Almanac

At the instance of several friends who feel a boding anxiety to know beforehand what sort of phenomena we may expect the elements to exhibit during the next month or two, and who have lost all confidence in the various patent medicine almanacs, because of the unaccountable reticence of those works concerning the extraordinary event of the 8th inst., I have compiled the following almanac expressly for this latitude:

OCT. 17—Weather hazy; atmosphere murky and dense. An expression of profound melancholy will be observable upon most countenances.

OCT. 18—Slight earthquake. Countenances grow more melancholy.

OCT. 19—Look out for rain. It will be absurd to look in for it. The general depression of spirits increased.

OCT. 23—Mild, balmy earthquakes.

OCT. 24—Shaky.

OCT. 25—Occasional shakes, followed by light showers of bricks and plastering. N. B.—Stand from under.

OCT. 26—Considerable phenomenal atmospheric foolishness. About this time expect more earthquakes, but do not look out for them, on account of the bricks.

OCT. 27—Universal despondency, indicative of approaching disaster. Abstain from smiling, or indulgence in humorous conversation, or exasperating jokes. . . .

OCT. 28—Misery, dismal forebodings and despair. Beware of all discourse—a joke uttered at this time would produce a popular outbreak.

OCT. 29—Beware!

OCT. 30—Keep dark!

OCT. 31—Go slow!

NOV. 1—Terrific earthquake. This is the great earthquake month. More stars fall and more worlds are slathered around carelessly and destroyed in November than in any other month of the twelve.

NOV. 2—Spasmodic but exhilarating earthquakes, accompanied by occasional showers of rain, and churches and things.

NOV. 3—Make your will.

NOV. 4—Sell out.

NOV. 5—Select your "last words." Those of John Quincy Adams will do, with the addition of a syllable, thus; "This is the last of earthquakes."

> Nov. 6—Prepare to shed this mortal coil.
>
> Nov. 7—Shed.
>
> Nov. 8—The sun will rise as usual, perhaps; but if he does he will doubtless be staggered some to find nothing but a large round hole eight thousand miles in diameter in the place where he saw this world serenely spinning the day before.
>
> —Mark Twain
> *Mark Twain's San Francisco*, 1863

of Honor were relatively unscathed. At the Asian Art Museum only 31 artworks were damaged—but the total value of the damaged objects was $10 million.

The commercial district hardest hit in Northern California was the Pacific Garden Mall in downtown Santa Cruz, the city closest to the earthquake's epicenter. A month later, more than thirty downtown merchants moved into covered pavilions nearby while the mall was being rebuilt.

The earthquake's dampening effect on tourism sent San Francisco Mayor Art Agnos to New York, Chicago, and Washington in December 1989, to reassure potential visitors that the city was back in business. He feared that shocking photographs on television and in magazines and newspapers had created the impression that the city lay in ruins. Most San Franciscans, grateful that the city was spared and their lives could return to normal so quickly, were more shocked by the reactions of anxious friends and relatives around the country. And there was hopeful news generated by the earthquake. The month-long closing of the Bay Bridge convinced thousands of commuters to rely on public transportation for the first time. The Bay Area Rapid Transit system flourished, and there were plans to continue the commuter ferry service between San Francisco and the East Bay cities of Oakland and Richmond.

Civic leaders and editorial writers immediately began to focus on the future. The *Examiner* recalled that the city's history was shaped by shared adversities and the overwhelming powers of nature, and that it should deal boldly with waterfront development, transportation, and plans for a regional park in the vast Presidio, soon to be abandoned as an Army base. Newspaper editorials touted the spirit of cooperation that pulled the city through this ordeal, much as it did in 1906. Today, it is with a historically proven sense of innovation and survival that the world's favorite city looks to its future.

Duck and Cover

Californians do not worry about earthquakes around the clock. For one thing, they have grown up with earthquake emergency drills in school, and reviews of safety procedures after every moderate quake.

These are the recommendations:

- If you are indoors during an earthquake, stay there. Get under a desk or table. Stay clear of windows.
- Do not attempt to use stairs or elevators while a building is shaking, or while there is any danger of being hit by falling debris.
- Do not rush outside, where you may be injured by falling glass or bricks.
- If you are outside during an earthquake, get into the open, away from buildings or power lines.
- If you are driving, stop the car but stay inside. Do not stop, however, on or under a bridge or overpass if possible.
- After an earthquake, indoors, beware of items that may fall when closets or cupboards are opened.

1

TRAVELING TO SAN FRANCISCO IN 1990

To me San Francisco is a city of romance. . .the romance of being in a city where a hint of adventure hangs tantalizingly in the cool air. Where a pale yellow light glowing at the end of a dark Chinatown alley can create a sudden feeling of mystery. Where a turn of a corner may bring you face to face with an unexpected vista that makes you stop and stare.

There is romance in a cable-car ride,over the hills and far away, with the city teeming at your very toes. Romance at Top o' the Mark at sunset, with the view more intoxicating than the drink in your hand. Romance in a little North Beach restaurant, with a candle glowing on your table and the wine encouraging you to call the waiter "Mario," as all the other customers are doing.

There is romance in the mighty bridges that "couldn't be built," and in the ageless Bay that brought the pioneers and the gold-seekers to the shores of an almost unknown village. And there is romance in the fog that slithers through the Golden Gate and creeps up the hills, drowning the neon lights and mantling the city with its gray majesty. Romance awaits the traveler in almost every corner of Baghdad-by-the-Bay. I hope you find it, so you can understand why we who live in San Francisco love San Francisco.

—Herb Caen, *Herb Caen's Guide to San Francisco,* Doubleday, 1957

San Francisco is perhaps one of the most livable cities in the world—even in the frantic 1990s it is never harsh or inhuman, but elegant and inviting. In a world determined to move at an ever faster clip, San Franciscans savor each foggy morning. Lumbering cable cars force visitor and resident alike to slow down and drink in the views. And this remains, blessedly, a city where it's easy to get lost on a coastal overlook or in a Japanese tea garden.

San Francisco is a city of grand parks and ferries, summer concerts in cathedral groves, hotels that entertain with magic shows, and restaurants that serenade guests with free operas. Not to mention the sourdough bread and Dungeness crab. You could travel all through China and have a hard time matching some of the dishes served at the city's Szechuan, Hunan, or dim sum palaces. A city dedicated to having a good time, San Francisco has a kind of carnival atmosphere, with baroque trios performing on street corners, free circus acts on the waterfront, and Chinese lion dances with firecracker accompaniment.

Collectively the city's cultural oddities, historical treasures, Asian masterpieces, and Victorian landmarks set against the deep blue backdrop of the bay make a compelling case to visit San Francisco again and again. Like the '49ers of the past century, who originally turned this sleepy outpost into a booming supply center for the Mother Lode gold rush, contemporary visitors will find themselves in the midst of a city in transition. Once a rough and tumble frontier town where vigilantes meted out justice on the spot, the city became the crown jewel of the West. Here businessmen dominating the Pacific trade dined in garden courts where glass roofs allowed the sun to shine in all day. Theaters with their gold ceilings offered seats of plush velvet and soft leather. And in the offices along Montgomery Street, Persian carpets stretched between tapestried walls.

Today much of that elegance remains, particularly in the swank aeries of Pacific Heights and Nob Hill. But the city that rose to world prominence in the Gold Rush now mines another kind of lode. It has become a crucial American base in the booming Pacific Rim economy. Indeed, San Francisco is truly a cultural crossroads. With its Mediterranean climate, Asian and Latin neighborhoods home to kosher burrito stands, Zen centers run by roshis from Brooklyn, and hotels that can accommodate guests in thirty languages, San Francisco offers a unique vision of the American melting pot. A city with a sense of humor, San Francisco has turned its most famous prison into a cultural attraction and has bridge tollbooth attendants who sing bebop to passing motorists.

If you have never seen San Francisco before, your expectations are probably already high. If you haven't been back in awhile, you'll discover the San Francisco of 1990 has become an even more compelling place to visit: a booming local theater scene, many new restaurants (particularly Asian and elegant Italian), a renaissance in luxury hotels and inns, as well as the eclectic night and dance clubs South of Market are all here to welcome you. Although a proliferation of high rises has altered the city's skyline, San Francisco now has even more fascinating public spaces, sunny sidewalk and terrace cafés, and public art such as Ruth Asawa's sculpture in the plaza at the Grand Hyatt.

While the city is renowned for its landmarks, monuments, and museums, the residential areas are its greatest strength. At heart, San Francisco remains a cluster of small neighborhoods, each with its own distinct personality. Renovated, remodeled, and rehabbed, these communities are a pleasure to explore in their own right. With the neighborhood bistros, shops, and bars, they even appeal to people who don't particularly like cities. And that, in the final analysis, may be San Francisco's trump card. Surrounded on three sides by ocean and bay, within minutes of the wilderness that is Golden Gate National Recreation Area, and blessed with the cultural variety of the world's great metropolises, San Francisco's neighborhoods make this a city as comfortable and charming as any small town.

This guide assures that you will see the city at its best. After a brief summary in the next chapter (*Orienting Yourself*) we'll help you get settled in as quickly as possible (see *Hotels*). You'll then reach a section we call *Priorities,* a subjective alphabetical listing that summarizes thirty stops that should be at the top of any San Francisco visitor's list. See as many as you can and save the rest for a repeat visit. After you've finished up on this primary list, and are well acquainted with the city's various modes of transportation (*Transportation*), continue on to the *Neighborhoods* chapter, where each area of the city is covered in greater detail. *Shopping, Restaurants,* and *Entertainment* follow. If you have time, visit one of the many beautiful areas near San Francisco, which are explored in *Excursions.* The *City Listings* chapter covers museums and other attractions. And don't worry if you can't see it all this time—relax, savor the city, and hurry back.

2

ORIENTING YOURSELF

Were it a flat city, which it's not, San Francisco would be a breeze to navigate. Much of the city, particularly its residential districts, consists of gridlike networks familiar to urbanites. A handful of major arteries, such as Geary Boulevard and 19th and Mission streets, link up the city's diverse neighborhoods. But there's a catch, and it's a big one—the city's forty hills which rise as high as 939 feet. While they add much to the city, they also make getting around a bit tricky; a direct connection between seemingly nearby spots can require advance planning.

Understanding how San Francisco works is relatively simple. First, familiarize yourself with the layout of this 46-square-mile city. A bird's-eye view of the Bay Area shows the city at the northern tip of San Francisco Peninsula with the bay to the east and north, and the Pacific to the west. Much of your time will be spent in the northeast corner of the city where the downtown district meets North Beach, Fisherman's Wharf, and Chinatown. The largest residential areas are to the west and south. And, of course, this city of seven hundred thousand is only one small part of the nine-county Bay Area that is home to more than four million.

Instead of a single geographic center, San Francisco has several hubs. Most important is Market Street, where BART (Bay Area Rapid Transit) and the city's bus lines meet. Geary Boulevard links downtown with the central and western districts such as Japantown, the Western Addition, and Richmond. Nineteenth Avenue runs through Golden Gate Park, connecting the northern and southern ends of the city's west side. Numbered streets begin at the Embarcadero and extend southwest out into the Mission District. The north/south avenues begin at Arguello and continue west towards the ocean. On streets running east to west, numbers go up as you head west. On streets running north/south, numbers increase as you head south. To avoid confusion, always ask for the cross street nearest your destination. One-way streets are rampant, making it vital to get specific directions. Because most of the city's streets are named rather than numbered, it's important to keep a good map, such as the ones in this book, with you at all times.

It's also good to inquire ahead of time about parking convenient to your destination. Downtown can be particularly tricky. In many neighborhoods, such as North Beach and Pacific Heights, only cars with a special permit are allowed unrestricted parking. Since permits are only sold to residents, nonresidents can only park for a few hours in these zones. Towing restrictions are vigorously enforced and can lead to steep fines.

Be sure to always curb your wheels, park in gear, and set your parking brake on hills to prevent runaways.

To get your bearings it's important to keep in mind that certain key arteries provide direct access to most of the areas you'll want to visit. For example, Market Street links up many downtown districts along a southwest/northeast axis. A good way to move north from downtown to North Beach is via Columbus Avenue. In the same direction, Sansome Street links downtown to the Embarcadero and Fisherman's Wharf. Geary Boulevard is a convenient east/west route from downtown to the ocean, while 19th Avenue is an easy way to go north/south between the Presidio, San Francisco State University, and the zoo.

Of course, if you're serendipitous and willing to experiment, there are many colorful alternatives. Naturally these byways that twist and turn their way through the city are ideal for pedestrians. But if you're driving, be sure to review your route with someone who knows the territory before setting off. Otherwise you may find your path altered due to unexpected dead ends.

SAN FRANCISCO'S NEIGHBORHOODS

DOWNTOWN

Likely to be your port of entry for San Francisco, the city's business and commercial center is not just another bland postmodern maze. Diverse enough to satisfy just about any taste, downtown is home to many of the city's leading commercial and cultural institutions. Of course, traffic here can drive you batty. Fortunately it's small enough to explore on foot. Often you'll discover it's quicker to walk than to drive, particularly during rush hour. With some help from the city's MUNI bus line, cable cars, BART, and an occasional cab, it's doubtful you'll even need a car to see this part of town. You'll be glad that all the downtown districts are within easy walking distance of one another. For convenience we've subdivided this area into **Market Street, Union Square, Chinatown, Financial District, South of Market,** and **Civic Center.**

Market Street is downtown's spine, providing a transit hub for BART and MUNI. One block south, at 1st and Mission, is the Transbay (bus and Amtrak) Terminal. The city's cable-car lines also begin at Market and Main streets (near Embarcadero Center) and Market at Powell. At the foot of Market Street, adjacent to the Ferry Building, is the terminal for Golden Gate Transit ferries to Sausalito and Larkspur. At Justin Herman Plaza, across the street from the Embarcadero, Market Street becomes a major commercial and retail corridor. One of the city's oldest retailing landmarks, Emporium-Capwell, is adjacent to San Francisco Center, home of the world's first circular escalator and Nordstrom's. The San Francisco Visitor Information Center is located at the intersection of Market and Powell on the lower level of Hallidie Plaza.

Union Square, two blocks north of Market, is easily reached via Stockton or Powell streets. The city's best known shopping district, the central plaza is surrounded by such stores as Macy's, I. Magnin's, Saks Fifth Avenue, and Sanrio, the Japanese store offering hundreds of "Hello Kitty" products. Anchored by the venerable

St. Francis Hotel, the square is alive with festivals and holiday celebrations. It's brightly wrapped at Christmas time and during the Hanukkah celebration a rabbi gets a lift from a cherry picker to light the giant menorah here. A hub for airline-ticket offices and home of a half-price theater-ticket service, this square is flanked by charming side streets such as Maiden Lane. Many hotels are located on or near the square.

Chinatown, which begins three blocks north of Union Square at Grant Avenue and Bush Street, is home to sixty thousand Chinese, making it America's second-largest Chinese community. This jam-packed 24-block area is best known for the many restaurants offering everything from dim sum to an eight-course banquet. Besides shopping for jade, celadon, porcelain, or silk, you can snack on rice candy and tour the **Tien Hou Temple, Buddha's Universal Church,** or the **Chinese Cultural Center.** The Chinese Kite Shop on Grant Avenue offers unique San Francisco souvenirs. Portsmouth Square at Kearny and Clay streets is a favorite gathering place of the Chinese community. This was the heart of Yerba Buena, the 19th-century pioneer settlement that became San Francisco. Two blocks east is Jackson Square, a Barbary Coast center of bars and brothels that has transcended its past to become a hot spot for interior designers and antique purveyors.

Adjacent to Chinatown is the **Financial District,** where skyscrapers box narrow streets into urban canyons. Extending roughly from Clay Street to Market Street between Kearny and Drumm streets, the area is home to numerous important architectural landmarks, such as the **Pacific Coast Stock Exchange** at 301 Pine Street. Communist muralist Diego Rivera provided the murals inside this capitalist temple. The black sculpture outside the **Bank of America** headquarters at 555 California Street is known locally as Banker's Heart.

Until a recent high-rise–population-control ordinance was passed, this region was wide open territory for developers who have added such modern monuments as the **Transamerica Pyramid,** the **Crocker Galleria,** and **Philip Johnson's cylindrical 48-story tower** at 101 California Street. The five towers and two hotels of **Embarcadero Center** form the eastern boundary of this busy commercial district.

South of Market—a booming downtown district that is home to the **Moscone Convention Center** and hotels such as the Meridien and the new mirrored San Francisco Marriott—is one of the city's fastest-changing neighborhoods. Many popular restaurants such as the Billboard Café and nightspots such as the DNA Lounge and Club DV 8 are found in this district just minutes from many of the city's major hotels.

Anchoring downtown's southwest corner, off Market Street between Leavenworth and Van Ness, is the **Civic Center** complex. Home to the city's domed **City Hall,** the **Brooks Exhibit Hall,** the **War Memorial Opera House, Louise M. Davies Symphony Hall, Herbst Theatre,** the **Museum of Modern Art,** and the Beaux Arts **San Francisco Public Library,** this is a major hub for cultural events and conventions. One of the city's most important jazz venues, Kimball's, is also in the neighborhood.

TELEGRAPH HILL/NORTH BEACH

Located between downtown and the city's northeast waterfront, this venerable district is one of San Francisco's must-sees. You can ride to the top of Telegraph Hill or hike up the Filbert Steps from Sansome Street. You'll be rewarded with one of the city's best views and a look at two dozen circa-1934 murals in the Coit Tower gallery. North Beach's busiest area is the intersection of Grant Avenue, Columbus Avenue, and Broadway. This is the gateway to the clubs, theaters, galleries, restaurants, shops, and bed and breakfasts found in one of the city's most celebrated neighborhoods. Although almost every road stop in the Bay Area (barring gas stations) now offers espresso, it's still fun to visit the old coffeehouses here in the neighborhood that was the birthplace of the Beats. **City Lights,** probably San Francisco's best known bookstore, is found here, along with **Club Fugazi** (home of the *Beach Blanket Babylon* review) and quintessential San Francisco spots such as **Caffé Trieste** with its Saturday concerts. **Washington Square,** on Columbus at Union, is an ideal spot to picnic with fare ordered up from a local Italian deli.

FISHERMAN'S WHARF

The city's leading tourist attraction and a priority for any visitor, the wharf is reached by continuing north on Columbus or via the Powell/Mason and Powell/Hyde streets cable-car lines. Here are the **San Francisco Maritime National Historical Park, ferries** to Alcatraz and Angel Island, and the popular shops of **Pier 39, Ghirardelli Square,** and the **Cannery,** as well as many hotels. **Aquatic Park,** which begins at Beach Street and the foot of Hyde Street, is the focal point for the wharf's historic ships. South of the ships is the **Maritime Museum.** To the west at Pier 3 is the *Jeremiah O'Brien,* the last of the World War II Liberty Ships built to ferry American soldiers to Europe. On the bluff above the ship is **Fort Mason,** a cultural and performing-arts center with several fine small museums and the city's best known Zen/vegetarian restaurant, Green's. You'll also probably want to visit (and perhaps even board) the *Pampanito,* a submarine berthed east of Aquatic Park at Pier 45.

RUSSIAN HILL/NOB HILL

The best way to ascend Russian Hill is via the Hyde Street cable car. At the top, a serpentine section of Lombard Street plunges down to Leavenworth. It's easier to walk this block than drive it. One block north, at 800 Chestnut, is the **San Francisco Art Institute** where galleries exhibit more Diego Rivera murals. The café here comes highly recommended. Next you'll want to head south to Nob Hill, home of four grand hotels: the **Huntington,** the **Fairmont,** the **Mark Hopkins,** and the **Stanford Court.** No visit to San Francisco is complete without a drink at one of these landmarks, a visit to **Huntington Park,** and a look at **Grace Cathedral.** Views from the Fairmont Hotel's rooftop Crown Room or the Top of the Mark are outstanding.

PACIFIC HEIGHTS/PRESIDIO HEIGHTS

Continue down California Street, turn right on Franklin Street and left on Broadway, and you'll soon come to Pacific Heights. This area and its western neighbor, Presidio Heights, are the city's premier residential districts with lofty views of the bay, Alcatraz, and Marin County. At the bottom of the hill, on the northern edge of Pacific Heights, is **Cow Hollow** and **Union Street,** a popular shopping, clubbing, and dining district. Here you can nosh on French or Italian pastries, shop for European toys designed for the gifted and talented, hit popular bars such as Perry's, or have brunch at Doidge's. Perhaps the most gentrified neighborhood shopping district in the Bay Area, it is the kind of place where you'd expect a mortuary to be called "Death and Things." Immediately north of Union Street across Lombard is Chestnut Street, the commercial heart of the **Marina District.** To the west is the **Presidio** and **Fort Point** where Jimmy Stewart fished Kim Novak out of the bay in *Vertigo.* Here, in the shadow of the Golden Gate Bridge, is a view you won't soon forget.

RICHMOND/GOLDEN GATE PARK/HAIGHT-ASHBURY

Drive west from Presidio Heights and you'll be in **Richmond,** a residential area focused around two primary arteries, Clement Street and Geary Boulevard. This is the place to find Russian restaurants, bagel emporiums, Greek delis, and some of the city's best Asian restaurants such as Fountain Court at 5th Avenue and Clement Street (see *Restaurants*). Continue south and you'll reach **Golden Gate Park.** On the east end are major museums such as the **M. H. de Young, Asian Art Museum,** and the **California Academy of Sciences,** which houses the **Steinhart Aquarium** and the **Morrison Planetarium.** Directly east of the park is the Panhandle strip leading into **Haight-Ashbury,** trendier now than in its sixties heyday. Bed and breakfasts such as the Red Victorian, dance clubs such as the I-Beam, coffee shops, and garden restaurants make this a blast from the past for natives and visitors alike. Return to the park and head west on John F. Kennedy Drive to the **Japanese Tea Garden, Stow Lake, Spreckels Lake,** the **Dutch Windmill,** and **Ocean Beach.** The Great Highway bounds the Park on the west, leading north to the **Cliff House** set above the ruins of the **Sutro House, Seal Rocks,** and **Point Lobos.** To the east is **Lincoln Park,** home of the **Palace of the Legion of Honor.** East beyond Lincoln Park is the posh **Seacliff** neighborhood. There are lifeguards at China Beach for the safety of those brave enough to try the frigid waters. You are probably better off hiking, fishing, or picnicking here and at nearby **Baker Beach.**

SUNSET/TWIN PEAKS

South of Golden Gate Park are the avenues leading into

the **Sunset District.** Some of the city's finest parks such as **Stern Grove,** where free classical and jazz concerts are offered in the summer, are found here. Located between Skyline Boulevard and Ocean Beach off Sloat Boulevard is one of the nation's best animal kingdoms, the **San Francisco Zoo.** It's adjacent to the city's largest body of water, **Lake Merced.** Sloat Boulevard and Portola Drive to the east are the way to ascend **Twin Peaks,** the city's commanding viewpoint. Here you can enjoy another look at some of the areas you've already explored. To the south and southeast are such residential neighborhoods as the **Ingleside** and **Glen Park.** Directly east is one of the city's most eclectic districts— **Upper Market, Castro,** and **Noe Valley.**

A trip down Twin Peaks back toward downtown brings you to the **Eureka** and **Noe** valleys, two residential neighborhoods filled with busy urban pioneers gardening, restoring old Victorians, and enjoying local bistros. While these communities have been gentrified with boutiques, cafés, and good restaurants, they are not overrun. Heart of the city's gay community, Eureka Valley's **Castro** is adjacent to **Corona Heights** and the **Vulcan Stairway,** considered to be one of the best of San Francisco's over two hundred staircase streets. Upper Market near Castro Street has been handsomely landscaped with magnolia trees.

MISSION/POTRERO HILL/BAYVIEW

East of Eureka Valley is the **Mission,** the city's Latin neighborhood that is also home to many Chinese, Filipinos, and Native Americans. The architectural landscape here is enhanced by murals that can be viewed with a self-guiding tour. Mission Street, the neighborhood's center, has some excellent and moderately priced restaurants serving Mexican, Salvadorean, and Italian specialties. After touring historic **Mission Dolores,** you can visit a Levi factory. East of the Mission is **Potrero Hill,** a relatively sunny Victorian-style neighborhood that does not cater to tourists. For those put off by the crowds on Lombard Street's famous curves, Vermont Street south of 20th offers another twisty downhill experience with no waiting. To the south is **Bayview-Hunters Point.** Located east of U.S. 101, this is a major residential and industrial area that includes **Candle-stick Park.** Adjacent to the stadium is a pleasant state recreation area offering fishing, swimming, and picnicking facilities. It's best visited early in the day, before the prevailing winds come up.

3

HOTELS

Probably no city in America offers a wider, more convenient range of comfortable accommodations than San Francisco. Whether you spend $200 a night to stay at the Huntington, where Queen Elizabeth resides when she's in town, or $35 to enjoy the many pleasures of the San Remo on Fisherman's Wharf, you will find yourself in a prime location. Most hotels are within twenty minutes of the main attractions; many are within walking distance.

San Francisco hotels can be expensive—$150 a night and more is not uncommon for first-class accommodations. But many establishments offer sharp discounts on weekends and during holiday seasons, particularly at Christmas. Family plans are also common. There's also been a surge in smaller elegant hotels, such as the Galleria Park, charging $90–$125. And there are many comfortable bargain establishments where a family suite starts around $77. The bed-and-breakfast boom, now a national phenomenon, took off early in the Bay Area. As a result you can find an eclectic variety of fine inns and homestays in some of the city's best neighborhoods such as Pacific Heights and Russian Hill.

We have bounced on the beds of each of the hotels listed below. In addition to passing the box spring test, these hotels all provide visitors with a glimpse of the city's character, whether that is elegant or charming, modern or Victorian.

To the right of each hotel name you'll find first the name of the neighborhood or area it's located in, then a key to the atlas in the back of the book—the map page number and the appropriate coordinates.

🧳 THE SELECTIONS

LUXURY HOTELS

For those who insist on 24-hour room service, a concierge, club floors, and first-class dining rooms, here you can order special candlelight dinners for two at any time of the day or night, you can enjoy baronial suites with fireplaces, television in the bathroom, and free games, toys, and books for the kids. These are the kind of hotel where a foreign dignitary would feel at home. Expect to pay over $150 a night for the experience.

Campton Place Hotel   UNION SQUARE, P. 3, D1
340 Stockton St., San Francisco 94108; (415) 781-5555, (800) 647-4007, in California (800) 235-4300; telex 6771185 CPTN; fax (415) 955-8536.
Singles or doubles, $190–$260; suites, $450–$850.

Located half a block from the Union Sq. shopping area, this hotel has 126 rooms with king or double beds, limited-edition art, baths with marble floors, and double glazed windows that slide open. If you're in a hurry, a valet will be pleased to unpack or pack your suitcase. The Campton Place Restaurant offers such breakfast specialties as crabmeat hash and eggs, Missouri ham served in an orange hollandaise, and yogurt granola parfait with fresh fruit. Valet parking, 24-hour room service. Wheelchair accessible. AE, D, DC, MC, V.

Claremont Resort Spa and Tennis Club
OAKLAND
Ashby at Domingo, Oakland 94623; (415) 843-3000; fax (415) 843-6239.
Singles, $135–$200; doubles, $155–$220; suites, $250–$650.

Readers of D.M. Thomas's *The White Hotel* will be pleased to find there is such a place in the Oakland Hills twenty minutes from San Francisco. This castle-like resort with its olympic-size swimming pool, ten tennis courts, spa facilities, sculpture garden, and extensive collection of Pacific Northwest art has been completely renovated. Although some rooms are small, many offer wonderful bay views. Wheelchair accessible. AE, CB, D, DC, MC, V.

Embassy Suites Burlingame   BURLINGAME
150 Anza Blvd., Burlingame 94010; (415) 342-4600, (800) EMBASSY; fax (415) 343-5137.
Suites, $119–$129.

This 344-suite hotel, convenient to San Francisco International Airport, is ideal for business or pleasure. One room comes with a king or two double beds and a second has a fold-out hideabed. Two televisions, microwave, refrigerator, two phones, complimentary breakfast and cocktail hour (both unlimited) are included. The nine-story atrium courtyard has carp pools, bridges, and parrots. There's an indoor pool, hot tub, sauna, health club, jogging path, and fishing pier. Bobby McGee's restaurant offers specialties such as prime rib and fresh fish. Wheelchair accessible. AE, DC, MC, V.

Fairmont Hotel
NOB HILL, P. 3, D1

950 Mason St., Nob Hill, San Francisco 94108; (415) 772-5000, (800) 527-4727; fax (415) 772-5026.
Singles, $140–$230; doubles, $170–$260; suites, $475–$5,000.

Built by the Fair family shortly after the turn of the century, the Fairmont Hotel is best known as the St. Gregory of the popular T.V. series "Hotel." Operated in the grand manner, the original Beaux Arts hotel has been supplemented by a new tower wing. The original building, with its carriage entrance, golden marble columns, and collections of historic photographs, is a popular tourist attraction for visitors to Nob Hill. The view from the Pavilion Room on the lobby level is great. Two sides offer panoramic views of San Francisco and a third opens out onto the hotel's roof garden and fountain. The Fairmont offers everything from standard singles to the eight-room suite with an outdoor terrace where the United Nations Charter was drafted. The price tag includes round-the-clock butler and maid, a grand piano, a two-story circular library with a celestial constellation in gold on the domed ceiling, a billiard room with Persian-tiled walls, stained glass skylight, baths with 24-karat, gold-plated fixtures, a secret passageway, and a burglar-proof vault. A special $20,000 a night package provides an elaborate dinner with wine for up to twenty guests, three Rolls Royces, and accommodations for six in the suite plus 14 friends in the adjoining tower.

For those who can't afford to stay in this suite, the Fairmont has many less expensive, extremely pleasing alternatives. Amenities in every room and suite include goosedown pillows, cotton Supercale sheets, electric shoe buffers, and 24-hour room service. Guests can work out at the Nob Hill Club. The hotel also has its own bank, travel agency, jade and antique shop, and florist.

Perhaps the most intriguing restaurant in the hotel is the **Tonga Room** which serves dinner and rum drinks on the deck of an old four-masted schooner. Dance to the strains of a Polynesian band while tropical storms rain down on a small lake that used to be the hotel swimming pool. Other popular night spots include the Art Deco **Cirque Room,** which is decorated with gilt carousel murals, and the tower's rooftop **Crown Room.** The latter offers drinks, a buffet, and great views of the bay. Other restaurants in the Fairmont include the **Squire,** which serves continental cuisine, and **Masons** for grilled entrées. Wheelchair accessible. AE, CB, D, DC, MC, V.

Four Seasons Clift Hotel   UNION SQUARE, P. 3, D2
495 Geary St., San Francisco 94102; (415) 775-4700, (800) 332-3442; telex 340647; fax (415) 441-4621.
Singles, $165–$210; doubles, $165–$210; suites, $295–$675.

With their pastel gray-blue decor, dark wooden ottomans, comfortable wing chairs, and marbleized bathrooms, rooms here offer all the amenities you would expect at a first-rate hotel. From its wonderful lobby with oriental rugs and exceptionally helpful staff, to fine dining at the Art Deco Redwood Room and French Room, this is a hotel that would make just about anyone feel at home. Extensively renovated a few years back, the Clift has more employees (359) than rooms (329) and is a favorite of the literary set. Although this is an ideal businessperson's hotel, guests can also take advantage of a special Cliff Dweller's program for families. Call ahead and your room will be stocked with baby bottles, childrens' books, strollers, diapers, and baseball cards. Oreo cookies and milk are on the room-service menu. Wheelchair accessible. AE, DC, MC, V.

Grand Hyatt on Union Square   UNION SQUARE, P. 3, D1
345 Stockton St., San Francisco 94108; (415) 398-1234, (800) 233-1234; telex 340592; fax (415) 392-2536.
Singles, $185–$238; doubles, $215–$268; suites, $300–$900.

With a staff that speaks 31 languages, nearly any traveler can expect to feel at home here. Convenient to the city's Union Sq. shopping area, the 693-room Grand Hyatt is built around a large open plaza deck whose bas-relief sculpture by Ruth Asawa depicts scenes of the city. The plaza also features a fine outdoor café that's delightful on a sunny day. The $900 suite on the 34th floor comes with a Roman-style tub that takes an hour to fill. Full health-club facilities and valet parking. Wheelchair accessible. AE, CB, D, DC, MC, V.

Holiday Inn Fisherman's Wharf   FISHERMAN'S
WHARF, P. 3, D1

1300 Columbus Ave., San Francisco 94133; (415) 771-
9000; telex 34494; fax (415) 771-7006.
Singles, $114–$127; doubles, $130–$140.

Within walking distance of all the major wharf attractions and cable-car lines, this 580-room hotel has comfortable rooms (some with views) and an outdoor pool.
It's close to the Alcatraz and Angel Island ferries, Ghirardelli Sq., and North Beach. Charley's restaurant serves
good buffets. Wheelchair accessible. AE, CB, D, DC, MC,
V.

The Huntington Hotel   NOB HILL, P. 3, D1

1075 California, San Francisco 94108; (415) 474-5400,
(800) 227-4683, in California (800) 652-1539; telex 857-
363; fax (415) 474-6227.
**Singles, $160–$220; doubles, $180–$240; suites,
$265–$640.**

With its one hundred oversize rooms and 43 suites, this
Nob Hill hotel overlooking Huntington Park and adjacent
to Grace Cathedral enjoys what is arguably the best location in town. The Huntington lobby resembles a private
library furnished with antique bookcases, deep red sofas,
and Ming Dynasty treasures. Every room is individually
decorated with imported silks, 17th-century paintings, and
Asian antiques. Named for Henry Huntington, another
member of the Central Pacific's Big Four, this hotel hosts
celebrities ranging from Queen Elizabeth to Luciano
Pavarotti. Guests receive breakfast each morning in the
Big Four restaurant, afternoon tea or sherry, and a complimentary chauffeured Rolls Royce limousine shuttle to
Union Square or the Financial District. Most rooms and
all suites have a wet bar. Room service is catered from
L'Etoile, a popular French restaurant located off the
lobby. Valet parking. AE, D, DC, MC, V.

Hyatt Regency San Francisco   NEAR MARKET
STREET, P. 3, D1

5 Embarcadero Center, San Francisco 94111; (415) 788-
1234, (800) 233-1234; telex 170698; fax (415) 989-
7448.
**Singles, $185–$218; doubles, $215–$248; suites,
$350–$995.**

Part of the Embarcadero shopping complex, this twen-
ty-story–high wedding-cake–shaped hotel is crowned by
a glass-walled revolving rooftop restaurant. The vast sky-
lighted lobby is a small arboretum of ficus trees, twelve

hundred flowering plants, and four thousand green plants hanging off interior balconies on each floor. The Other Trellis is the only cocktail lounge in town where you can sit next to a running stream and cages of live doves. Because of the hotel's unusual acoustics, guests in any of the 803 rooms may be lulled to sleep by music from one of the lobby lounges. Valet parking. AE, DC, MC, V.

Mark Hopkins Inter-Continental Hotel   NOB HILL, P. 3, D1

999 California St., San Francisco 94108; (415) 392-3434, (800) 327-0200; telex 340809; fax (415) 421-3302. **Singles, $165–$225; doubles, $195–$255; suites, $375–$900.**

Named for one of the Big Four railroad barons who parlayed a Sacramento hardware business into a major stake in the Central Pacific line, the Mark Hopkins has one of the finest locations in the city. Ornamented with terracotta, this combination French chateau/Spanish Renaissance tower has welcomed the past ten American presidents, General De Gaulle of France, and Soviet Premier Khrushchev. The 19-story hotel has 393 rooms offering panoramic views of both city and bay. Ample, high-ceilinged rooms with marble bathrooms have been recently remodeled in neo-classic style with large writing desks and cherrywood armoires. Twenty-four–hour room service, complimentary overnight shoeshine, terrycloth robes, health-club privileges, and express video checkout are standard. The Nob Hill Restaurant menu features French cuisine made with fresh California produce and herbs from the hotel's own garden. Views from the Top of the Mark cocktail lounge are memorable. Valet parking. Wheelchair-accessible. AE, D, DC, MC, V.

Le Meridien Hotel   SOUTH OF MARKET, P. 3, D2

50 3rd St., San Francisco 94103; (415) 974-6400; telex 176910; fax (415) 543-8268. **Singles, $162–$202; doubles, $188–$228; suites, $350–$1200.**

Convenient to Union Sq., the Moscone Convention Center, and the Financial District, Le Meridien's 675 rooms showcase the city's skyline with floor-to-ceiling windows. Guests enjoy services such as complimentary shoe shine, cable movies, video check-in/out, and mini-bars. The Pierre combines traditional French cooking with California seasonal recipes. The hotel occasionally brings in Michelin-award–winning French chefs to cook a fixed-price dinner. After the guest chef heads home, this meal remains on the regular menu at a price less than you would pay for the same dinner in France. The hotel's Sun. Champagne Jazz Brunch is one of San Francisco's best. Valet parking. Wheelchair accessible. AE, CB, D, DC, MC, V.

Miyako Hotel   NEAR PACIFIC HEIGHTS, P. 3, C2
1625 Post St., San Francisco 94115; (415) 922-3200, (800) 533-4567; telex 278063; fax (415) 921-0417.
Singles, $95–$135; doubles, $115–$155; suites, $155–$300.

Located in Japan Center, about 2 miles west of downtown, the Miyako is a well-priced hotel offering a choice between western and Japanese-style rooms. The latter provide comfortable futons and traditional shoji-style screens. Many of the 208 rooms and suites offer deep tubs where you can soak Japanese style. A dozen rooms and two suites, starting as low as $155, have private redwood saunas. As you'd expect, there's a tranquil Japanese garden and the restaurant offers a choice between Continental and Japanese cuisine. Especially recommended during the Apr. cherry-blossom season. Wheelchair accessible. AE, D, DC, MC, V.

Hotel Nikko   NEAR UNION SQUARE, P. 3, D2
222 Mason St., San Francisco 94102; (415) 394-1111; telex 204910; fax (415) 394-1156.
Singles, $150–$190; double, $175–$215; suites, $325–$900.

A minimuseum of Asian arts, this 525-room hotel is ideal for a stopover en route to the Far East. A few days at the Nikko, with its white marble staircase and bilevel water sculpture spilling over a shaft of patterned glass, will acquaint you with service in the Japanese tradition. Nikko meeting rooms come with a personal computer and document shredder. The Benkay restaurant here has an excellent sushi bar. There's a tanning salon in the fitness center. Valet parking. Wheelchair accessible. AE, CB, DC, MC, V.

The Stanford Court Stouffer Hotel   NOB HILL, P. 3, D1
905 California, San Francisco 94108; (415) 989-3500, (800) 227-4736, in California (800) 622-0957; telex 34-0899; fax (415) 391-0513.
Singles, $155–$215; doubles, $185–$245; suites, $385–$550.

Built on the site of the Big Four rail magnate and university founder Leland Stanford's mansion, this 402-room hotel is located at the crossroads of the California and

Powell sts. cable-car lines. Reached via a courtyard carriage entry domed with Tiffany-style stained glass, the hotel lobby is furnished with Empire period settees, carrara Italian marble, and fine antiques. Rooms come with two televisions (one in the marble-walled bath), bathrobes, an armoire offering extra storage space, and fine city views. Many are done in an Asian motif with antique Tansu dynasty chests, while others have a French country look. Café Potpourri will redefine your notion of a coffee shop with homemade pastries, blue-cornmeal waffles, and Black Forest ham and melted fontina on dark rye. Fournou's Ovens serves French provincial cooking. Valet parking. AE, CB, D, DC, MC, V.

Westin St. Francis   UNION SQUARE, P. 3, D2

335 Powell, Union Sq., San Francisco 94102; (415) 397-7000, (800) 228-3000; telex 278584; fax (415) 774-0124.

Singles, $145–$270; doubles, $175–$300; suites, $290–$1,725.

Big Four member Charles Crocker, joined by millionaire friends, financed this Union Sq. landmark that has remained at the center of the city's social and business scene since opening day in 1904. The great magenta clock in the vast rosewood lobby has been a favorite downtown meeting place for generations. Traditionalists will prefer the original building, with its travertine marble floors, oak columns, and gilded ceilings. Many of the European-style rooms have crystal chandeliers hanging from their high ceilings. Private bars are standard. The tower offers more contemporary design with pastel color schemes and excellent views from the upper floors. Ride the outside elevator 32 stories to Victor's restaurant or the Oz dance club for a panoramic look at the city. With its soaring fluted columns, carved ceiling, oak paneling, and antique furnishings, the Compass Rose is ideal for a drink or afternoon tea. This is the only hotel in the world that launders its money with a special machine designed to spruce up dirty coins. The St. Francis always tries to be accommodating. On her last San Francisco engagement, actress Anna Held demanded and got a daily room-service allotment of thirty gallons of milk for her bath. Valet parking. Wheelchair accessible. AE, CB, D, DC, MC, V.

INNS AND SMALL HOTELS

Offering many of the amenities found in the luxury hotels, these establishments provide possibilities for every kind of traveler. From the businessperson who prefers the

peace and quiet of a small inn, to the couple seeking a
romantic getaway, these establishments are an inviting
alternative to large hotels.

Alta Mira Hotel   SAUSALITO
125 Bulkley Ave., Sausalito 94965; (415) 332-1350.
Single and doubles, $70–$125; suites, $110–$145.

Outstanding views of Marin, the bay, and San Francisco
come with many of the 28 Victorian-style rooms, furnished
with brass beds and period antiques. Some offer balconies and fireplaces. Located just a block from downtown
Sausalito, the Alta Mira's continental restaurant has terrace dining. Be sure to try the Sun. brunch. AE, DC, MC,
V.

The Archbishops Mansion Inn   NEAR HAIGHT-
ASHBURY, P. 3, C2
1000 Fulton St., San Francisco 94117; (415) 563-7872,
(800) 543-5820.
Singles and doubles, $100–$159; suites, $189–$285.

This 15-room inn, built for the city's archbishop in 1904,
is located on Alamo Sq., a handsome Victorian neighborhood. The paneled rooms, named after 19th-century operas, are decorated around a French-country-castle
theme complete with European antiques, flowers painted
on ceilings, and crystal chandeliers. The house is distinguished by Corinthian columns crafted from virgin redwood and a three-story carved staircase crowned by a 16-
foot stained-glass dome. During the afternoon there's
wine service in the French Parlour and entertainment is
provided on a grand piano that once belonged to Noel
Coward. Guests receive an expanded continental breakfast. Free parking. AE, MC, V.

Aston Regis Hotel   NEAR UNION SQUARE, P. 3, D2
490 Geary, San Francisco 94102; (415) 928-7900, (800)
345-4443, in California (800) 854-0011; fax (415) 441-
8788.
**Singles, $99–$225; doubles, $105–$250; suites,
$140–$190.**

Close to the theater district and Union Sq., this 86-room
Renaissance/Baroque hotel has been renovated in Louis
XVI splendor. All rooms are furnished with antiques and
have beds with either a Marie Antoinette half-crown canopy or full four-poster canopy. There's 24-hour room service and jazz five days a week at Regina's, which serves
French creole cuisine. Late-night theater suppers are offered until 1 A.M. Free taxi service to the Financial District
in cabs imported from London. AE, CB, D, DC, MC, V.

Casa Madrona Hotel   SAUSALITO
801 Bridgeway, Sausalito 94965; (415) 332-0502, (800)
288-0502; fax (415) 332-2537.
Singles and doubles, $80–$175; suites, $175–$300.

Overlooking the Sausalito harbor, this luxurious hillside
hotel offers 32 rooms and three cottages done in your
choice of Victorian, country French, Art Nouveau, Asian,
or nautical decor. The Renoir Room has a clawfoot tub
surrounded by a hand-painted garden scene, fireplace,
and deck. Free continental breakfast. The restaurant features California cuisine. AE, DC, MC, V.

Cornell Hotel   NEAR UNION SQUARE, P. 3, D1
715 Bush St., San Francisco 94108; (415) 421-3154; fax
(415) 399-1442.
Singles, $50–$65; doubles, $55–$70.

Located between Nob Hill and Union Sq., this European-style hotel offers sixty comfortable contemporary
rooms with private bath. The ground-floor Jeanne d'Arc
restaurant has a rustic medieval decor surrounded by tap-
estries, statues, and artifacts that tell the story of Saint
Joan. A special package offers seven nights, seven
breakfasts, and five dinners here for just $350. AE, CB,
DC, MC, V.

Grant Plaza Hotel   CHINATOWN, P. 3, D1
465 Grant Ave., San Francisco 94109; (415) 434-3883,
(800) GRANT-99, in California (800) GRANT-05.
Singles, $32; doubles, $37; suites, $77.

This centrally located 72-room Chinatown hotel with a
Tiffany-style dome is an outstanding value for budget-
minded travel. Rooms are small, but immaculate. All have
color TV, private bath, phone, and wall-to-wall carpeting.
The suites, an excellent value, are recommended for families. Rooms fronting on the Grant Ave. side are quieter
than those on Bush St. MC, V.

Hotel Juliana   NEAR UNION SQUARE, P. 3, D1
590 Bush St., San Francisco 94108; (415) 392-2540,
(800) 382-8800, in California (800) 372-8800; telex
470733; fax (415) 391-8447.
Singles and doubles, $98; suites, $125–$135.

In 1980, entrepreneur Bill Kimpton began transforming
older, historic downtown San Francisco into European-
style accommodations. Today there are seven properties
in his Kimco Hotel group including the Hotel Vintage
Court, Galleria Park, Villa Florence, Monticello Inn, Pres-
cott, Hotel Bedford, and Juliana. Like the other properties,

this 107-room hotel has a well-known restaurant (the Palm), sound-proof windows, minirefrigerators, complimentary limo service to the Financial District, afternoon wine service, and a multilingual staff. The homey rooms are done in a pastel decor with floral-print drapes and bedspreads. A rotating artwork collection supplied by galleries is available for purchase by guests. You can book any of the other Kimco properties through the Juliana's numbers above. Wheelchair accessible. AE, CB, D, DC, MC, V.

The Mansion Hotel   PACIFIC HEIGHTS, P. 3, C1
2220 Sacramento St., San Francisco 94115; (415) 929-9444.
Singles, $74–$150; doubles, $89–$200.

Walk into this Pacific Heights Queen Anne and you may be greeted by a macaw backed up by the strains of Bach. Choose among 19 rooms, all furnished with Victorian treasures and historic memorabilia. Some come with terraces or views of the Golden Gate Bridge. Full breakfast is complimentary, and, if you wish, served in bed. Tues. through Sat. a full dinner is offered in the dining room for $35. The Mansion's Cabaret Theater offers classical concerts with silent-movie horror show overtones, magic shows, and performances by the nation's leading classical saw player. Concierge, gift shop, valet, and laundry service. Close to the cable-car line; parking available. AE, D, DC, MC, V.

Obrero Hotel   CHINATOWN, P. 3, D1
1208 Stockton St., San Francisco 94133; (415) 989-3960.
Singles, $35; doubles, $42–$45.

Located in Chinatown just one block from North Beach, this 12-room hotel and Basque restaurant serves guests a complimentary breakfast of ham, cheese, eggs, fruit, hot bread, and coffee. Dinners served family-style include specialties such as oxtail stew, shepherd's pie, and cassoulet. Originally a Barbary Coast bordello, the hotel offers small rooms that are bright and cheery. Adjoining rooms available. Shared bath. Traveler's checks or cash only.

Petite Auberge   NOB HILL, P. 3, D1
863 Bush St., San Francisco 94108; (415) 928-6000; fax (415) 775-5717.
Singles and doubles, $105–$155; suite, $195.

If you're seeking a room done in a country-French decor, look no further than this 26-room inn. While the rooms are small, they are elegantly furnished in a pastel

Laura Ashley motif. Full breakfast with homemade muffins as well as complimentary afternoon wine and cheese. Suite comes with sundeck, Jacuzzi, fireplace, wet bar, and private garden. AE, DC, MC, V.

Red Victorian Bed and Breakfast Inn

HAIGHT-ASHBURY, P. 2, C2

1665 Haight St., San Francisco 94117; (415) 864-1978. **Singles and doubles with shared bath, $50–$78; doubles with private bath, $93; suites, $125.**

What looks like a classic Victorian hotel from the outside is a beehive of creativity and colors. Designer and artist Sami Shepard converted the 1904 Haight-Ashbury inn into a bed-and-breakfast that offers some highly unusual accommodations. Each room is individually designed and decorated, often by theme. Stay in the Flower Child Room, with rainbows and clouds on the ceiling and psychedelic sixties posters on the walls, or Gigi's Room, with the life-size doll G. G. Brown who will keep you company. Also available—Transformational Art, massage, and MacIntosh computer rental. Rooms and decor change constantly, making each visit a new discovery into the depths of the imagination. Continental breakfast and afternoon tea is served in the pink parlor, where you may run into psychic healers or chat with animal-rights activists. After a hard day of sightseeing, you can unwind in the meditation room. During the summer months, the inn can arrange a walking tour of the historic Haight-Ashbury. AE, MC, V.

San Remo Hotel

FISHERMAN'S WHARF, P. 3, D1

2237 Mason St., San Francisco 94133; (415) 776-8688. **Singles, $35–$55; doubles, $55–$75; weekly rates Oct.–May, $100–$175.**

This historic 1906 Italianate Victorian has been restored into a comfortable Fisherman's Wharf hotel. The 62 rooms, all with shared bath, cater to the traveler with a sense of history and romance. Stained-glass skylights, leaded glass windows, restored redwood wainscotting, brass lights, antique furniture and art, oak armoires, pedestal sinks, and clawleg tubs add to the turn-of-the-century ambience. Many rooms offer views of such landmarks as Coit Tower and the spires of St. Peter and Paul Church. The San Remo serves moderately priced five-course family-style dinners 5–10 P.M. Close to shopping plus a park with indoor pool, tennis courts, playground, bocci ball, and library. Parking. MC, V.

Victorian Lodgings

For a special overnight stay, experience one of these San Francisco Victorians turned guesthouse.

Alamo Square Inn, 719 Scott, 922-2055. An 1895 mansion that brings together the Queen Anne and neoclassical revival styles.

Archbishops Mansion, 1000 Fulton Street, 563-7872. A 1904 Belle Epoque villa that served as a residence for archbishops. (See review.)

Bed and Breakfast Inn, 4 Charlton Court, 921-9784. A pair of Victorians converted into an inn.

Grove Inn, 890 Grove Street, 929-0780. An 1870s shingled Italianate.

The Majestic, 1500 Sutter Street, 441-1100. A quasi-Victorian opened in 1902.

The Mansion, 2220 Sacramento Street, 929-9444. An 1887 Queen Anne. (See review.)

Queen Anne, 1590 Sutter Street, 441-2828. An 1890 girls' school that later became a men's club.

Red Victorian Inn, 1665 Haight Street, 864-1978. A turn-of-the-century hotel that keeps the Haight tradition alive. (See review.)

Sherman House, 2160 Green Street, 563-3600. An Italianate mansion and carriage house built in 1876.

Victorian Inn on the Park, 301 Lyon Street, 931-1830. An 1895 Queen Anne Victorian.

4

PRIORITIES

From the fifth-generation San Franciscan you met on the plane to the concierge at your hotel, everyone has good suggestions on how to see the best of the city. So do we.

Alphabetized and keyed to our maps for your convenience, these listings help you see the essential San Francisco. It would take more than a week to enjoy all these recommendations. If your time is limited, why not concentrate on one part of the city. At the end of each listing you'll find suggestions on other sights close at hand.

To get oriented, you might want to consider a city tour that can run anywhere from a couple of hours to an entire day. Some of the best are outlined in our *Traveler's Information* (see the "Tours" section). After getting an overview, you can return to explore the best sights, attractions, museums, restaurants, and clubs at your own pace. While many of our recommendations are popular destinations, a number are off the beaten track. Collectively they offer an insider's look at a city that you may have trouble leaving.

THE BEST OF SAN FRANCISCO

To the right of each entry you'll find, where applicable, a neighborhood name and a key to the atlas section: a page reference number followed by map coordinates.

Alcatraz
Now part of the Golden Gate National Recreation Area, this island prison closed in 1963. Today ranger-led or

27

audio tours of the rock take you from its early days as an army fort to the cellhouse completed in 1912. Built by convicts who were later incarcerated here, this army prison became one of the FBI's first penitentiaries in 1933. During the tour you'll have a chance to visit the cell blocks and even get locked up in solitary. The tables are still set in the dining hall that served some of the best food in the federal prison system. Along the way you'll have a chance to see a slide show, take a self-guided audiocassette tour narrated by former prisoners, and learn about the 37 convicts who attempted escape. Five were successful and three are still unaccounted for. Wear warm clothing and good walking shoes. This trip, which takes about three hours, is not recommended for visitors with heart or respiratory problems. Reserve by phone or in person at the pier at least a day ahead for this popular tour.

Red and White ferry (546-2896 or 800-445-8880 in California) departs every half hour from Pier 41, 8:45 A.M. to 4:15 P.M. late May to early September; 9:45 A.M. to 2:45 P.M. mid-September to mid-May. Ferry is $7.50 for adults, $4 for children ages 5 to 11, $7 for seniors. For ferry reservations call 392-7469.

Nearby: Angel Island, Fisherman's Wharf, Fort Mason, Ghirardelli Square.

Angel Island

Just half an hour from Fisherman's Wharf is the best view of San Francisco Bay. Once home of four Indian villages, Angel Island has served as a prison, missile launch pad, fort, and kind of west-coast Ellis Island. A military outpost in the Civil War, it later served as a quarantine and immigration station, a World War II prisoner-of-war camp for the Japanese, a Nike missile base, and, finally, a state park. Today it is a 740-acre wildlife sanctuary. Ayala Cove, a popular fishing and picnicking site, is the island's port where you'll find a visitors center and small museum. After a two-hour walk on the trail around the island, you will be rewarded with views of the city along with the Golden Gate, Bay, and Richmond–San Rafael bridges plus Marin County and the Eastbay. En route you'll pass Perles and Quarry beaches. Swimming is not recommended at these idyllic spots because of cold temperatures and rough surf.

The circular route also takes you to the 19th-century West Garrison where you'll see such buildings as the old schoolhouse and hospital. There are also docent-led tours of a historic home during the summer. At the North Garrison another small museum on the history of the immigration station is open May to September. Also consider hiking the cove-to-crest nature trail up 781-foot Mt. Caroline Livermore. This walk leads through a live oak and pine forest where you're likely to spot bush lupine, French broom, mule deer, hummingbirds, owls, and egrets. Allow at least half a day for your visit.

Reached via Red and White ferry from Pier 43½ (546-2896) or the state ferry from Tiburon (435-2131); 456-5218 for park information. Park open 8 A.M. to sunset. Free.

Nearby: Alcatraz, Fisherman's Wharf, Fort Mason, Ghirardelli Square.

At press time, Red and White ferry was in the process of merging with Blue and Gold ferry. Call the San Francisco Convention and Visitors Bureau for updated information.

Beach Blanket Babylon/Club Fugazi NORTH BEACH, P. 3, D1

The San Francisco treat, *Beach Blanket Babylon* is the city's longest-running musical review and a haberdasher's nightmare. This is a unique Bay Area institution that incorporates popular advertising icons such as Mr. Peanut and the walking Old Gold cigarette packages into a memorable show. The wild and crazy guys and gals upstage one another with Carmen Miranda hats, crazy lyrics, and clever satires. Some fans have seen this 15-year-old show more than three hundred times. Pencil it into your schedule right now.

678 Green Street near Columbus Avenue, 421-4222. Wednesday and Thursday at 8 P.M., Friday and Saturday at 8 and 10:30 P.M., Sunday at 3 and 7:30 P.M. $14 to $28.

Nearby: dim sum, cable cars, Filbert Steps.

Cable Car P. 3, D1

There are three cable-car routes in San Francisco and we recommend riding them all as frequently as possible.

Invented here in 1873 by Andrew S. Hallidie, this type of cable-driven vehicle was once found on the streets of New York, Seattle, Denver, London, and even Sydney, Australia. Today they survive only in San Francisco. The ride, which costs $2, can take you up California Street, or out to Fisherman's Wharf via the Powell/Mason line or the Powell/Hyde line. Although they operate at just 9.5 miles per hour, this is one of the most exciting rides in town. The biggest thrills are on the Hyde Street slope to Fisherman's Wharf or the California Street descent from Nob Hill. Most passengers board at either Powell and Market, Fisherman's Wharf, or the Embarcadero Center. To avoid these queues, you might try boarding a few blocks up from one of the busy turnaround points. Besides providing easy access to many of the city's best neighborhoods (such as Chinatown, Nob Hill, North Beach, and Fisherman's Wharf), the cable car leads to many museums including the Cable Car Museum (474-1887) on the Powell/Hyde line at Washington and Mason streets. In a basement room you can see how the cables actually operate.

Nearby: Nob Hill, Fisherman's Wharf, Fort Mason, *Beach Blanket Babylon,* dim sum.

California Academy of Sciences GOLDEN GATE PARK, P. 2, B2

If you only have time for one major museum in San Francisco, let this be it. The Roundabout at the **Steinhart Aquarium** is one of the city's best attractions. Instead of simply walking from tank to tank, as at most aquariums, you stand on a platform completely surrounded by a circular tank with more than fourteen thousand specimens including sharks, yellowtail, and sea bass. The only way to get closer to an underwater environment such as this is to go scuba diving. Also at the aquarium is the new living coral reef, dolphins, seals, penguins, and a California tidepool where you can pick up a starfish.

Elsewhere in this science complex you'll find the **Natural History Museum,** the **Morrison Planetarium,** natural-history exhibits, an imitation trek through the Australian outback, and, for those who can't wait for the next Richter event, a free ride on an earthquake simulator in the Earth and Space Hall. Don't miss cartoonist Gary Larson's Far Side Gallery. Do your shopping at the

Nature Company, a store specializing in goods, games, and tools of the natural world.

Golden Gate Park, 221-5100. Open daily 10 A.M. to 5 P.M., summer till 7 P.M. Admission $4 adults, $2 seniors and youths ages 12 to 17, $1 children ages 6 to 11.

Nearby: Stern Grove.

Dim Sum   CHINATOWN, P. 3, D1

One of the best reasons to visit San Francisco is Chinatown's dim sum restaurants, probably the finest in the world outside Hong Kong. If you're the kind of person who likes to see what's on the menu, literally, this is the ideal Chinese lunch. Just take your seat and soon waiters will drift by pushing carts full of steamed pork buns, spring rolls, pot stickers, shrimp dumplings, braised fried chicken feet, deep-fried crab balls, turnip cakes, fried taro cakes, shark's-fin dumplings, lion's-head meatballs, or western sea vegetables. The prices are very fair and quality is high. Every visitor should try establishments such as Chinatown's **Hong Kong Tea House,** 835 Pacific Avenue (391-6365) or **Ocean City,** 640 Broadway (982-2328). For elegant dim sum, go to **Harbor Village** at 4 Embarcadero Center (781-8833). **Nearby:** North Beach, *Beach Blanket Babylon,* Wells Fargo Bank History Room, cable cars.

Exploratorium   MARINA, P. 2, C1

After the popular 1915 Panama-Pacific Exposition, one building, Bernard Maybeck's **Palace of Fine Arts,** was saved for posterity. This Roman rotunda, in the midst of a park with a small lake, now houses a remarkable science museum. Children and adults learn chemistry, geology, physics, biology, geometry, and much more through hundreds of hands-on exhibits. Visitors become active participants in demonstrations that teach and entertain. One such exhibit is the Listening Vessels, designed by artist Douglas Hollis. Visitors sit at the focal point of a parabolic dish and talk to another person thirty feet away. Even at a whisper, the sound is so focused it is possible to hear someone far away. To get inside the one-of-a-kind Tactile Dome, make reservations well in advance. Allow about two hours.

Palace of Fine Arts, 3601 Lyon Street at Marina Boulevard, 563-7337; 561-0362 for Tactile Dome. Open Thursday to Sunday, 10 A.M. to 5 P.M.; Wednesday, 10

A.M. to 9:30 P.M. Admission $5 adults, $2.50 seniors, $1 youth ages 6 to 17.

Nearby: Fort Point, Fort Mason, Fisherman's Wharf.

Filbert Steps   NEAR FINANCIAL DISTRICT, P. 3, D1

With more than two hundred stairway streets, San Francisco offers the visitor a unique opportunity to get off the busy thoroughfares and explore old neighborhoods. An ideal way to escape the traffic, these lanes make the city a kind of urban village where you can find hidden parks, historic cottages, wildflowers, and blackberries. Your reward for heading up the down staircase is splendid views minus the crowds that sometimes overpopulate better-known destinations. Among the finest stairways is the **Filbert Steps.** It begins just minutes from downtown. Follow Sansome Street north across Broadway. After parking near Levi Plaza, walk up the stairs. A platform network leads up wooden steps to the top of Telegraph Hill. Benches along the way are an ideal spot to rest and enjoy the harbor view. There's even a small garden park along the way as well as numerous Gold Rush–era frame homes along narrow byways. On top you'll reach Coit Tower. Walk back down the hill via parallel Greenwich Stairs. Or you may want to continue down the west side into North Beach. Allow about an hour for your walk and a visit to Coit Tower.

Nearby: Fisherman's Wharf, Wells Fargo Bank History Room, dim sum.

Fisherman's Wharf   P. 3, D1

The city's leading tourist attraction is headlined by the one-of-a-kind **San Francisco Maritime National Historical Park.** Located at Hyde Street Pier, this floating park has six historic ships including three you can board. They include the **Balclutha** (a square-rigged Cape Horn sailing ship), a lumber schooner called the **C.A. Thayer,** and an old sidewheeler ferry, the **Eureka.** Besides visiting these ships you'll want to see the Maritime Museum building on Beach Street at Polk. This structure's distinctive boat shape makes it easy to find. Nearby at Pier 45 is the **Pampanito.** An audio tour, narrated by crew that served on this vessel during World War II, is an ideal way to round out your visit to the maritime park. There's an excellent gift shop on the Hyde Street Pier where you can find souvenirs a cut above the typical tourist schlock.

While in the wharf area you'll probably want to explore shopping venues such as Pier 39, the Cannery, or Ghirardelli Square. During the Christmas season, a special Dickens Fair is staged on the wharf. This traditional English celebration features period entertainment, games, food, and shops. A good place to take a break or picnic is Aquatic Park on the waterfront below Ghirardelli Square.

Nearby: Alcatraz Ferry, Angel Island Ferry, Coit Tower, Russian Hill, North Beach.

Fort Mason   FISHERMAN'S WHARF, P. 3, C1

Located in a park setting adjacent to Fisherman's Wharf, the fort has been demilitarized into a major San Francisco cultural center. The youth hostel here is one of the best deals in town. The old barracks and office buildings are now home to fine drama companies, restaurants, and art galleries. Many of Sam Shepard's plays have debuted at **The Magic Theatre** here (441-8001). The Mexican Museum, African-American Historical and Cultural Society, and the Museo Italo-Americano are located here along with many environmental and public-interest groups. For lunch you'll want to try Green's, a popular vegetarian restaurant (see *Restaurants*). On the way down to the wharf, along the city's freeway, you'll find a wonderful mural featuring animal life. Fort Mason is also home of the *Jeremiah O'Brien,* the last of 2,751 Liberty Ships built for World War II. It's located at Pier 3. Allow an hour or two for your visit.

Marina Boulevard and Laguna Street, 441-5705.
Nearby: Fisherman's Wharf, cable cars, Exploratorium.

Fort Point   P. 2, B1

Built in the mid-19th century, Fort Point, located near the south anchorage of the Golden Gate Bridge, was meant to protect the San Francisco harbor. It was a great posting for the Civil War soldiers who served here as they were never called on to defend the city by the bay. This classic seacoast fort, with its granite spiral staircases, red brick walls, muzzle-loading cannons, and their supporting casements, has been restored by the National Park Service. A delightful place to picnic, the wheelchair-accessible fort is the perfect approach to the Bay Bridge. Guided tours and cannon demonstrations are available. Allow about an hour for your visit. The fort is part of the **Presidio of San Francisco,** surely

' most picturesque military installations in the
' small museum showcases military attire,
,unry, and a well-preserved hardtack biscuit. One
of the best ways to see it is to hike the coastal trail beginning at the fort and continuing south for a little over
a mile to Baker Beach. You can also hike the 3.5-mile
Golden Gate Promenade through the Presidio back to
Fisherman's Wharf.

Marine Drive via Lincoln Boulevard north exit off
U.S. 101, 556-2857. Open daily 10 A.M. to 5 P.M. Free.
Nearby: Exploratorium, Fort Mason, Golden Gate
Bridge.

Golden Gate Bridge   P. 2, B1
The 1.7-mile-long bridge is an inviting spot to linger,
particularly when the fog starts rolling past to tuck the
city in for the night under a white blanket. Drive it, bike
it, or walk it, but don't miss it. This turbulent entrance
to the bay, buffeted by high winds, strong currents, and
powerful tides, seemed an improbable construction site.
But builder Joseph Strauss was determined to make
good on an idea first floated by the city's unofficial em-
peror, Joshua Norton, in 1870. The bridge-construction
project, which took the lives of ten workers, was completed in May 1937 after four years of building. Opening
festivities included four hundred planes flying overhead
and every fire siren, church bell, and foghorn in San
Francisco and Marin County resounded. In May 1987,
the fiftieth anniversary celebration included over eight
hundred thousand people walking across, flattening the
bridge's central arc. Walking is the best way to appreci-
ate this often chilly and windy span. At the end of your
two-mile-long trip you'll want to pause at **Vista Point**
and enjoy the city views. Nearby are beautiful walks in
the **Marin Headlands** and the popular town of **Sausalito.** Be sure to dress warmly for this excursion that
will take about two hours. The trip is best made on
weekday mornings when adjacent highway traffic is
light.

U.S. 101 North, toll $2 southbound; free northbound.
Nearby: Fort Point, Fort Mason, Fisherman's Wharf.

Golden Gate Park   P. 2, B1
It would take a day just to sample this 1,017-acre refuge
that has 27 miles of hiking trails, 11 lakes, a Japanese
tea garden, an aquarium, and a planetarium. Built on

sandy dunes more than a century ago, the three-mile–long park offers tulip fields, a rhododendron dell, redwood groves, and the **Strybing Arboretum** featuring more than six thousand species. Take away the palm trees in front of the **Conservatory** and you might think you're in London's Kew Gardens. Nearby are the **M.H. de Young** and **Asian Art** museums. Strawberry Hill, an island in Stow Lake, is easily reached by paddle or row boat. Huntington Falls is the highest manmade falls in the west. Plan to spend at least three or four hours here.

West of Stanyan between Lincoln Way and Fulton. **Nearby:** Stern Grove.

Mission Murals   MISSION, P. 3, D3

The great names in Mexican art such as Rivera, Orozco, and Siqueiros are all part of the Mexican Museum in Fort Mason. But to see some of the best local muralists, you have to be willing to walk. A good starting point is the **Galeria de la Raza** at 24th and Bryant. Here you can pick up a walking-tour map and begin the ten-block walk trip from Mission to York on 24th Street. Along the way you'll see murals in a pre-Columbian motif, others honoring the tradition of such Mexican masters as Rivera, and several dedicated to the theme of international peace. You can sample one of the city's Latin restaurants and explore local markets. Don't miss Balmy Alley off 24th. It's the site of the Mission's first community mural, created in 1973. Today there are 28 murals spread across garage doors and fences in this colorful street of San Francisco.

24th Street from Mission to York, begin at 24th Street BART station.

Nob Hill   P. 3, D1

Even if you only have one day in San Francisco, don't miss Nob Hill. Come on foot, by car, limo, or cable car, but by all means, do see this grand aerie with its famed hotels, Gothic churches, Art Deco apartment houses, and rooftop lounges at the Fairmont and Mark Hopkins hotels, as well as great views of the surrounding city. This is old San Francisco. Come at sunset and you'll see why all the Big Four railroad barons (Charles Crocker, Leland Stanford, Mark Hopkins, and Collis Huntington) built their mansions on Nob Hill.

Nearby: Cable cars, dim sum, Wells Fargo Bank History Room, *Beach Blanket Babylon.*

Oakland Museum   OAKLAND

A pleasant twenty-minute BART ride from San Francisco is the state's leading museum of California. Come for lunch overlooking the sculpture gardens. Then visit the galleries offering an overview of the state's political, cultural, environmental, and social history. From California's geologic origins, through the Gold Rush to the Depression Era photography of Dorothea Lange and paintings of Richard Diebenkorn, this is an outstanding collection. The Cowell Hall of California History recreates settings ranging from a Victorian sitting room to a 1940s kitchen. This is one of the best regional museums in America, while the parklike environment, with its terraces and garden walks overlooking Lake Merritt, makes it a welcome place to spend two or three hours.

1000 Oak Street, Oakland, 273-3401. Open 10 A.M. to 5 P.M. Wednesday to Saturday, noon to 7 P.M. Sunday. Free admission; charges for some special exhibits. BART: Lake Merritt Station.

Stern Grove   SUNSET, P. 2, B3

There are many fine parks in San Francisco, but this Sunset District spot near the zoo is one of the best. Pack a picnic and head here on a summer Sunday afternoon to enjoy free jazz, classical, or operatic performances. For information on these events call 398-6551. A jacket or sweater is good insurance against prevailing winds and coastal fog. The cute little gingerbread cottage in the grove was once a gambling den and hideout for one of the city's most infamous political wheeler-dealers, Abe Ruef. Two bullet holes blasted in the door on the day of his capture still remain.

Sloat Boulevard and 19th Avenue.
Nearby: Golden Gate Park, Zoo.

Wells Fargo Bank History Room   FINANCIAL
                                        DISTRICT, P. 3, D1

The Gold Rush of 1849 instantly brought remote California into the American mainstream. This museum tells the story of that Gold Rush through artifacts, paintings, photographs, and documentary materials. Various forms of mining technology ranging from panning to hydraulic methods are explained. A beautiful brass and bronze gold scale used to weigh the real gold at the assay office is on display as are gold nuggets and gold dust. In addition, there are extensive exhibits of vintage banking equipment, a replica of a pioneer branch office, and many rare gold pieces. Among the museum's treasures is an original Concord stagecoach. Visitors are welcome to bounce around on another model stage.

420 Montgomery Street at California Street, 396-2619. Open 9 A.M. to 5 P.M. Monday to Friday except bank holidays. Free.

Nearby: Cable cars, dim sum, *Beach Blanket Babylon,* Filbert Steps.

5

TRANSPORTATION

Thanks to cable cars, ferries, BART, trains, light rail, and buses, San Francisco is an easy city to explore. But from the foot of Fisherman's Wharf to the top of Nob Hill, you'll find the best way to see this town is to take a hike. Popular neighborhoods such as Chinatown and North Beach are within easy walking distance of the downtown hotels. Even if you do drive, you'll find some of the city's more unique attractions—for example, the Filbert Steps on Telegraph Hill—reserved for walkers.

Of course cars are convenient for longer journeys. But given the congestion downtown and rush-hour jams in and out of the city, you'll want to consider the alternatives. Take a cable car to Fisherman's Wharf or the MUNI light rail out to the beach. BART will whisk you to the first-rate Oakland Museum, while CalTrain is an ideal way to reach Stanford. Two ferry lines, Red and White and Golden Gate, sail regularly to the Sausalito harbor. Cabs are ideal for short trips. But you'll often find public transit equally convenient. Transferring between systems is a relatively simple matter once you learn how they dovetail. And because distances are short—no point in the city is more than half an hour from another—you'll find San Francisco is an easy city to explore.

ARRIVING

BY AIR

The San Francisco Bay Area is served by three airports. Most passengers land at **San Francisco International,** 14 miles south of the city. With expansion complete after years of terminal construction, SFO is only twenty minutes from the city during off-peak periods. A cab into the city runs about $25. Outside the lower-level baggage claim, blue pillars mark the pickup location for numerous van and bus services to communities throughout the greater Bay Area. Schedules are posted at the pickup location. The Airporter bus provides service from the lower level to a downtown San Francisco terminal every twenty minutes, 5 A.M.–midnight. The fare is $5. For $9 you can take advantage of Super Shuttle's 24-hour shared-ride service to any location in the city. (They will also take you to the airport.) Call (415) 871-7800 to arrange pickup on the upper level. The cheapest way to get downtown is the $1.25 SamTrans 7F bus departing from the upper level in front of Delta (south terminal) or United (north terminal) to the Transbay Transit Terminal. Call 761-7000 for schedule details. If you're driving, take U.S. 101 north to downtown and exit at 4th St.

Oakland International Airport is the Bay Area's sleeper. Named by the *Los Angeles Times* as one of the nation's best airports, it is located 19 miles southwest of San Francisco. A five-minute AIRBART shuttle-bus ride (fare: $1) links you up with the 71-mile BART rail system at the Coliseum station. The ride into downtown San Francisco takes just 27 minutes. BART also provides convenient access to many other Bay Area destinations including Oakland, Berkeley, Walnut Creek, Fremont, Hayward, Richmond, and Daly City. If your primary destination is in the Eastbay or Contra Costa County, Oakland is the airport of choice. Unlike at San Francisco International, air-traffic delays here are unusual. Baggage facilities are also efficient. **San Jose International Airport** is convenient to the South Bay region as well as Palo Alto, Fremont, and popular resort destinations such as Monterey and Santa Cruz. This is a good way to beat the heavy rush-hour traffic that can slow your progress between San Francisco Airport and the Silicon Valley area. New flights added in recent years make this airport a convenient point of entry from many destinations around the country. The airport's central location, just five minutes from downtown San Jose, is ideal. The cab trip will run $5–$8.

BY TRAIN

What better way to enter the Bay Area than via the western terminus of the original transcontinental railroad. Oakland's last operating station, this Beaux Arts **Southern Pacific terminal** is considered one of the finest depots in the West. Restoration plans are currently in progress. Unfortunately it's located in a rather shaky industrial neighborhood. Buses pick up all San Francisco–bound passengers here for the twenty-minute shuttle across the bay to the Transbay Terminal in downtown San Francisco. If you're not going to San Francisco, catch a cab to your destination or the Oakland City Center BART station. All Amtrak trains to Oakland, except the northbound Coast Starlight, stop en route at the BART station in suburban Richmond. If you're not carrying a lot of luggage, this is a convenient place to detrain and connect to points along the local rail network. (Likewise you can take BART to the Richmond Amtrak station when you're ready to head home on Amtrak.) Coast Starlight passengers may detrain in San Jose. Martinez and Antioch Amtrak stations serve northern Contra Costa County. In addition, passengers arriving on the San Joaquin trains from the central valley and Southern California can take advantage of direct bus connections from the Martinez station to Napa and Sonoma counties points. Phone 982-8512 for more information.

BY BUS

Greyhound's downtown terminal is at 50 7th St. (558-6789). Trailways provides service to the **Transbay** bus terminal in downtown San Francisco (982-6400). There are direct connections here to points throughout the Bay Area. BART is just one block away on Market St. Taking a taxi to your hotel, particularly after dark, is an excellent idea. Like many urban bus terminals, this one is located in an area you wouldn't want to explore nocturnally.

BY CAR

Interstate 80 from the east and U.S. 101 from the north and south are principal motor routes into the city. If you're driving in from the San Francisco Airport or other points south on U.S. 101, exit downtown at 4th St. If you're coming from the north, you'll come off the Golden Gate Bridge on Doyle Dr. (U.S. 101 South). At Van Ness, turn left to North Point and then turn right on Columbus, which takes you into downtown. If you're coming from the Eastbay via Interstates 80 or 880, take the Bay Bridge to the Main St. exit for downtown or the Broadway exit for North Beach, Russian Hill, and Fisherman's Wharf. (Note: Due to the earthquake, there is a detour on 880 in Oakland that takes you to Interstate 580, which runs directly into the Bay Bridge.) Avoid the morning rush hour on all these routes.

In the downtown area, expect to pay $8–$15 a day for parking. On-street parking is difficult and don't even think of parking in a restricted zone. Enforcement by police is aggressive and it can cost $100 to get your car released from the impound lot. Also don't try to park your car on the street all day in northside neighborhoods such as

North Beach and Pacific Heights. Residential permit parking in these areas means that you, a nonresident, are generally restricted to two-hour parking. After that, it's another ticket. You'll find parking lots at popular destinations such as Fisherman's Wharf running $6–$10. With cable cars, ferries, buses, BART, and trains available, you may find it easier to use transit for many local sightseeing trips. For example, the Sausalito ferry is a delightful way to reach Marin and there's even a ferry from Fisherman's Wharf to Vallejo's Marine World. The University of California at Berkeley and the wonderful Oakland Museum are both easy to reach via BART. Of course, you'll also enjoy exploring the city's convenient neighborhoods, such as North Beach and Chinatown, by foot.

HOW TO USE LOCAL TRANSIT

Purchase a copy of the Official San Francisco Street and Transit Map available from the Visitor Information Center on the lower level, Hallidie Plaza, 900 Market St. It's at the Powell St. BART station exit, 5th and Mission. The San Francisco MUNI bus and light-rail system blankets the city at a flat adult rate of $.85. Youths age 5–17 pay $.25. Cable car adult fare is $2; $1 for youths age 5–17. Seniors pay $.15 on both systems. Exact change is required. Caution is advised when riding the system at night; cable cars are safer then. For specific information, check with your hotel front desk to find the safest route to your destination. For route information, call 673-MUNI.

The comfortable BART system serves 34 stations along a 71-mile route in San Francisco, Alameda, and Contra Costa counties. A relatively safe and efficient transit network, BART is often the fastest way to reach many major destinations such as the Oakland Coliseum or the University of California at Berkeley campus. One-way fares range from $.80 to $3. BART operates 6 A.M.–midnight, Mon.–Sat., and 9 A.M.–midnight, Sun. Purchase your magnetically encoded fare card at the station, using it for exit at your destination. Buy a card with a high enough value to see you through your route for the day. That way you'll avoid the necessity of purchasing additional cards. Serious transit buffs may want to purchase the $2.60 round-trip excursion fare that lets you explore the entire system, as long as you exit from the station you entered. Keep in mind that this is not an unlimited pass; you must stay within the system. Passengers are allowed to detrain and look around the BART stations at no extra charge. The best BART-system view of San Francisco is on the MacArthur station platform. There's also nice scenery on the Concord line between Orinda and Pleasant Hill. In downtown San Francisco, MUNI's light rail and BART trains share stations below Market St. In addition, many MUNI and suburban bus lines offer direct connections to BART. For BART information, call 788-BART.

Several bus lines and CalTrain provide extensive service from the Transbay Terminal at 1st and Mission to suburban destinations. SamTrans (761-7000) covers peninsula routes in San Mateo county south of San Francisco. CalTrain (557-8661) runs trains south from its terminal at 4th and Townsend to peninsula points and San Jose. AC Transit (839-2882) operates in Alameda and Contra Costa counties. Golden Gate Transit (332-6600) buses connect with Marin and Sonoma counties. In addition, Golden Gate vessels provide service from the ferry building at the foot of Market to Sausalito and Larkspur. These ferries are a delightful way to travel about the bay. The Red and White Fleet at Pier 41 on Fisherman's Wharf (546-2896) serves Tiburon, Sausalito, Angel Island, and Marine World Africa USA in Vallejo.

Taxis are convenient for short trips with fares running $2.75 for the first mile and $1.50 for additional miles. The best place to catch a cab is a major hotel taxi stand. Hailing a cab can be problematic during rush hour or inclement weather. If you're not in the downtown area, your best bet probably is to call for a cab from a taxi company such as Veteran's (552-1300) or Allied (826-9494).

6

NEIGHBORHOODS

Any doubts in the minds of the pioneering '49ers who made the difficult, and at times terrifying, trip around Cape Horn or crossed the isthmus at Panama to get to California must have quickly vanished as they sailed through the Golden Gate. One of the world's most picturesque natural harbors was dominated by the masts of sailing ships that had rushed here from all over the world to join the Gold Rush. Later in the 19th century the railroad replaced the steamship as the principal means of transportation. But ferries remained an important common carrier for many residents commuting into the city from outlying communities until the Bay and Golden Gate bridges were built in the thirties. Today the **Ferry Building,** designed to resemble a Spanish cathedral tower, continues to welcome daily arrivals from the ports of Sausalito and Larkspur. From here travelers can transfer on Market Street to buses, the MUNI System, BART, or simply walk to their offices. This transit hub also makes it easy for visitors to take the ferry to Marin, the MUNI out to the ocean, or BART over to the University of California campus at Berkeley. At Market and California you can also catch the cable car up Nob Hill.

Justin Herman Plaza, across from the Ferry Building, offers free entertainment during the summer months in the plaza theater. While joggers make their way through the Parcourse here, you can browse at handicrafts offered by street vendors or simply relax next to Armand Vaillancourt's free-form, walk-through fountain.

Directly behind the plaza is the **Hyatt Regency San Francisco,** the atrium hotel with a glass-walled escalator that rises to the Equinox, a revolving rooftop restaurant. This hotel—with its reflecting pools, birds, trees, hanging gardens, and conversation pits—is a major tourist destination, whether or not you're staying here.

Embarcadero Center

Adjacent to the Hyatt Regency San Francisco is this office complex with more than 135 shops and forty restaurants. Linked by pedestrian bridges, the center includes the new **Park Hyatt** hotel, sidewalk cafés, and specialty shops such as the **Nature Company** where you'll find an excellent collection of prints, posters, gifts, and books on the natural world. (A sister store is located at Ghirardelli Square.)

Concerts, dances, and special events are frequently held at the center. As you stroll through Embarcadero Center you'll find more than a dozen major works of art including Willi Gutman's *Two Columns with Wedge,* Jean Dubuffet's *La Chiffonniere,* and Louise Nevelson's *Sky Tree.* To locate these and other pieces as well as restaurants and shops, consult the directories at the foot of each escalator.

From the Hyatt you can walk up Market past some of the city's most important landmarks such as the **Sheraton Palace** (at New Montgomery). This local landmark, home of the famous Garden Court restaurant, is being renovated and will reopen sometime in 1990. With its vast glass skylight, the Garden Court is one of the city's most elegant dining rooms.

Across the way from the hotel at 39 New Montgomery is the **House of Shields** (392-7732) saloon, a onetime men's club that now welcomes women but refuses to change the decor for them. Paneled in oak and mahogany, the stand-up bar here retains its brass spittoons, chandeliers, stuffed steer heads, and nymph statuettes. There are no television sets, clocks, or ferns anywhere in sight.

Continue on to the **Emporium-Capwell** at 835 Market and you can explore one of the city's grandest retail establishments. A skylit rotunda dome illuminates the main floor of this department store that connects to **San Francisco Centre** at 870 Market Street. A circular escalator winds up through the first four floors of this vertical mall. Adults and children alike will want to enjoy the ride on this conveyance, the first of its kind ever built in the United States. On the top four floors is **Nordstrom's,** the specialty fashion store so obsessed with pleasing that they operate on the policy, if the customers are wrong, they won't hear it from us.

Note: If you need to get your shoes heeled, are looking for a toothbrush, need an inexpensive suitcase to take your purchases home, or simply want to pick up some postcards, consider the giant Woolworth's across the street next to the cable car turnaround.

That escalator on the left side of the cable car stop descends to One Hallidie Plaza and the **San Francisco Convention and Visitors Bureau,** a handy source of maps and advice.

Union Square

A cross between New York's Fifth Avenue and London's Hyde Park Speaker's Corner, and the heart of San Francisco's major-league shopping, the park is a 2.6-acre crossroads in this fascinating city. Whether you want to buy, dine, see a play, stroll, or just get a good night's sleep, this part of downtown tries to offer the city's best—and often succeeds. From coffee-shop fare to California cuisine, the square can satisfy any taste or pocketbook. For more than a century, Union Square has been a San Francisco hub covered by passionate shoppers in search of the city's finest goods. While some customers do pause here periodically for a break from their rounds of the racks, the square is usually populated by lunching office workers, strolling couples, bongo players, impromptu public speakers holding forth on the issues of the day, and of course, sunbathers who prefer to tan in the public eye. From the violent pro-Union army demonstrations that gave the park its name on the eve of the Civil War to more recent protests dealing with wars in Southeast Asia and Central America, Union Square has always been crucial to the city's political life. The dominant 97-foot-high Corinthian column in the center of the park commemorates Commodore George Dewey's victory over the Spanish fleet at Manila in 1898. This monument to U.S. imperialism was financed by public donations and survived the 1906 earthquake.

During the four-day fire that followed the calamity, this verdant plaza became a busy campsite. First to arrive were displaced residents of the crumbled St. Francis Hotel, including actor John Barrymore. The performer, who'd tied one on the night before, was immediately recruited by the militia into stacking fallen bricks. Watching the famous actor do blue-collar labor, another actor commented, "It took an act of God to get Jack out of bed and the United States government to get him to work." Restored in 1907, the St. Francis is the best known of forty hotels within a three-block walk of the square.

Boasting the fourth-largest retail-sales volume in the country, this plaza surrounded by Geary, Powell, Post, and Stockton streets includes such well-known establishments as Saks Fifth Avenue, Burberry's of London, Macy's, Bally of Switzerland, I. Magnin, and Neiman Marcus. In the nearby blocks are other well-known shops such as Gucci, Tiffany & Co., Jaeger, Brooks Brothers, Louis Vuitton, Wedgwood, Celine, Herme's, Laura Ashley, and Cartier.

Many special events are staged at Union Square including Rhododendron Days in late April, the summertime Cable Car Bell-ringing Competition, national holiday observances, fashion shows, fund-raisers, sports rallies, band concerts and, of course, political demonstrations. A giant menorah is lit for Hanukkah and during Christmas the square is illuminated with colored lights. There's also a big Chinese New Year pageant staged between mid-January and late February. Whenever you come, count on being in the midst of San Francisco's finest shops, hotels, theaters, and streetlife.

THE SQUARE

One of the busiest corners in town is Geary at Stockton. Flower vendors, limousines, hawkers, police directing traffic, and countless shoppers crowd this intersection. You may even see A.S.P.C.A. workers busy trying to persuade locals to adopt adorable little puppies. Also here is **I. Magnin & Co.** (362-2100), ten stories of designer fashion for the whole family. Built in 1876, this white marble landmark has a gallery-like cosmetic hall on the entry level and spectacular chandeliers on the third floor. When it's time to take a break you can snack at Narsai's Café.

Note: The ultimate ladies' lounge is located on I. Magnin's fifth floor. It's beautifully decorated and offers chairs where you can rest up before returning to the racks.

Next door is **Macy's** (397-3333), an eclectic, much remodeled building that is one of the city's most important retailing centers. If you continue walking up Geary you'll be at the heart of the city's theater district. The **Geary Theatre,** home base of the **American Conservatory Theatre** (at 415), sustained substantial damage during the earthquake. While repairs are underway, A.C.T. will be performing at various venues. Call the American Conservatory Theatre at 749-2228 for information. Be sure to check out the **Curran Theatre,** 445 Geary, with its beautiful mansard roof for local productions and road shows. Continue up the block to 495 Geary and the **Four Seasons Clift Hotel.** Probably the loveliest spot in the city for a lunch break, or drinks after a hard day of shopping, is this establishment's Redwood Room. With the redwood-paneled walls, brass-railed bar, and very comfortable upholstered chairs, this room is one of the city's finest examples of Art Deco. At the least, be sure to drop in and have a look before returning down Geary to Union Square.

Reading Material

If you're looking for something to read try one of the fine bookstores in the vicinity:

B. Dalton, Sutter and Kearny, 956-2850.
Books Inc., 140 Powell, 397-1555.
Doubleday Book Shop, 265 Sutter Street, 989-3420.
Hunter's Bargain Bookstore, 151 Powell Street, 397-5955.

Continuing left around the square on Powell you'll come to the **Westin St. Francis Hotel,** where many visitors like to stop for tea at the Compass Rose room.

Another popular attraction is the exterior glass-walled elevator. Ride up to the 31st floor for a great view of Union Square and the downtown area. You reach the elevator by proceeding to the back of the lobby (past the reception desk) and turning right. Incidentally, the Oz, a bar/disco on the top floor, is an ideal place to enjoy this commanding view. Or you may want to dine at the adjacent Victor's rooftop restaurant.

Clean Cash

Laundering money isn't a crime at the St. Francis, it's an institution. For the past thirty years, 85 year-old Arnold Batliner has been washing all the hotel's change on a regular basis. During his career he has cleaned $15.5 million in coins, more than $500,000 a year. The St. Francis initiated this custom in 1938 to help female guests avoid soiling their white gloves with dirty coins. Batliner gets the job done at his money laundry which includes a silver-burnishing machine that washes the coins with White King cleaning compound. The machine rotates the money for ninety minutes and then it is transferred to a dryer before being recounted and returned, spanking clean, to the cash drawers.

Across the way at Powell and Post is **Saks Fifth Avenue,** the high fashion store serving women, men, and children with fine apparel, accessories, gifts, and chocolates. There's also a restaurant here. Down the block at 360 Post is the Quantas Building where you'll find the offices of many foreign-government tourist offices and consulates, a real blessing if San Francisco is a stopover en route to an overseas destination.

After passing the **Bullock and Jones** emporium you'll come to the **Grand Hyatt on Union Square.** The plaza here is dominated by sculptor Ruth Asawa's fountain featuring wraparound bronze friezes. More than 250 San Franciscans from ages three to ninety collaborated with her on these bas-reliefs originally molded in bread dough. Outside tables on the plaza here make an inviting place for lunch on a sunny day.

Continue down Post Street toward Stockton and you'll come to one of San Francisco's most elegant stores, **Gump's.** Whether you want to buy a small gift or a fine antique, this is an ideal place to shop for oriental

Bay Area Mysteries

Here are ten mysteries with a Bay Area setting. Some are famous, some are not, but all will add to your enjoyment of the San Francisco Community.

"Behind That Curtain" by Earl Derr Biggers. Charlie Chan, the great Chinese detective solves two murders, one in San Francisco and one in London, 16 years apart.

"The Cable Car Murder" by Phoebe Taylor. A recovering alcoholic and a gruff old-fashioned S.F. detective uncover a trail of murder and deceit in San Francisco.

"The Case of the Seven of Calvary" by Anthony Boucher whose real name was William Anthony Parker White. For many years he wrote the influential *New York Times* mystery book review column from his Berkeley home. This book, his first novel, is set on the University of California at Berkeley campus with a professor of Sanskirt as its witty hero.

"Doctor Lawyer . . ." by Collin Wilcox. One of the Lt. Frank Hastings series, this police procedural follows the SFPD officer through several layers of San Francisco's population in his search for an extortionist.

"Edwin of the Iron Shoes" by Marcia Muller. Sharon McCone, a no-frills private investigator, knows the underside of the Bay Area as she searches for clues to the murder of an antique shop owner.

"Grave Error" by Stephen Greenleaf. A follower of the Hammett tradition, Greenleaf's private detective hero John Marshall Tanner investigates the blackmail of a consumer advocate and is soon embroiled in murder.

"Hammett" by Joe Gores, a writer who emulates the Hammett-Chandler tough guy school of writing, has re-created the wide-open San Francisco of the twenties with his fictionalized story of Dashiell Hammett's Pinkerton days.

"The Maltese Falcon" by Dashiell Hammett. The definitive San Francisco mystery, wherein Sam Spade unravels the enigmas within enigmas surrounding the beauteous Brigid O'Shaughnessy.

"Murder on the Air" by Ralph Warner and Toni Ihara. An unlikely pair of Berkeley Police Department detectives—a Japanese-American woman and an ex-sixties radical—trail through the ins and outs of the Eastbay's new age culture to trap a murderer.

"Random Access Murder" by Linda Grant. A feisty San Francisco private investigator tackles murder and mayhem in Silicon Valley.

goods, jewelry, accessories, china, crystal, and carved objects. There's also an excellent art gallery. At Christmas time, Gump's decorated windows literally stop traffic—they install everything from Victorian wind-ups in timely settings to A.S.P.C.A. puppies and kittens up for adoption. After visiting this lovely store return to Stockton Street and turn left to **Sanrio,** purveyors of the popular "Hello Kitty" line and other popular Japanese toys, clothes, and games. This shop is always a big hit with kids and an easy place to find little gifts for the folks back home. Across the street (Stockton between Post and Geary) is the **San Francisco Ticket Box Office Service.** You'll enjoy substantial discounts on plays and musicals by shopping for tickets good for that day's performance. It's open Tuesday through Thursday from noon to 7:30 P.M., and Friday through Saturday noon till 8 P.M. You must pay in cash. Phone 433-STBS for details.

MAIDEN LANE

Originally known as Morton Street, the former heart of the city's red-light district changed both its name and its image after the 1906 fire. Long gone are the prostitutes operating out of windows and the murders that plagued this overgrown alley—today, you'll see that Maiden Lane, which begins off the Stockton Street side of Union Square, has gentrified considerably. Sycamores line the sidewalks and old-fashioned street lamps add a note of class to this two-block area that bans traffic from 11 A.M. to 4 P.M. You can shop here for gifts at **Orvis,** print dresses at the **Diane Freis** boutique, classy sportswear at **Canterbury of New Zealand,** or traditional and contemporary art at the **Maiden Lane Gallery** (986-7475) at 111 Maiden Lane, Suite 310. The hours are Monday through Saturday, 10 A.M. to 5:30 P.M. Across the street, the **Circle Gallery Building** (designed by Frank Lloyd Wright in 1949) offers paintings, graphics, and exceptional jewelry designed by a variety of artists. The gallery's spiral interior ramp is a miniversion of the one he later brought to fruition at the Guggenheim Museum on New York's Fifth Avenue. The gallery is open Monday through Saturday, 10 A.M. to 6 P.M.; and Sunday, 11 A.M. to 4 P.M. Phone

989-2100 for details. **Hanson Galleries** (956-4338) at 153 Maiden Lane is a good place to look for paintings and sculpture by prominent contemporary artists. The gallery is open daily 10 A.M. to 7 P.M. For American impressionist prints try the **Richard Thompson Gallery** (956-2114) at 80 Maiden Lane. The gallery hours are Monday through Friday, 10 A.M. to 5 P.M.; Saturday, 10 A.M. to 3 P.M., but always call in advance.

Among the restaurants offering sidewalk tables on Maiden Lane is the **Nosheria.** This is a good place to lunch on gourmet salads and sandwiches. The marinated eggplant is a particular favorite.

By the way, if you need film or camera service, visit **Brooks Cameras** (392-1900) at Maiden Lane and Kearny Street. Incidentally, **Robinson's** (421-0310), the oldest business on Maiden Lane, got its start importing produce during the Gold Rush of 1849. After monkeys began leaping out of the banana crates, the company went into the pet business and has been there ever since.

Passionate shoppers in the Union Square area revive themselves with tea. Best known is the **Compass Rose** (397-7000) at the Westin St. Francis where a classical trio serenades guests while they sip Russian caravan, select cakes, or sample offerings from the caviar cart. Tea is served Mon.–Sat. 3–5 P.M. Arrive early to avoid the wait. At **Neiman Marcus's Rotunda** restaurant (362-4777) tea time is Thurs.–Sat. 3–5 P.M. Sandwiches, tarts, and muffins are all offered. A petit cream tea consisting of scones and tea is served during the same hours. Just off the square at 334 Mason St. between Geary and O'Farrell, the **King George Hotel** (781-5050) serves guests in the Bread and Honey Tea Room. In the true British manner guests enjoy finger sandwiches, crumpets, muffins, scones, tipsy trifle, and fresh breads. There's a classical pianist at the keyboard for this cozy event held Mon.–Sat. 3–6:30 P.M. **Campton Place** (781-5155), just off the square at 340 Stockton between Sutter and Post, serves tea in the bar every day from 2:30–4:30 P.M. Menu items include ice cream, fresh fruit sorbets, and the inimitable cucumber and watercress sandwiches. Other downtown hotels offering tea include the **Mandarin Oriental** and the **Park Hyatt.** On Nob Hill the **Mark Hopkins Inter-Continental** serves farmhouse fruitcake and scones on Wedgwood china while the nearby **Stanford Court** offers nine teas, cookies, pastries, and fresh fruit as an alternative to cocktails.

For tea in the true oriental tradition, try the **Japanese Tea Garden** in Golden Gate Park. Fortune cookies and tea are served here from 10:30 A.M. to 5:30 P.M. It's located off John F. Kennedy Drive.

SUTTER STREET

Just one block from Union Square, this is one of the city's most important commercial arteries. One way to reach Sutter is to walk from Union Square down Maiden Lane to Grant and turn left. Continue down Grant past Tillman Place to Sutter. On the way, stop in at the oldest established bar in San Francisco. **Templebar** at One Tillman Place boasts a beautiful rosewood and birch bar that has been in the city since 1853, and at its current address since 1907. Turn right on Sutter and continue across Kearny to the **Crocker Galleria.** This glass-domed mall is an inviting place to shop. Be sure not to miss **Japonesque,** a wonderful Japanese art store located on the third story. Directly across the street is architect Willis Polk's **Hallidie Building.** This landmark, which commemorates the inventor of the cable car, pioneered the glass-curtain-wall facade and is an important element of San Francisco's architectural makeup.

Continuing up Sutter past Kearny, you'll pass prominent clothing stores for women such as **Jeanne Marc** (262 Sutter) and **Jessica McClintock** (353 Sutter). **Wilkes Bashford,** offers designer-label clothing for men and women at 375 Sutter. For leather goods try **Portico d'Italia** at 469 Sutter. Across the street is one of the city's most important Art Deco landmarks, the **450 Sutter** building.

If you feel a sudden urge to crawl into a cave, consider **Lascaux** at 248 Sutter. A creation of the city's leading restaurant designer, Pat Kuleto, this basement-level establishment pays tribute to ancient cave art and offers European country food.

Chinatown

Most visitors to Chinatown look upon it as a foreign enclave in the midst of an American city. In fact, the heart of the original San Francisco, a tiny settlement known as Yerba Buena, was built around Portsmouth Square, the center of what is today the city's Chinatown. The first of a steady stream of immigrants from impoverished southern China's Guangdong Province arrived here in 1848. To them California was the Land of the Golden Mountain, the place where they could build a new life in the boomtown culture of the Gold Rush. The good news spread quickly as the new arrivals sent money home to impoverished relatives eager to escape China. As boatloads of Chinese arrived during the height of the Gold Rush, they became an important part of the local labor force and established a major commercial district focused around Grant, Kearny, and Stockton streets.

Portsmouth Square, which was called Little Canton, was an important and controversial part of bohemian San Francisco with its prostitution houses, opium parlors, bars, and gambling spots. Vigilante committees tried to put a stop to some of these practices by lynching suspected Chinese criminals on Portsmouth Square. As this racist hysteria subsided, the Chinese began to expand out into the Mother Lode to seek gold. They prospered in the mines and opened stores in the new towns springing up in the Sierra foothills. Later the Chinese were indispensable in the difficult job of constructing the transcontinental railroad route across the rugged Sierra Nevada. But their willingness to work for a dollar a day, a third to a fifth of what whites earned, led to strife in the labor market.

When the rail project was over and the job market tightened up, unemployed white laborers went on a vendetta against the Chinese, trying to drive them out of San Francisco. These sentiments were strong enough to prompt the writing and passing of the Chinese Exclusion Act, an 1882 federal bill designed to end the immigration of Chinese. The Chinese tongs, operating like syndicates to protect themselves, ran prostitution rings, controlled gambling parlors, and dealt opium. However, the tongs usually ended up fighting one another. Finally, after the 1906 earthquake leveled Chinatown, the district was rebuilt into its present form and as soon as the twenties tourism began here.

The Chinese were effectively segregated into this neighborhood until the end of World War II. Finally, with the lifting of the Exclusion Act and other restrictions, and the advent of fair-housing legislation, the Chinese-Americans were able to break down the segregation barriers. As the Chinese families spread out into other parts of the city, tourists began to come in ever larger numbers to sample the district's restaurants and shops. Glamorized in films such as *The Flower Drum Song,* this area is now the heart of the second-largest Chinese community in America. A large share of the city's 140,000 Chinese live in this 18-square-block district and adjacent streets in North Beach, and on Russian and Nob hills.

GRANT AVENUE

The oldest street in San Francisco, Grant Avenue was laid out in 1834 as part of the Yerba Buena pueblo. On the waterfront the first settlers built a group of New England–style frame buildings. And along the street known today as Grant Avenue, a group of small adobes was built. In early 1848, when Mexico ceded California and much of the southwest to Washington D.C., San Francisco remained an obscure coastal settlement. But, by the spring, news of John Marshall's discovery of gold at Coloma on the American River made San Francisco into the greatest boomtown the west had ever seen.

Today Grant Avenue, the city's first artery, stretches 1.6 miles from Market Street to Pier 39 and is one of the most popular walks in town. On the way to Chinatown from Market you'll pass such well-known establishments as Brooks Brothers, Tiffany & Co., Shreve & Co., Fila, Crate & Barrel, and Eileen West. At Bush Street an ornamental, green tiled gate welcomes you to Chinatown.

Kites, basketry, fabrics, foodstuffs, herbs, curios, and trinkets, many of them not made in China, are offered at shops along this famous street. Like all tourist zones,

Chinese Heritage Walk

One of the best ways to see Chinatown is to take the Chinese Culture Foundation walks. There's a **Chinese Heritage Walk** at 2 P.M. on Saturday or if you are a group of five or more you can take the **culinary walk** (which includes a luncheon) Wednesday at 10:30 A.M. For information and reservations call 986-1822. Another tour with "Wok Wiz" Shirley Fong-Torres, who is also an author and restaurant critic, runs daily at 9:30 A.M. and 2 P.M. for large groups. A dim sum lunch is included. Reserve by calling 981-5588.

much of the emphasis is on bargains. But you can also find exquisite jade, cultured pearls, fine silk, or antiques ideal for your home. The vast **Canton Market** at 111 Grant Avenue (362-5588) is a good bet for cloisonné enameled boxes, embroidery, china, and glassware. If you're looking for glorious kites to fly out by the ocean, try **Chinatown Kite Shop** at 717 Grant Avenue (391-8217). **Dai Fook Jewelry** at 848 Grant Avenue (391-1502) is an excellent place to shop for jade. **Far East Fashion** at 953 Grant Avenue (362-8171) has fine silk. For tea, try the **Ten Ren Tea Company** at 949 Grant Avenue (362-0656).

Our top restaurant choice is the **Hong Kong Tea House** at 835 Pacific Ave. (391-6365). A short walk from Grant, this is a great place to go for dim sum, which you select off bountiful rolling carts. **Yuet Lee** at 1300 Stockton St. (982-6020) serves excellent seafood. **Celadon** at 881 Clay St. (982-1168) is a good choice for entertaining, with a handsome dining room offering Cantonese specialties, Peking duck, and very good seafood. If you're just looking for a moon cake or sesame cookies head for the **Eastern Bakery** at 720 Grant (392-4497).

Chinatown also has many architectural landmarks. **St. Mary's Church** on the corner of Grant and California was built in 1854 out of brick brought around Cape Horn and granite cut in China. Diagonally, across California, is **St. Mary's Square,** where you'll find a statue of Sun Yat-sen, founder of the Chinese Republic.

Walking up Grant, it's fun to look at the gold dragons guarding the **Bank of America** branch at number 701 and temple dogs protecting **Citicorp Savings** at 845. The former **Chinatown Telephone Exchange** (now the Bank of Canton) is located near Grant at 743 Washington Street. Until 1949, when the dial system was introduced, this exchange was staffed by twenty operators fluent in five Chinese dialects. By memorizing the numbers of over 2,100 subscribers, they were able to assist numerous Chinese customers who asked for patrons by name rather than phone number.

One of the best places to get an overview of the region's past is the **Chinese Historical Society of America** (391-1188) at 650 Commercial. Here you can learn about the Chinese migration to California and the Asian community's role in the evolution of the West's mining, rail, and fishing industries. Hours are Tuesday through Saturday, 1 to 5 P.M. The **Chinese Cultural Center** (986-1822), located inside the Holiday Inn at 750 Kearny, also offers background on this community. It's across the street from Portsmouth Square. The span linking this historic spot with the hotel has been nicknamed "the Bridge over the River Kearny," although Kearny and the River Kwai bear little resemblance. A statue dedicated to Robert Louis Stevenson, who lived for a time in this area, can be found on the square's upper level. There's a parking garage beneath the square that is often difficult to get into. You're better off walking here, or taking a bus or taxi.

Back Alley

To get away from the tourist crowds, duck into one of the many alleyways that quickly put you in touch with old Chinatown. Here you get the feel of this district where, in the thirties, as many as twenty thousand people lived in a ten-block area. A good example is Wentworth Street, the little byway that connects Washington and Jackson streets. Another nice walk leads down Waverly Place from Sacramento Street to Washington Street (half a block west of Grant). The **Tien How Temple,** located on the top floor of 123 Waverly Place, is open 10 A.M. to 5 P.M. and 7 to 9 P.M.; it's just steps from the main tourist route but most visitors never get here. Built in 1852, the temple building has been ornamented with loggias, balconies, and bright lights.

Across from the plaza at 720 Washington is **Buddha Universal Church.** This white temple has beautiful mosaics, murals, and an interior richly ornamented with teak. There's also a little chapel with a pool of purifying water and a rooftop lotus pool. Phone 982-6116 to arrange a tour.

STOCKTON STREET

While Grant is the region's most heavily touristed street as it continues on across Broadway into North Beach, the Chinese community does much of its marketing in the 1000–1200 blocks of Stockton Street. Families come from all over the Bay Area to patronize the specialty shops here. Just one block over from Grant, this is the place to find glazed ducks, whole pigs, sharks' fins, and boxes of ginger roots and bamboo shoots. Check out the **Wo Soon Produce Company** (989-2350) at 1210 Stockton, and the **Canton Market** (982-8600) at 1135 Stockton, which sells fish. The market scene here is exactly what you'd expect to find in China. Also in this area, at 1208 Stockton, is the Obrero Hotel, one of the city's better lodging bargains. Call 989-3960. Another popular, moderately priced place to stay in Chinatown is the **Grant Plaza** (434-3883) at 465 Grant Avenue.

Financial District

The commercial heart of northern California, the financial district grew up with the Gold Rush and is now a major base for Pacific Rim trade. Within this skyscraper zone are the giants such as Bank of America, Wells Fargo Bank, and Pacific Stock Exchange, plus such multinationals as Transamerica, which occupies a pyramid-style building on Montgomery at Columbus Avenue. There are important architectural landmarks here, some of the city's best restaurants and hotels, compact urban parks, and museums. The best place to begin your visit is on the northern border in the Jackson Square Historic District.

JACKSON SQUARE

This square, formed by Jackson, Montgomery, Gold, and Sansome streets, is now an elegant spot with classy offices, shops, and restaurants. Jackson, between San-some and Hotaling Place, has become a center for art galleries and antique shops. But the square was not al-ways such a classy place. During the Gold Rush era this was a dangerous spot where the Argonauts ('49ers en-gaged in the quest for gold) fought it out at an intersec-tion called Murderer's Corner. Miners fresh from the Mother Lode stepped up to the counters of Gold and Balance streets where their nuggets and gold dust were weighed and assayed. The muddy streets were crowded with stagecoaches, hansom cabs, and drays. Miraculous-ly spared by the fire that consumed much of the city after the 1906 earthquake, this area fell into disrepair as the center of downtown shifted to the south.

Fortunately, in the early fifties, restoration work began and today you can tour fine landmarks on Jackson between Sansome and Montgomery. Among them are 415 Jackson Street (where Domingo Ghirardelli started his chocolate business) and 470 Jackson, former homes of the Spanish and Chilean consulates. Also here is the old **A.P. Hotaling and Co.** whiskey distillery at 451 Jackson.

Hotaling Place, a charming alley that retains its old hitching posts, is one of the best reasons to visit Jackson Square. It provides rear access to the 722–728 Mont-gomery Street building, the office of attorney Melvin Belli. The buildings in this block between Washington and Jackson streets are some of the oldest in town, red brick classics that you won't want to miss. Just two blocks east of Jackson, in the Golden Gateway residen-tial complex, is **Sidney Walton Park,** distinguished by the **Fountain of Four Seasons.** From this point you can walk up to Whaleship Plaza and then take a series of pedestrian bridges to reach the heart of today's finan-cial district. Alternatively you can walk up to Montgom-ery Street, to stroll down one of the district's most important corridors.

The **Transamerica Pyramid** at Clay and Montgom-ery is one of San Francisco's best-known landmarks. But most visitors miss the company's great gift to the finan-cial district, a redwood grove directly behind the build-ing—a great place to enjoy lunch or simply take a break. The **Pacific Heritage Museum,** entered just off Montgomery at 608 Commercial, is part of the Bank of Canton. This impressive collection focuses on Pacific

The High and The Mighty

For great views, drinks, dinner, and entertainment, try these sky rooms:

Carnelian Room—52nd floor, restaurant and cocktail lounge, Bank of America Building, 555 California Street, 433-7500.

Cityscape—46th floor, San Francisco Hilton, One Hilton Square, 776-0215.

One Up—Hyatt on Union Square, Stockton and Sutter, 398-1234.

Victor's restaurant and the **Oz** nightclub—32nd floor, Westin St. Francis, Powell and Geary, 956-7777.

S. Holmes Esq.—30th floor, Holiday Inn Union Square, Sutter and Powell, 398-8900.

Crown Room—24th floor, Fairmont Hotel, 950 Mason Street, 772-5131.

Starlite Roof—21st floor, Sir Francis Drake, Sutter and Powell, 392-7755.

Top of the Mark—19th floor, Mark Hopkins Inter-Continental, California and Mason, 392-3434.

Equinox—18th floor, Hyatt Regency San Francisco, 5 Embarcadero Center, 788-1234.

trade, culture, and history. It's open Monday to Friday, 10 A.M. to 4 P.M. Call 362-4100, extension 715 for information. Continue south to the **Wells Fargo Bank History Room** at 420 Montgomery Street. (See *Priorities.*) This is the city's best monument to the Gold Rush, with good exhibits on mining, commerce, and, of course, stagecoach transportation. Kids will love riding in the model coach. You can also look at a real Gold Rush era stage, one of the few that still survives. The museum is open Monday through Friday, 9 A.M. to 5 P.M. Nearby at 45 Kearny Street and Post is the **Joseph Dee Museum of Photography** (392-1900). The museum has an impressive collection of rare and antique cameras as well as interesting photo exhibits. Hours are Monday through Friday, 9 A.M. to 5 P.M.

There are many architecturally significant buildings in the financial district such as the **Russ Building** at 235 Montgomery, the **Mills Building and Tower** at

220 Montgomery, the **Hallidie Building** at 130 Sutter Street, the **Shell Building** at 100 Bush Street, and the Willis Polk–designed **Merchants Exchange** at 465 California Street. The black sculpture in front of the Bank of America building at 555 California Street is nicknamed "Banker's Heart."

☕ Some of the city's classiest restaurants are located in or adjacent to the financial district. They include the **Pierre** at the Meridien Hotel, 50 Third St., **Circolo** at 161 Sutter St., **Ernie's** at 847 Montgomery, **Masa's** at 648 Bush, and **Postrio** at 545 Post. (See *Restaurants*.)

South of Market

While it is not as well known as some of the city's residential neighborhoods, South of Market ("SoMa") is a favorite of locals who flock to its nightclubs, moderately priced restaurants, intriguing galleries, museums, experimental theaters, and discount stores. Roughly bounded by Market Street, the Embarcadero, China Basin, and Division Street, this onetime industrial area is just minutes from Union Square, yet it allows visitors a chance to get away from the busy tourist scene and join the locals in discovering a new area.

The newest waves in San Francisco nightlife are breaking right here. Every night of the week you can choose from jazz, blues, and rock entertainment. Restaurants and bars such as singer Boz Scaggs's Slim's, Julie's Supper Club, Hamburger Mary's, and the Paradise Lounge are all popular. At the Oasis, a two-level nightclub, the Jungle Room houses a 20-by-40-foot swimming pool that converts into a dance floor.

There are about twenty art galleries here and more than fifty discount shops offering savings of thirty to seventy percent on high-quality apparel. SoMa is also the home of the city's Moscone Convention Center and the city's first planned development, South Park, which was created in 1850. This oval park at Brannan and 3rd streets is surrounded by a variety of homes, studios, and shops.

MISSION STREET

Running parallel to Market Street, this main arterial begins at the Embarcadero, heads west, and then swings south into the Mission District. The SoMa portion of this street is a primary transportation hub beginning with the Transbay terminal (the city's main bus station) and Amtrak terminal. (Buses connect the city to the railhead to Oakland, twenty minutes away.) Just a block away from BART, Mission Street has traditionally been the line of demarcation between downtown and the city's industrial district to the south. That distinction is blurring as new hotels, office buildings, residential centers, and nightclubs spring up along the Mission corridor and points south.

Because of its proximity to the financial district, this is an excellent place to sample the San Francisco that standard tours don't show you. Mission and adjacent side streets are the place to find anything slightly funky, New-Wave, or revived from the fifties. From gay dance palaces to some of the best Mexican food in town, the Mission is a fascinating place. It's also an area in transition, which means that you're well advised to travel here by taxi or car during the evening hours.

Beginning at the bay, the Mission area caters heavily to office workers who enter the city through the Transbay terminal. East of the terminal at 121 Steuart Street (between Mission and Howard streets) is the **Jewish Community Museum** (543-8880) which showcases Jewish art and culture both past and present in a series of changing exhibits, lectures, and multimedia presentations. Open Tuesday, Wednesday, Friday, and Sunday 10 A.M. to 4 P.M.; and Thursday till 8 P.M. If you walk west up Mission you'll see some of the city's discount outlets and off-prices stores specializing in apparel and accessories. For menswear, check out the **Kutler Bros.'** racks at 585 Mission Street (543-7770). The **Van Heusen Factory Store** (243-0750) at 601 Mission and 2nd streets offers shirts for men and women as well as sportswear.

In this same area just off Mission Street at 140 New Montgomery Street (between 2nd and 3rd) is the **Pacific Telephone Building.** This modern classic is one of the finest skyscrapers in the city, a handsome tower sheathed with terra-cotta. Don't miss the lobby with its Chinese ceiling decor. There's a modest **Telecommunication Museum** (542-0182) here, open weekdays 10 A.M. to 2 P.M., run by the Telephone Pioneers of America.

A few blocks away is the **Moscone Convention Center** at 747 Howard Street between 3rd and 4th streets. Named for George Moscone, who was assassinated by former city supervisor Dan White in 1978, this complex was the site of the 1984 Democratic National Convention. It's part of the Yerba Buena redevelopment area which includes private residences, new hotels such as the San Francisco Marriott (the controversial new jukebox-style building between Market and Mission), and office buildings.

Nearby at 665 Third Street and Townsend is the **Cartoon Art Museum** (546-3922). Located on the fifth floor, this museum exhibits a wide variety of cartoon art and artifacts including works from newspapers, magazines, comic books, and animation art. Open Wednesday through Friday, 11 A.M. to 5 P.M.

Another popular spot in this area is the **Hotel Utah** at 500 4th St. (421-8308). Owned by Paul Gaier who wrote the script for *The Electric Horseman*, this is an eclectic place patronized by a cross section of humanity. White- and blue-collar patrons flock to this establishment. It features a bar that was brought around Cape Horn to help promote a Belgian brewery in the 1850s—a gift to the saloon operator who agreed to stock this European import. From 1946 to 1978 this spot was known as Big Al's Transbay Tavern and patrons included the likes of Joe DiMaggio and Marilyn Monroe. This is the bar of choice for people who like to look at the mounted heads of trophy animals and bus-route signs.

At 5th Street and Mission is the **Old Mint** (744-6830), a classical-revival landmark done in granite. Once the nation's leading mint, this museum offers tours on the hour that include a look at rare-coin collections, gold nuggets, and minting. A film, *The Granite Lady,* tells the building's history. The free museum is open weekdays 11 A.M. to 4 P.M.

Continue up Mission to 7th Street and turn right to the **Tattoo Art Museum** (864-9798). Located at 30 7th

Street, this museum and tattoo parlor tells you everything you'd want to know about the craft of tattooing from the tools of the trade to a gallery of famous tattoos. It's open daily, noon to midnight; no charge. The museum is owned by Lyle Tuttle, possibly the world's most tattooed man.

SoMa Nightclubs

If you like to party, look no further. Just take a taxi from your hotel over to one of these establishments all located just minutes from major downtown hotels:

The Oasis Nightclub and Grill, 11th and Folsom, 621-8119, is the only nightclub in America with a swimming pool that converts into a dance floor. There's open swimming here Sunday through Wednesday and sometimes during Friday happy hour. In the evening the plastic dance floor goes back on top of the swimming pool so you can literally dance on water. Happy hours Friday afternoon and all day Sunday offer free drinks. There's a cover charge of $8 after 9 P.M. This is also a pleasant spot for lunch on a sunny day.

The DNA Lounge, 375 11th, 626-1409, is a good place to sample local rock in a warehouse setting. The decibel level is high and there's a big bar scene. Fashion shows and poetry readings are staged here.

Club DV8, 540 Howard Street, 957-1730, is another popular dance palace in a warehouse renovated with ersatz marble columns. This is the place to catch rock and New Wave.

Slim's, owned by singer Boz Scaggs, at 333 11th, 621-3330, emphasizes New Orleans music: blues, rock, R&B, jazz, and Cajun, all served up with California cuisine.

Another possibility is **Lipp's Underground** (Howard and 9th, 552-3466). Popular gay clubs include the **Endup** (401 6th Street, no phone listing) and the **Stud** (3999 9th Street, 863-6624).

For Mexican food there are two good possibilities. **Chevys** (543-8060) at 150 4th St. serves great fajitas. The Rube Goldberg–style tortilla machine is fun to watch. Another popular spot is **Cadillac Bar** (543-8226) at 1 Holland Court, whose vast menu includes many seafood specialties.

  Max's Diner (546-6297) at 311 3rd St. also offers American cuisine in a crowded deli setting. Across the street from Moscone Center, this establishment serves good buffalo chicken wings, short ribs in Russian cabbage soup, and chicken fried steak. There's also the inevitable corned beef, pastrami, and chicken liver. If you're not maxed out here you can also try sister establishments such as **Max's Opera Café** (771-7300) at 601 Van Ness Ave.

Moderately priced **Eddie Jacks** (626-2388) at 1151 Folsom is a good place at happy-hour time when you can get an alternative to french fries called fried polenta sticks. For lunch or dinner the seafood stew here is great, as is the mixed grill.

To enjoy SoMa's waterfront ambience, why not try **The Sailing Ship Restaurant** (777-5771) at Pier 42, the Embarcadero. This old lumber schooner is a fine place to enjoy the bay. As you'd expect, the emphasis is on seafood. In the same neighborhood at 817 China Basin Rd. is the **Mission Rock Resort** (621-5538). Located on Mission Creek, this is a great, sunny spot to sample their lunch fare of burgers, fish, and salads. Few tourists find the Mission Rock even though it's just five minutes from downtown by taxi.

South Park Café (495-7275) at 108 South Park St. is a Parisian café adjacent to an English-style park in the midst of an industrial neighborhood. For basic fare, two SoMa establishments are recommended. **Hamburger Mary's** (626-5767) at 12th and Folsom sts. has a saloon-style atmosphere, excellent bloody Mary's, and a classic jukebox. For coffee-shop fare try the **Rite Spot Café** (552-6066) at 2099 Folsom St.

When the tour buses start showing up at factory outlets, you know SoMa has made it as a discount-shopping mecca. But this district is more than just a place to save money off the retail sticker. At the **Butterfield and Butterfield auction house** (861-7500), 220 San Bruno Street, you can bid for Warhol prints, rare triple slot machines, English antiques, and other one-of-a-kind items.

The **Galleria Design Center** (431-2321) at 101 Henry Adams and **Showplace Design Center** (864-2400) at 2 Henry Adams, near 8th and 9th streets, are fine examples of adaptive reuse. These two warehouses have been turned into handsome showrooms for home furnishings. Another complex worth visiting is the **San Francisco Jewelry Center** (552-5272) at 101 Utah Street. Thirty stores here cater to every taste.

Of course bargains are the red meat that draws thousands of shoppers south of Market every day. More than fifty stores offer great deals for the fashion-conscious. Companies such as **Esprit, Wilkes Bashford, Grodin's,** and **Burlington** all operate outlet stores. Many of them are clustered in the area between 2nd and 5th, and Bryant and Townsend streets. Shop here for a day and you may need another suitcase to take home all your bargains.

Although not technically South of Market, the neighboring complex known as the **Civic Center** is a cultural cornucopia ranging from the ballet to major jazz joints.

The Civic Center

Architect Daniel Burnham, whose impressive list of accomplishments ranges from Washington D.C.'s Union Station to the Manila Hotel in the Philippines, came up with the concept for this cultural arena. The centerpiece is the domed **City Hall** located between Polk, Van Ness, Grove, and McAllister. Directly behind City Hall are the San Francisco **Opera House** and **Museum of Modern Art.** The museum's highlights include paintings by Picasso, Kandinsky, Matisse, and Braque. Among the Latin American artists featured are Diego Rivera and his wife Frida Kahlo. Some North American works displayed are by Jackson Pollock, Jasper Johns, and Robert Rauschenberg. The museum is open Tuesdays, Wednesdays, and Fridays from 10 A.M. to 5 P.M. Thursdays hours are 10 A.M. to 9 P.M. Weekends the museum is open from 11 A.M. to 5 P.M. Admission is $3.50 for adults. Seniors and children under 16 are $1.50. Call 863-8800.

Louise M. Davies Symphony Hall at Van Ness and Grove (431-5400) is home of the San Francisco Symphony. Many other concerts are held nearby at **Herbst Theatre** (552-3656), 401 Van Ness Avenue. Near Davies Symphony Hall is the **San Francisco Opera Shop** (199 Grove Street, 565-6414), a must for music buffs in need of souvenirs ranging from music boxes to opera glasses. The **War Memorial Opera House,** at 301 Van Ness Avenue, is a gem. Ballet, as well as opera, is performed here. Call 864-3330 for information.

Also in the neighborhood is one of the city's leading jazz venues, Kimball's at 300 Grove Street (861-5555).

North Beach

You may be wondering where this celebrated neighborhood's name came from. Over a century ago, before the bayfront was filled in, North Beach was the city's northern waterfront. Today it's the city's café front—and a rapidly gentrifying one, at that. While its ethnic heritage is predominantly Italian, escalating rents and the gradual encroachment of the financial district have pushed out many of the old-timers. This region has been the center of much that's new and hot, from Carol Doda, pioneer of the Broadway topless nightclub scene, to Lawrence Ferlinghetti, in San Francisco. Joe DiMaggio began playing sandlot ball here. The Beats got their start at the local coffeehouses. And today, restaurants include amateur operas with the price of a meal.

An indispensable part of any visit to San Francisco, North Beach is the natural gateway to Telegraph Hill, Coit Tower, and the often overlooked Filbert Steps, one of the city's finest walks. For breakfast, lunch, or dinner, nightlife, shopping, or just about anything else you might care to try, North Beach is the perfect San Francisco neighborhood.

COLUMBUS AVENUE (SOUTH OF BROADWAY)

The place to begin a tour of North Beach is **Columbus Tower** at 906 Kearny Street (and Columbus). This green flatiron building, built by political boss Abe Ruef following the 1906 earthquake, was a major San Francisco power center. With the help of his political front man, mayor Eugene Schmitz, Ruef milked the public trough until finally, in 1907, he was convicted and sent to jail. This political scandal triggered a reform movement that led to the election of Governor Hiram Johnson in 1910. The building is now owned by film producer Francis Ford Coppola.

City Lights Bookstore (362-8193) at 261 Columbus Avenue near Broadway is another North Beach landmark. Poet Lawrence Ferlinghetti owns the shop and publishing company that gave such poets as Allen Ginsberg their start. Enjoy the wonderful selection of poetry, fiction, Californiana, political works, and everything else you'd expect to find in a classy bookstore. Try to come for an evening poetry reading. By the way, this is not a high-pressure, hard-sell environment. Tables on the lower level make it possible for you to read as much as you want before taking any book home. For used books and some new titles, walk across to **Columbus Books** (986-3872) at 540 Broadway.

Next door to City Lights, at 255 Columbus Ave., is **Vesuvio Café** (362-3370). Once favored by the Beats, Vesuvio continues to attract the young, restless, blue-collar types and the arts crowd. Like such former patrons as Jack Kerouac, Dylan Thomas, Bob Dylan, and physicist Robert Oppenheimer, they consider it the bar of choice in a city with very stiff competition.

You're now in the heart of silicone valley—the topless joints made famous by the likes of Carol Doda. Back before blue movies gave way to X-rated videos and live sex shows, like those at Mitchell Brothers' Theater and the O'Farrell Theater, appeared on the scene, the topless and bottomless parlors were the place aspiring performers tried to undress for success. Today establishments such as the **Condor** (392-4443) at 300 Columbus Avenue and Broadway continue to offer these so-called love acts. Down at 506 Broadway the tour buses continue to flock to **Finocchio's** nightclub (982-9388), the drag-queen capital of North Beach.

GRANT AVENUE

The North Beach section of this street ascends Telegraph Hill. Once an Italian stronghold, this eclectic neighborhood has caught some of the spillover from Chinatown. The 1200 to 1500 blocks are the place to find interesting shops, stores, clubs, and restaurants. **Figoni Hardware** (392-4765) at 1351 Grant Avenue is the kind of neighborhood-oriented retail business that dominated this street before North Beach became a trendy destination. Peek inside for a look at a traditional hardware store that offers houseware, hardware, and gifts. The **Panama Canal Ravioli Factory** (421-1952) at 1358 Grant is typical of the venerable shops serving the Italian community. For bread try the **Italian French Baking Co.** (421-3796) at 1501 Grant Avenue. **R. Iacopi and Co. delicatessen** (421-0757) at Grant

Lost In A Fog

It was one of those good San Francisco days—gray and misty. If you could keep from looking at the Bank of America Building, it could have been a day in the 1930s, the city's last golden age. Drench coat weather. Dashiell Hammett might have been puttering around at Bush and Stockton, setting the scene for Miles Archer's murder in *The Maltese Falcon.* Jake Ehrlich and his latest girl, a blonde nine feet tall, should have been drinking Cutty in the far corner of Fred Solari's bar. Bill Saroyan, in sneakers, sneaking up to Anita Zabala Howard's penthouse at 1001 California? At John's Grill in the Tenderloin, the bookies are gathering for a 2 P.M. breakfast, dividing the spoils over steak and eggs (hi Marty, hello Benny).

A day to churn memories and stomachs. At Fifth and Mission—Filth and Mish' to the regulars—Mel Ravella, the good traffic cop, was dodging signal jumpers and muttering, "They're crazy, they're all crazy." A Volkswagen jumped the light and swerved left, narrowly missing two pedestrians, Mel whistling at the driver in vain. What makes it funny is that the driver was wearing a safety harness. And he had a Flag decal on the back window to show he's a good American light jumper.

Like a homely pigeon, I headed northward, toward all that is left of the old town, if you don't count the back yards of the Deep Mission and the Victorians of the Western Addition. I walked along Grant Avenue, past the ornate lampposts with their dragons entwined around tourists. Grant *Avenue,* young-timer. Just because City Hall is so chintzy these days that the street signs don't tell you whether you're on a street, avenue, boulevard or what is no excuse for not remembering it's Grant *Avenue.* Still sniffling 1930, I kept trying to avert my eyes from B of A, Crocker, Alcoa and all those other dark buildings thrown up by newcomers with cold New York hearts who think this town is Chicago. It's hard to measure how much damage they've done to San Francisco, but it's considerable. The old-timers, who knew what San Francisco was all about, built their buildings to scale and made the city grow beautiful. The giants have passed on and now we have rich pygmies with ego problems.

I slid down the Chinatown hill toward Kearny, past crated ducks and winter melons, staring at a freighter moving slowly across the leaden Bay. . . .

Lost in a foggy memory, I wandered around North Beach, reliving the vanished summertimes. Past La Tosca (uptight Italian, where Allen Ginsberg was once thrown out), past Vesuvio (where Ginsberg licked his wounds) . . . On Columbus, Carol Doda came swinging past, jaunty in brown tam, jacket and bell-bottoms; with her clothes on, she's one pretty girl. Across from the Gold Spike, the tiny shoeshine stand run by a sad-looking woman and today she looked even sadder—who gets a shine on a drizmal day? I stepped into the little Italian newsstand nearby and bought an *Oggi* and a *Domenica del Corriere.* I don't read Italian but it seemed the thing to do and besides somebody has to keep these little places alive.

Back on Broadway, I felt a pang that could have been nostalgia or hunger. Deciding it must be the latter, I fell into Yank Sing, which the most knowledgeable Chinese favor for dim sum (teahouse-style food). The place was crowded with knowing-look Chinese, chattering at round tables. And prebeatnik bohemians who know where to shop for a buck. Also some straight Montgomery Streeters with their secretaries, smugly sure they wouldn't bump into anybody who knew them. You can imagine how delighted they were to see me. Yank Sing. It sounds like the title of a World War II movie about a GI stool pigeon caught by the Japanese. In my phony phonetic Chinese, I ordered Poy Nay tea, steamed pork buns (it's the same in English), Hai Gow, Sei Chai, Sei, Sei Mai and Chai Sei Bow. French touch in this very Oriental place: at the end of the meal, the waiter counts the plates—just as a waiter does in a Parisian sidewalk cafe—and figures out your check.

It was less than an hour later that I felt hungry again, so I stopped at an Italian bakery and bought a cream puff. There is only one way to eat a walking-around cream puff without getting goo all over yourself: you take off the top and use it as a spoon to scoop up the cream. That's the way we did it in the thirties, when spring came every day to San Francisco, and it still works here in the winter of the malcontents.

—Herb Caen
One Man's San Francisco, 1976

and Union shares a storefront with an intriguing second-hand store called the **Schlock Shop** (781-5335). At 1441 Grant, **Quantity Postcards** (986-8866) is a good place to find something a bit more distinctive than another panorama of the Golden Gate Bridge.

Turn at Union Street to walk down to Stockton Street

North Beach Café Society

North Beach is loaded with cafés ideal for watching the passing scene. Among them are:

Caffé Gaetano (397-0435) at 348 Columbus Avenue serves excellent cappuccino, Italian fare, wine, and beer.

Caffé Puccini (989-7033), 411 Columbus Avenue. The opera-oriented decor is complemented by excellent baked goods, desserts, beer, and wine.

Caffé Roma (391-8584) at 414 Columbus Avenue is perfect for patio dining. It serves pizza, pasta, and desserts.

Caffé Malvina (391-1290) at 1600 Stockton has a good view of Washington Square. Serves pizza and pastries.

Caffé Freddy's (922-0151), 901 Columbus Avenue. More views of Washington Square Church with Mediterranean fare.

Savoy Tivoli (362-7023), 1434 Grant Avenue. Filled with artwork and antiques, this venerable establishment, serving paella and sangria, is ideal for patio dining.

Caffé Trieste (392-6739), 601 Vallejo. If you're in the neighborhood on Saturday afternoon, stop by, have a drink, and enjoy the free opera performance. A real San Francisco treat!

and **Washington Square.** The statue of Benjamin Franklin was donated by H.D. Cogswell, the eccentric dentist and prohibitionist who fought the good fight in the late 19th century to make this hard-drinking town dry. On the park at 666 Filbert Street is the **Saints Peter and Paul Church** (421-0809). The annual October parade to bless the fishing fleet departs from this Romanesque landmark.

To get a sense of the area's history, walk to the **North Beach Museum** (626-7070) at 1435 Stockton. The museum is located on the mezzanine level of the Eureka Federal Savings. Hours are Monday through Thursday, 10 A.M. to 4 P.M.; Friday, 10 A.M. to 5:30 P.M.; Saturday, 10 A.M. to noon. A few doors away at 1441 Stockton Street is **A. Cavalli and Co.** (421-4219), an Italian bookstore in a distinguished century-old building.

Continue on to Greenwich and turn left to **Columbus,** this time to the north of Broadway. The North Beach playground spawned many star athletes such as

Joe DiMaggio and Hank Luisetti. There's a swimming pool here open to the public.

Walk back up Columbus toward downtown to try some of the popular cafés and local favorites such as **Molinari's Deli** (421-2337) at 373 Columbus Avenue, which has been serving customers since the turn of the century. Not far away at 678 Green Street, between Columbus Avenue and Powell Street, is **Club Fugazi** (see *Priorities*), an Italianate theater offering the city's venerable musical revue, *Beach Blanket Babylon*.

TELEGRAPH HILL

Return to Grant Avenue and head north to Filbert Street, which takes you to Telegraph Boulevard. From here it's a healthy walk up to the top of Telegraph Hill and **Coit Tower**. After enjoying the view and seeing the Tower murals you can walk down the **Filbert Steps** on the east side of the hill to Sansome Street and **Levi Plaza**. Headquarters of the Levi Strauss jeans empire, this is a pleasant place for lunch.

If you're looking for ambience in a restaurant, **Julius Castle** (362-3042) at 1541 Montgomery is a Telegraph Hill tradition with terrific views. The **Washington Square Bar and Grill** (982-8123) at 1707 Powell St. is the city's best-known literary/culinary hangout.

Fisherman's Wharf

Each spring, the busy wedding season in Japan, travel agents sell their engaged clients the ultimate vacation. It begins with a honeymoon-night red-eye flight to San Francisco. Once there, all the newlyweds are immediately taken to the city's ultimate tourist destination— Fisherman's Wharf.

Like the cable cars and Coit Tower, Fisherman's Wharf is a must-see, a place where all visitors have to help themselves to a walking shrimp cocktail, eyeball Alcatraz through the $.25 telescopes and check out the fleet. Of course some of what's purveyed on the wharf— the fudge shops, tacky souvenir stands, artists who sketch your portrait in two minutes, and wax museum— are hardly unique to this city. But with just a minimum of effort you can turn a casual visit to the wharf into a highlight of your trip. As noted in the hotel section, the wharf has one of the city's best hotel bargains (the San Remo) and many other establishments are a pleasant alternative to the popular downtown hotels. Excellent dining spots offer everything from light snacks to Hungarian cuisine. Easily reached by cable car, this area also boasts some of the best street theater in town as well as a fleet of historic ships, jazz and comedy clubs, calypso music, and sailboat, helicopter, and ferry rides that show off the bay.

THE EMBARCADERO

This bay-front boulevard was once the center of Bay Area maritime activity, welcoming both passengers and freight to the city. Most of the freight business has moved to Oakland and other ports while only a handful of ocean liners call here. But several of the piers have destinations of major interest to visitors. On the way to Fisherman's Wharf, near Lombard Street, is **Pier 23** (362-5125), a popular restaurant and jazz club with good views of the bay. Continue up Embarcadero to **Pier 39.** Here adaptive reuse has created a shopping plaza where you can buy T-shirts, luggage, cookies, music boxes, leather goods, and major-league baseball caps. From churro stands to restaurants such as Swiss Louis and the Eagle Café, there are dozens of eating options. One stand that didn't make it was the Hot Potato. It was owned by San Francisco Supervisor Dan White who, after resigning his position in 1978, murdered Mayor George Moscone and fellow Supervisor Harvey Milk (a gay-rights leader). At his trial White's attorney claimed that excessive quantities of Hostess Twinkies elevated the defendant's blood-sugar level, leading to temporary insanity. This so-called "Twinkie defense" led to a relatively light sentence and prompted gay riots in protest. After serving seven years in jail White was paroled, finally committing suicide a few years later.

Continuing past the Alcatraz ferry dock at Pier 41, you'll soon come to the **U.S.S. Pampanito** berth at Pier 45. A fascinating audio tour is narrated by sailors who served on this World War II sub. (As of this writing, the Pampanito is temporarily closed due to earthquake damage to the pier building. There is a good possibility that the sub will be moved to a different location in the

Street Theater

You can find street performers all over town, but the city's mecca for jugglers, mimes, musicians, and magicians is Fisherman's Wharf between Aquatic Park and Pier 39. Many of the best acts are found along Jefferson and Beach streets or on the outdoor stages of Ghirardelli Square, the Cannery, Pier 39, and the Anchorage. Stage shows at the shopping centers usually run from noon to 9 P.M. weekdays, and hours are extended to as late as midnight on weekends. These scheduled acts change every twenty to thirty minutes. On the street, performers work their own schedules. Tips are always welcome.

Among the performers you might catch on any given day are:

Silky the Clown, a one-man band who plays drums, banjo, harmonica, and slide whistle.

Ray Jason, a juggler who also does half-time shows at San Francisco 49ers football games.

John Park and Scott Meltzer, the American Dream Juggling Team, who sit on unicycles and munch apples while juggling cleavers and machetes.

Many performers have gone on to higher callings after breaking into the entertainment world on the wharf. They include Harry Anderson of TV's "Night Court," A. Whitney Brown of "Saturday Night Live," and Michael Davis who now does commercials. Others such as magician Robert Kirk, who liked to lie on a blanket covering 1,600 screws piercing a plate of Plexiglas, have left the scene. The highlight of Kirk's act came when he placed a cinder block on his chest and then asked an audience volunteer to smash it with a twenty-pound sledgehammer.

Fisherman's Wharf area. Call 929-0202 for information.) The vessel neighbors one of the city's most notable attractions—the **San Francisco Maritime National Historical Park.** If you continue walking along the wharf to Hyde Street Pier, you'll find six ships that are floating historic landmarks. They include the square-rigged Cape Horn ship *Balclutha* and the *C.A. Thayer,* a classic lumber schooner. Also here is the *Eureka,* one of the many ferries that served the bay earlier in the century. All three vessels are open to visitors who can see them on self-guided tours. Also berthed here, but not open to the public, are the tug *Hercules* (currently under restoration), the paddle tug *Eppleton Hall,* and the *Alma,* a scow schooner. If you walk across Aquatic Park, you'll come to the boat-shaped Maritime Museum building which houses an extensive seafaring collection. You can visit the Hyde Street Pier (556-6435) daily from 10 A.M. to 5 P.M.; till 6 P.M. in summer. Admission is $2 for adults, free for children and seniors. The museum building (556-2904) is open daily 10 A.M. to 6 P.M. May to October and 10 A.M. to 5 P.M. November to April. There's wheelchair access at both sites. Next door at Fort Mason is the World War II Liberty Ship freighter, the *Jeremiah O'Brien* (441-3101). Open daily 9:30 A.M. to 3:30 P.M. Admission is $2 for adults, $1 for children and seniors.

For Japanese food on Fisherman's Wharf, try **Tokyo Sukiyaki** (775-9030) at 225 Jefferson St. On Pier 39, **Swiss Louis Restaurant** (771-4383) offers Italian cuisine. Also part of this complex is the venerable Eagle Café. When Pier 39 was built in 1978, this restaurant was literally kicked upstairs to a second-story location. Fortunately none of the memorabilia or formica tables were tampered with when the restaurant was hoisted to the upper level. Today the **Eagle Café** (433-3689) is a good spot for breakfast or lunch. Try the cornbeef hash and enjoy nice views of the waterfront. The bar, open until 1:30 A.M., is one of the best in town. **Pier 23** (362-5125), down the Embarcadero near Lombard, is a good bet for American home cooking. It has an excellent outdoor dining area and jazz.

Two shopping venues worth visiting on the wharf are the **Cannery** and Ghirardelli Square. The former, at Leavenworth and Jefferson streets, is an old Del Monte packing plant with courtyard restaurants, a movie theater, and specialty shops. On the Cannery's ground level, at 2801 Leavenworth, is one of the city's best comedy clubs, **Cobb's** (928-4320). The **San Francisco International Toy Museum** (441-TOYS) is another Cannery hit; open Tuesday through Saturday, 10 A.M. to 5 P.M., it features toys from all over the globe. Not far from the Cannery, at 2552 Taylor Street, is **Cost Plus Imports** (928-6200), a bazaar offering everything

from basketry and toys to clothes and cookware imported from 35 countries around the world.

Carousel Country

Across the street from the Cannery at 633 Beach Street
is the **American Carousel Museum.** The 75 animal artifacts found here were handcrafted in the golden age of carousels between 1880 and 1920. Two glassed-in workshops
give visitors a chance to watch restoration work. The museum is open from 10 A.M. to 6 P.M. daily. Phone 928-0550.
Admission is $2 for adults, $1 for seniors and youths 13
to 17; under 12 admitted free.

If you'd like to ride a carousel try one of the 52 animals
on the merry-go-round at the **San Francisco Zoo.** Tickets are $.75 unless you can fit on one of your parents' lap.
The wooden roundabout at the **Children's Playground**
in Golden Gate Park has 62 nicely restored animals. It is
open daily 10 A.M. to 5 P.M. in the summer, and Wednesday
through Sunday from October to May. The carousel is located in the park's southeast corner. Adults pay $1, chil-
dren $.25. Kids under 39 inches are free with an adult.

On Fisherman's Wharf there's a 24-pony, double-deck
carousel at the end of **Pier 39.** It operates from 9:30 A.M.
to 9:30 P.M., Sunday through Thursday, and until 11:30 P.M.
on Friday and Saturday. Rides are $1.

Other carousels in the region are located at Berkeley's
Tilden Park, the Oakland Zoo, Kennedy Park in Hayward,
Happy Hollow Park and Zoo in San Jose's Kelley Park,
Great America in Santa Clara, the Santa Cruz Beach Board-
walk, and The Edgewater Packing Company on Cannery
Row in Monterey.

Ghirardelli Square (900 North Point), the first
American industrial plant to be made over into a retail
complex, has a perfect location below Aquatic Park.
Kites, clocks, hammocks, model ships, and gifts are sold
here. The **Ghirardelli Chocolate Manufactory**
(771-4903) offers ice cream sodas, hot fudge sundaes,
and other confections. Even if you're not hungry, come
in for a look at the antique chocolate-making equipment
at the rear of the manufactory. The **San Francisco
Craft and Folk Art Museum** (775-0990) at Fort
Mason Center brings international folk art to the square.
Hours are Tuesday through Sunday, 11 A.M. to 5 P.M.;
Saturday, 10 A.M. to 5 P.M.

☕ The best restaurant view on Fisherman's Wharf is at Ghirardelli Sq.'s **Paprikas Fono** (441-1223) at 900 North Point. Here's your chance to try Hungarian specialties such as gulyas soup and *palacsintas* (Hungarian crepes). The langos bread is great. Also in the square is the **Gaylord Indian** restaurant (771-8822). For light sandwich fare try the **Boudin Sourdough Bakery and Café** at Ghirardelli Sq. (928-7404) or 156 Jefferson St. (928-1849) in the heart of the wharf area. Just down the street from Ghirardelli, at 2765 Hyde St., is the **Buena Vista Café** (474-5044), the very crowded establishment that invented Irish coffee.

Nob Hill

An easy cable-car ride up California Street from downtown, Nob Hill is an essential part of any visit to San Francisco. Some people love it so much they insist on staying in one of the hotels perched atop this small summit. Once home to the city's wealthiest residents, Nob Hill is now hotels and restaurants, apartment buildings and clubs, and auditoriums and shops which cater to a cross section of San Franciscans. You don't have to be rich to live here, but it certainly helps.

Nob Hill's story begins with the Gold Rush. Winners in this mining sweepstakes built their baronial mansions, splendid adobe-style homes, and wooden villas in this prime location. European castles were unburdened of their treasures by agents acting for these new Nob Hill millionaires who shipped fine art back to the wharves of San Francisco. Ordinary citizens, many of them in dire straits, watched in amazement as workmen carried these spoils into the mansions by the crateload. Eager to ease the uphill load on their horses, the people of Nob Hill anted up for their own cable-car line which continues to climb California Street today.

Rich in symbolism, Nob Hill was, in a sense, the aerie of the Gold Rush, a place where the haves could look down on those who wished they were there. Perhaps the richest symbol of all was James Flood's $30,000 brass fence, brightly polished every day of the week. As lawsuits and muckrakers would ultimately prove, the outrageous fortunes of the great men of Nob Hill were the product of white-collar crime. As dramatized in the film *San Francisco* (where a wealthy matron watches her mansion being dynamited by fire-fighting crews), the great earthquake and fire leveled much of the hill—some San Franciscans believed they were seeing divine retribution at its finest. But the barons of Nob Hill were also the city's leading philanthropists, endowing some of today's most important institutions, museums, and parks. Their enterprises also grew to become major employers in San Francisco and the rest of California.

Today Nob Hill is one of the best places to stay in San Francisco. It is also a great way to round out a day here. At twilight it is one of the city's magical spots. Even 15 minutes on the hill is worth the climb from Union Square or the financial district.

CALIFORNIA STREET

California Street is Nob Hill's main line. Powell Street, where the city's three cable-car lines intersect, is an ideal point to begin your visit. The Stanford Court, at 905 California; the Mark Hopkins Inter-Continental, at 999 California; the Fairmont Hotel, at 950 Mason; and the Huntington Hotel, 1075 California, are four of the city's best-known hotels (see *Hotels*).

The Stanford Court, located on the site of railroad baron Leland Stanford's famous mansion (only part of the original walls remains), has a very pleasant, albeit expensive, spot for breakfast called **Café Potpourri** (989-3500). For a change of pace, why not try the blue-cornmeal waffle? This is also a good choice for lunch. If you only have a minute, at least peek in to see the hotel's architectural highlight, a courtyard domed with Tiffany-style glass.

The Mark Hopkins is best known for its rooftop lounge, with great views of the city. Built on the site of the architecturally controversial home built by Mark's widow, Mary, this hotel was frequently chosen by Barbara Hutton for her honeymoons. Before they shipped out for the Pacific campaigns, many sailors spent their last night stateside toasting at the Top of the Mark. The terra-cotta ornamented entryway may look familiar to Hitchcock fans. That's because this hotel was featured in *Vertigo*. Be sure to visit the Room of the Dons where the story of California is told in the mural art of Maynard Dixon and Frank Van Sloun. All the fanciful figures stand in relief against a solid gold background.

The Fairmont, featured in the television series "Hotel," offers two contrasting environments. The lobby of the original building is dominated by golden marble columns. Ride the elevator to the top of the tower and enjoy a drink in the Crown Room. You'll be rewarded with one of the best views in town. The Fairmont is also home of the Tonga Room, the only nightclub in town that actually delivers a tropical rain shower nightly. The water pours into an indoor lake that used to be the hotel's swimming pool. By the way, if price is no object, you can choose the penthouse suite where $5,000 a day gets you a butler, maid, and limo.

The fourth major hotel on Nob Hill is the Huntington. This elegant spot (no two rooms are the same) welcomes celebrities such as Princess Margaret, Prince Charles, Luciano Pavarotti, and Leontyne Price. The lobby atmosphere here is far quieter than at the other Nob Hill hotels. Never a big convention.

A good place to see memorabilia on this quartet is in the **Big Four** restaurant at the Huntington Hotel. Across the street is **Huntington Park** where you can relax by the marble fountain and watch the passing scene. Across Taylor Street to the west of the park, visit **Grace Cathedral.** This towering Gothic church has beautiful gilded bronze doors created for a 15th-century baptistery in Italy. Michelangelo thought they looked like the gates of Heaven. Ten rectangular reliefs depict scenes from the Old Testament. The church also has beautiful stained-glass windows featuring everyone from Einstein to Henry Ford. Across the street from the cathedral at 1111 California Street is the **Masonic Auditorium** (776-4917). It's worth stopping in here to see the **Masonic Museum** and the colorful glass mural telling the story of masonry. Also worth a stop is the **Cable Car Museum** (474-1887) at the corner of Mason and Washington. From the mezzanine you can watch the machinery that actually pulls these classic cars around town. Historic exhibits offer a look at the life and times of these motorless vehicles. Hours are daily, 10 A.M. to 5 P.M. October 31 to April 1; till 6 P.M. April 2 to October 30.

If you're looking for a change of pace on the restaurant scene, why not try the **California Culinary Academy** (771-3500) at 625 Polk St. It's a good idea to call for lunch

The Big Four

From Levi Strauss to George Hearst, California has long been seen as the promised land for the upwardly mobile. But the state's most famous period of economic expansion, the Gold Rush, was a big disappointment to most who came here; few of the '49ers actually fulfilled the California dream. Most returned home with little more than was in their pockets when they arrived. Others stayed on and struggled to begin a new life farming, running small shops, or working in the emerging California industries such as lumber, fishing, or construction. But for four men—Collis P. Huntington, Leland Stanford, Mark Hopkins, and Charles Crocker—the California dream wasn't a come-on, it was an easy catch.

Why did these four men flourish in the midst of the abject poverty that characterized so much of the Gold Rush? Their story, really the tale of California's birth, is a lesson for anyone who dares to be rich. In a nutshell, here's what happened. While miners worked away with pick, axe, and sluice box, the Big Four (as they are now known) prospered, like many Sacramento merchants, by overcharging for drygoods. Then in 1863, when the federal government decided to build a transcontinental railroad, these four men eagerly volunteered for the job. Besides getting free land for the railbed, the men maximized government subsidies for mountain construction by declaring that the Sierra Nevada actually started six miles east of Sacramento (though fifty miles would have been more precise).

Hiring Chinese workers at ridiculously low wages, the four men made a fortune on the building of the Central Pacific railroad. After driving the golden spike in 1869, Stanford went on to become a U.S. Senator and founder of the university that bears his son's name. Huntington is best known for the library and gardens he created in Pasadena as well as San Francisco's Huntington Park. Crocker founded one of the city's leading banks. And Hopkins left behind a vast fortune for his young widow. She used a good share of it to build what many San Franciscans believed to be the most garish mansion on Nob Hill. History's verdict on the Big Four, amply documented by court records, shows how these men used bribery to try to turn California into a kind of Banana Republic. Today the memory of the so-called "four-armed cuttlefish" is thoughtfully preserved in the philanthropic works they left behind in gratitude to the state that served them so well.

or dinner reservations because meals prepared by student chefs are very popular. **Nob Hill Café** (776-6915) at 1152 Taylor is a small French restaurant. For moderately priced Italian food, try **Vanessi's** (741-2422) on Nob Hill at 1177 California St., across from Grace Cathedral. Arrive early or expect to wait.

RUSSIAN HILL

While the Spanish and the Mexicans dominated California until the great mid-19th–century migration west, the Russians also played a significant role in California history. Busy fur traders along the northern California coast, they created an ambitious base at Fort Ross on the Mendocino coast. Although their colonization efforts failed, the city still has its **Museum of Russian Culture** (921-4082) at 2450 Sutter Street and Divisadero (near Presidio Heights), Russian restaurants and, of course, Russian Hill. Museum hours are Wednesday and Saturday, 11 A.M. to 3 P.M.

Named for Russians buried here, this residential neighborhood is home to a major cultural center, the **San Francisco Art Institute** (771-7020) at 800 Chestnut Street. Murals by Diego Rivera are one of the rewards of a visit. Hours are Tuesday through Saturday, 10 A.M. to 5 P.M. The district's other claim to fame is snakelike **Lombard Street** which weaves its way down the hill from Hyde to Leavenworth.

Thanks to its dramatic views of the bay and wonderful old homes and cottages, the hill also has other delights for those strolling through San Francisco. Long a cultural meeting place for the likes of Jack Kerouac and poet George Sterling, the hill features a number of architectural landmarks such as the **Feusier House,** one of two surviving octagon houses in San Francisco located at 1067 Green Street.

One of the hill's most important architectural legacies is found at Jones and Vallejo streets. Here Willis Polk, the architect who designed the James Flood home on Nob Hill (now the Pacific Union Club) and the Hallidie Building on Sutter, created a handsome 1915 neighborhood with attractive retaining walls, ramps for vehicles, and walkways. Just off Vallejo is **Russian Hill Place,** home to an exceptional quartet of Mediterranean-style

The Cool, Gray City of Love
The City of Saint Francis

Tho I die on a distant strand,
  And they give me a grave in that land,
    Yet carry me back to my own city!
    Carry me back to her grace and pity!
  For I think I could not rest
  Afar from her mighty breast.
  She is fairer than others are
  Whom they sing the beauty of.
  Her heart is a song and a star—
  My cool, gray city of love.

Tho they tear the rose from her brow,
  To her is ever my vow;
    Ever to her I give my duty—
    First in rapture and first in beauty,
  Wayward, passionate, brave,
  Glad of the life God gave.
  The sea-winds are her kiss,
  And the sea-gull is her dove;
  Cleanly and strong she is—
  My cool, gray city of love.

The winds of the future wait
  At the iron walls of her Gate,
    And the western ocean breaks in thunder,
    And the western stars go slowly under,
  And her gaze is ever West
  In the dream of her young unrest.
  Her sea is a voice that calls,
  And her star a voice above,
  And her wind a voice on her walls—
  My cool, gray city of love.

Tho they stay her feet at the dance,
  In her is the far romance.
  Under the rain of winter falling,
  Vine and rose will await recalling.
  Tho the dark be cold and blind,
  Yet her sea-fog's touch is kind,
  And her mightier caress
  Is joy and the pain thereof;
  And great is thy tenderness,
  O cool, gray city of love!

—George Sterling
Sails and Mirage and Other Poems, 1921

homes designed by Polk. At 1013 Vallejo Street is the
brown shingle home Polk designed for himself.

While you're on Russian Hill, take time to explore
Macondray Lane. One of the city's finest pedestrian
paths, it runs from Leavenworth to Taylor. Charming
cottages, homes, flats, and apartment houses line this
classic San Francisco street.

For Italian food on Russian Hill, try **Ristorante Milano**
(673-2961), a small trattoria at 1448 Pacific St.

Pacific Heights, Presidio Heights, and the Marina

This region, which extends roughly from Van Ness out
to the Presidio between California Street and the bay,
is one of America's most beautiful urban neighborhoods.
You'll have to use all your willpower to spend only an
hour in this delightful area; you'll be tempted to stay all
day shopping on Union Street, trying the vegetarian
dishes at Greens, picnicking on the lawn in front of the
Palace of Fine Arts, or simply enjoying the Victorian
landmarks that are home to the likes of Gordon Getty,
son of oil billionaire J. Paul Getty.

San Francisco has changed in many significant ways
in the past few decades. But one thing that has not
changed much is the feel of this area that is home to
some of the city's most interesting museums, stately
mansions, churches, and Beaux-Arts apartment houses.
This is San Francisco just the way you imagined it: steep
streets lined with Queen Anne's, carpenter Gothic, and
Renaissance revivals that look out toward the shipping
lanes coming into San Francisco Bay.

PACIFIC HEIGHTS

Union Street

The commercial heart of Pacific Heights, Union Street
is known for its specialty shops, galleries, antique
stores, bars, and restaurants. Arguably the most gentrified neighborhood in town, this district grew up around

an old dairy-farming region known as Cow Hollow. After the cows were banished by the Board of Health in 1891, this street filled up with service businesses. Then in the late fifties antique shops, furniture stores, and boutiques began to displace the old groceries, hardware stores, and five-and-dimes. Today Union Street offers art objects, imports, gifts, linens, specialty foods, and handicrafts. The old Victorians have been dolled up and turned into minishopping malls complemented by sidewalk restaurants.

A good place to begin your exploration of Pacific Heights is the **Octagon House** (441-7512) at the corner of Gough and Union streets. Like more than five hundred other eight-sided houses built across America in the 19th century, it was inspired by a book called *A Home for All,* whose author, Orson S. Fowler, believed octagonal residences led to good luck and had a positive impact on unborn children. It's open from noon to 3 P.M. on the second Sunday, and second and fourth Thursdays of the month. Also on the corner of Union and Gough is **Heffalump** (928-4300) which specializes in expensive European toys.

Pasand Madras Lounge (922-4498) at 1875 Union is a good place to catch live jazz acts. Nearby at the Charlton Court cul-de-sac, off the south side of the 1900 block of Union, are a pair of Victorians that have been converted into the **Bed and Breakfast Inn** (921-9784).

One of the street's most popular bars, **Perry's** (922-9022), is at 1944 Union St. Nearby at 1979 Union is the **Blue Light Café** (922-5510), owned by singer Boz Scaggs.

Across the street at 1980 Union is a matching trio of 1870 Victorian residences known as the Wedding Houses (legend has it that a dairy farmer sold the houses to a father as wedding presents for his daughters). Inside is a variety of shops and restaurants. To get a look at the sole survivor of Cow Hollow's milk industry, visit **Earthly Goods** (922-0606) at 1981 Union Street, which is housed in the former Laurel Vale Dairy building.

Other shops worth seeing in this neighborhood are **Images of the North** (673-1273) offering folk art at

1782 Union Street, **Made in USA** (885-4030) for handi-crafts at 1749 Union Street, and **Fumiki's Fine Asian Arts** (922-0573) at 1894 Union Street. For classy sec-ond-hand clothes including sought-after his-and-her Ha-waiian shirts, check **Masquerade** (567-5677) at 2237 Union Street.

Pacific Heights has a number of impressive residential streets. Take a look at Broadway beginning in the 1700 block or the beautiful homes around Alta Plaza park at Steiner and Jackson. There are a number of other impor-tant architectural and historic landmarks worth seeing in Pacific Heights. Perhaps the most visited is the **Haas-Lilienthal House** (441-3004) at 2007 Franklin Street. This Queen Anne mansion is open Sunday 11 A.M. to 4:30 P.M., and Wednesday noon to 4 P.M. The **Vedanta House** at 2963 Webster is an eclectic structure that combines Moorish domes, cusped arches, and crenellat-ed towers. The California Historical Society's **Whittier Mansion** (567-1848) at 2090 Jackson Street is a blend of Edwardian, Classical, and Baroque with a beautiful paneled interior. Cruise by the **Spreckels Mansion** at 2080 Washington Street for a look at the legacy of sugar baron Adolph Spreckels. This palatial home is one of the largest in town.

Fillmore Street

A late bloomer, the Fillmore shopping district between Post Street and Pacific Avenue is a popular commercial area with San Franciscans. Here you'll find antiques at **Glen Smith Galleries** (931-3081), 2021 Fillmore, or literature at **Browser Books** (567-8027), 2195 Fill-more. It's a healthy mix of neighborhood businesses, art galleries, thrift shops, bakeries, delis, and markets.

For a quick bite, try Brazilian pizza served up at **De Paula's** (346-9888), at 2114 Fillmore.

PRESIDIO HEIGHTS

Directly west of Pacific Heights, this district overlooks the city's parklike military base. Perhaps the finest home in this neighborhood is the mansion at **3778 Washington.** Across the street at Washington and Maple is a 38-room replica of the Petit Trianon. Another important landmark is **Temple Emanu-El,** the city's best-known synagogue at Arguello Boulevard and Lake Street.

The major draws to this area are the Exploratorium (see *Priorities*) and the **Palace of Fine Arts.** You'll find these two between Pacific Heights and the Marina. Located at Baker Street between Marina Boulevard and Bay Street, the Bernard Maybeck–designed palace was created for the 1915 Panama-Pacific Exposition. The Roman rotunda provides a classy background to lakefront picnics. Inside the palace is the **Exploratorium** (563-7337), one of the best science museums in the world. There are hundreds of hands-on exhibits perfect for the whole family. It's open Wednesday 10 A.M. to 9:30 P.M., Thursday to Sunday 10 A.M. to 5 P.M. Adults pay $5; $2.50 for seniors, $1 for youths age 6–17.

THE MARINA

Pick up Marina Boulevard and drive past the **Marina Green,** one of the city's popular waterfront parks, to Fort Mason. Headquarters of the Golden Gate National Recreation Area, this is also home of a wide variety of artistic, theatrical, environmental, and community groups. You can also visit the **Mexican Museum** (441-0404), the **Museo Italo-Americano** (673-2200), the **San Francisco African-American Historical and Cultural Society** (441-0640), and the **San Francisco Craft and Folk Art Museum** (775-0990).

San Francisco/Bay Area TV Series
"Streets of San Francisco"
"San Francisco Beat"
"Midnight Caller"
"Trapper John M.D."
"Wolf"
"Hotel" (exteriors)
"Falcon Crest"
"Hooperman"

Chestnut Street
The commercial hub of the Marina is Chestnut Street between Fillmore and Broderick streets. The **Red Rose** (776-6871) at 2251 Chestnut is a metaphysical shop with offerings as diverse as Buddha figurines to hand-woven

Moroccan dresses to massage tables. Step into **Ovation** (931-5445) at 2124 Chestnut. This women's boutique stocks clothing and accessories ranging from casual wear to party dresses for all ages. Ovation also specializes in California designers. Nearby **Solo** (567-4020) showcases ethnic artifacts from 21 countries including China, Russia, and Guatemala. Jewelry, statuettes, and purses are just some of the handmade items available for purchase. The **House of Magic** (346-2218) is at 2025 Chestnut Street.

☕ Among the many popular restaurants on this side of town are **Tortola** (see *Restaurants*) at 2640 Sacramento, **Doidge's** (921-2149) at 2217 Union St., the **Blue Light Café** (922-5510), 1979 Union St., **Green's** (see *Restaurants*) at Fort Mason, **Bechelli's** (346-1801) at 2346 Chestnut St., and, for diner fare, **Johnny Rockets** (931-MALT) at 2201 Chestnut.

Golden Gate Park and Haight-Ashbury

San Francisco's west side story embraces the city's major park, important commercial districts, and leading sixties landmark—the Haight-Ashbury. Some of the city's best restaurants are located along Clement Street and when it comes to museums, Golden Gate Park can keep you busy for days. The Haight has changed a great deal since the flower-child revolution took place in its own backyard. It has, shall we say, gentrified. But it still retains a distinctive flavor. Most visitors begin a visit to this region in the park's east end.

GOLDEN GATE PARK

Designed by William Hammond Hall out of a wasteland, this 1,017-acre park is a place where the buffalo still roam. You can find them among the park's many other beautiful sights—tea gardens, conservatories, lakes, waterfalls, over five thousand kinds of plants, one hundred species of conifers, and three hundred species of rhododendron. For more than a century the park has been the city's backyard. A grassroots (literally) center of the arts, Golden Gate Park also serves as a spawning

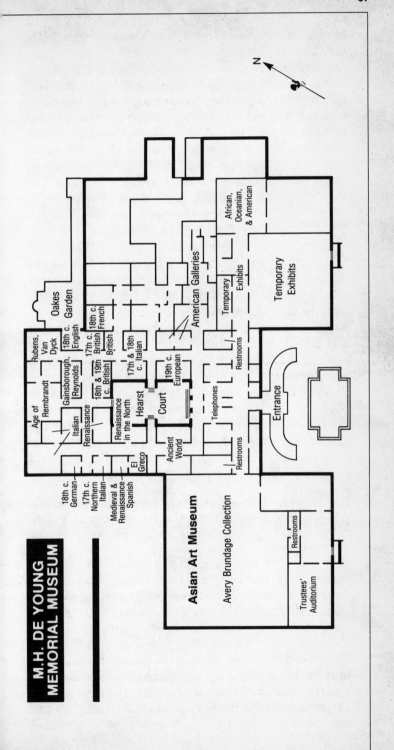

ground for musicians, artists, actors, and mimes who try out their acts on the public.

The **Asian Art Museum** (668-8921) with its Avery Brundage Collection of jades, bronzes, and ceramics, and the **M.H. de Young Memorial Museum** (see *Priorities*) are located at the east end of the park off John F. Kennedy Drive. Both are open Wednesday through Sunday, 10 A.M. to 5 P.M. Admission covers both: $4 for adults; $2 for seniors and youths 12–17; free for children under 12. The **Japanese Tea Garden** is located at the west end of the Asian Art Museum. Also on this side of the park is the botanic **Conservatory** that looks as if it came out of London's Kew Gardens.

Nearby, between Middle Drive East and Concourse Drive (off John F. Kennedy Drive) are the **California Academy of Sciences** (see *Priorities*) which includes the **Steinhart Aquarium** and **Morrison Planetarium.** Among the highlights is the Fish Roundabout, where hundreds of species move through a circular tank that surrounds the audience. There are also tidepool exhibits, an earthquake simulator, and a special collection of cartoons by "Far Side" creator Gary Larson.

Stow Lake in the middle of the park offers boating. Farther down John F. Kennedy Drive are riding stables, the buffalo paddock, fly-casting pools for fishermen to practice their craft, and a nine-hole golf course. At the far west end of the park, near the Great Highway, two windmills add a Dutch accent to the park.

Just north of the park at 1090 Point Lobos Ave. is the **Cliff House** (386-3330), a restaurant where you can look out at the sea lions and birds on Seal Rocks.

Before or after your meal, stop in at the visitors center here with a shipwreck guide as well as the **Musée Mécanique's** (386-1170) collection of penny-arcade machines. Hours are Monday through Friday, 11 A.M. to 7 P.M.; Saturday, Sunday, and holidays, 10 A.M. to 8 P.M.

A short walk east on Point Lobos Avenue from the Cliff House takes you to the ruins of the **Sutro House and Baths.** It was here that Adolph Sutro operated half a dozen pools in Pompeiian splendor. The parklike setting adjacent to the house ruins is a good place for a picnic.

Cradle of the Slot

San Francisco is well known for popularizing steam beer, sourdough bread, and denim jeans. It has also made some important contributions to the industrial revolution. According to Marshall Fey, author of *Slot Machines* (Nevada Publications, Las Vegas), the city midwifed two of the most important genres of slot machines. It was Charles Fey who created the three-reel Liberty Bell, the slot machine that created an entire industry, with millions of units manufactured around the world. This creation as well as Gustav Schultze's automatic paying wheel machines were soon found at saloons, cigar stands, pool halls, and other businesses across the land. "From the ubiquitous slots," says author Fey, "have come such household phrases as 'it's a lemon,' and 'jackpot.'" The slots, which helped thousands of small businesses survive the Depression, were banned by Congress in 1951 but still survive in Reno, Las Vegas, and Atlantic City, as well as in museum settings and private collections in other states.

From here drive east along Point Lobos Avenue (follow the 49-mile scenic-drive signs) to the **California Palace of the Legion of Honor** in Lincoln Park (750-3600), a French collection of 18th-, 19th-, and 20th-century arts as well as special exhibits ranging from Greek icons to Japanese woodblock prints. A short walk north of the Palace is the ocean and **Land's End,** a coastal overlook. Continue east on the 49-mile drive to see the handsome Seacliff residential area before heading back into the Marina and downtown.

While you're in the area, visit **Clement Street.** Named after a San Francisco supervisor, this neighborhood district is now home to some of the city's best restaurants as well as trendy stores. Among the shops you may want to visit is **Haig's Delicacies** (752-6283), a Middle Eastern food shop at 642 Clement Street.

THE HAIGHT

Thanks to Anna Boothe and Fiesta Tours (648-3352) it's now possible to take a professionally guided $15 walk back through time. The three-hour tour "San Francisco and the Hippie Haight-Ashbury," which includes coffee at the Haight Street Deli, runs June through August on weekends only. It has introduced an entire new generation to the story of the Haight. If you can't connect with Anna Boothe, she'd still like to tell you about her route so you can follow it on your own:

Begin at the **Red Victorian** (see *Hotels*), a 1904 Victorian B&B at 1665 Haight Street that offers every guest a mantra with his or her pass key, complimentary use of the meditation room, Pink Parlour discussions of subjects such as the Sandinistas at tea time, and an on-call masseuse.

Boothe admits that gentrification has taken its toll on the Haight. Among the victims is the late, great Haight coffeehouse, the Grand Piano, now a Round Table pizza parlor. The Eye of the Beholder, another coffeehouse, has become Happy Donuts. And the Straight Theater, onetime stage for Janis Joplin, Jimi Hendrix, and the Grateful Dead, has become yet another casualty of urban renewal.

Approaching her subject like a Renaissance scholar leading a tour of Florence, Boothe points out landmarks such as the **Haight-Ashbury Community Radio** (648-8213) at 1130 Treat Avenue and **Haight-Ashbury Produce** (861-5672), an organic market located at 1615 Haight Street where you can see huge bins of grains, lentils, fresh fruits, and vegetables. Boothe says, "This was the kind of diet the hippies were on. You won't find a single piece of meat around here. Vegetarianism was very big and it also saved them a lot of money."

Although Boothe finds a few people with long hair and headbands on Haight Street, sixties couture is clearly the province of used-clothing stores. Boothe says fur pieces were very popular; you can still find them at **Held Over** (552-3733), the second-hand clothing establishment at 1599 Haight Street. "Janis Joplin loved to perform in various stoles. You can see the hippies preference for colorful attire, sequins, beads, and lace in that rack of old dresses up there. There was sort of a childlike quality in the way they dressed."

Strolling across Stanyan into Golden Gate Park, she leads the way to **Hippie Hill,** the tour's grand finale. This was headquarters for the 1967 Summer of Love—for San Francisco, an event of historic importance second only to the Great Earthquake.

"On weekends there were so many people parading down Haight that they stopped traffic. And this is where they came, 20,000 of them, blanketing the hill in their rainbow-colored garb. It was the height of the hippie culture. They were free to play their music and smoke marijuana in an arrest-free zone."

The Victorians on 700 Steiner provide one of the best photographic backdrops in town. Just get a good angle from up on the Square and fire away.

Sunset/Twin Peaks

This district, which begins south of Golden Gate Park and includes one of the city's best viewpoints, encompasses the San Francisco Zoo, Lake Merced, and some of the city's finest residential districts such as St. Francis Wood. There are great parks in this part of town, a fine concert venue called Stern Grove, and the city's largest college, San Francisco State University. The best place to begin your tour is at the zoo.

Located at Sloat Boulevard and the Great Highway, the **San Francisco Zoo** (753-7083) can easily occupy a family for the entire day. Newer exhibits such as the Primate Discovery Center, Gorilla World, and Koala Crossing complement established domains such as the hippo and polar-bear areas. Don't miss the rain-forest aviary, Big Cat House, or night gallery which simulates nocturnal conditions. In the children's petting zoo be sure to ride the carousel. The zoo is open daily from 10 A.M. to 5 P.M. Admission is $5 for adults, $2 for seniors and youths 12–15, children under 12 free.

Adjacent to the zoo is **Lake Merced,** the city's largest body of water, where you can rent boats and enjoy trout fishing. Off Sloat Boulevard at 19th Avenue is the **Stern Grove** (see *Priorities*). If you're in town on a summer Sunday be sure to attend one of the free concerts. On a sunny day this is one of the city's great pleasures. Bring a picnic lunch.

Drive east on Sloat Boulevard and Portola Drive, and take a left on Twin Peaks Boulevard to ascend **Twin Peaks,** one of the city's most popular viewpoints. Also worth a visit, and nowhere near as crowded, is lesser-known **Tank Hill.** The easiest way to find it is to drive up Castro to 17th Street and then follow Twin Peaks Boulevard to its junction with Clarendon Avenue. Look for a flight of stairs to the right of a brown-shingle at

192 and then walk uphill to a small ridge for your memorable view.

The San Francisco Sound

If you've got a boom box or a Walkman you can tune in to the local scene by listening to Bay Area performers. All either grew up locally or got their first big break in this community.

Metallica	Graham Central Station
M.C. Hammer	Sly and the Family Stone
Too Short	Doobie Brothers
Sheila E.	Pointer Sisters
Tony! Tone! Toni!	Tower of Power
Pete Escovedo	Steve Miller
John Fogerty	Tracy Nelson and Mother Earth
Creedence Clearwater Revival	Quicksilver Messenger Service
Grateful Dead	Beau Brummels
The Hawkins Family	We Five
Hot Tuna	Dave Brubeck
Jefferson Airplane	Cal Tjader
Janis Joplin	

Upper Market, Castro, and Noe Valley

Beginning on the fringe of downtown, these are three of the city's most diversified neighborhoods. From old Italian families to the gay community to yuppies who want to be close to central-city jobs, this district has an excellent mix of shops, cafés, restaurants, theaters, and community parks. Italianate, Stick, Queen Anne, and Edwardian homes add to the local charm. Handy to downtown, all these areas offer a look at the less touristed side of town.

Located at the border of the Eureka Valley, Buena Vista, and Duboce Triangle neighborhoods, the **Upper Market** district was largely built between the 1880s and the end of World War II. The adjacent **Castro** neighborhood, which centers around Castro and 18th streets, is thick with bars, nightclubs, restaurants, and clothing stores. Before its urbanization, this district was dominated by breweries, cow ranches, livery stables, and the West's largest brickyard. Today it's the heart of San Francisco's gay community.

There are some fine shops in the Castro area including **Chocolates from Chocolates** (431-3640) at 218 Church Street. The area's most important architectural landmark is the **Castro Theatre** at 429 Castro Street. Close to this neighborhood at 199 Museum Way off of Roosevelt Way is the **Randall Museum** (554-9600). The labs and hands-on exhibits are ideal for young science buffs. Hours are Tuesday through Saturday, 10 A.M. to 12:30 P.M., and 1:30 to 5 P.M.

A restaurant worth trying here is **Le Piano Zinc** (431-5266) at 708 14th St. Excellent prix fixe meals are served. Moderate to expensive.

Noe Valley centers around the 24th Street commercial district that extends from Diamond Street to Chattanooga Street. For visitors, this area is best known for its bars.

Within Noe Valley you'll find such popular spots as the **Meat Market Coffeehouse** (285-5598) at 4123 24th St. and **Latin Freeze** (282-5033) at 3338 24th St., home of the finest fruit Popsicles in town. A popular gay bar in the Castro is the **Twin Peaks Tavern** (864-9470) at 401 Castro St.

Mission/Potrero Hill/Bayview

Mission Dolores, where Father Junipero Serra colonized this city in 1782, is the natural place to begin a visit to this part of town. Located at 16th and Dolores streets, this historic spot has a modest museum and graveyard dedicated to the memory of thousands of Indians buried here. Phone 621-0203 for information. Close at hand is **Mission Dolores Park** where the nearby skyscrapers loom over the little neighborhood Victorians. Convenient to the Mission at 250 Valencia Street is the historic **Levi Strauss and Co. factory.** You'll enjoy touring this pants factory that has made few architectural concessions to modern times. The tour is conducted every Wednesday at 10:30 A.M. and lasts approximately one hour. There is no admission fee, but reservations are required. Call 565-9153 for reservations and information.

The best reason to visit this area is the **Mission Murals** (see *Priorities*). Beginning at the 24th Street BART Station, walk down 24th Street between Mission and York streets. You can pick up a map of the murals at the gift shop **Galeria de la Raza** at 2851 24th Street (826-8009). Along the way you'll see 28 murals painted on neighborhood garages and fences.

For Latin nightlife try **Cesar's Latin Palace** (648-6611) at 3140 Mission Street. Also popular is **Bajones** (282-2522) at 1062 Valencia Street. One of the Mission's most intriguing bars is **La Rondalla** (647-7474) at 901 Valencia Street. Visit during the Christmas season to enjoy the beautiful holiday displays including a shrine to the Virgin Mary. Entertainment is provided by a strolling mariachi band. During the rest of the year you can dine amongst the mounted animal heads and African masks which decorate the bar.

South of the Mission is the **Potrero Hill** District, a residential area with a curvy street similar to Lombard—Vermont, between 20th and 22nd. The advantage to this one is that it lacks the heavy traffic found on the Lombard Hill. **Bayview** is home to **Candlestick Park** and the **Hunter's Point Naval Shipyard.**

For Salvadorean food try **La Olla** (282-6086) at 2417 Mission St.; for Italian food go to **La Traviata** (282-0500) at 2854 Mission St. In the Candlestick Park area **Dago Mary's** (822-2633) at Hunter's Point Naval Shipyard is an offbeat spot that serves up Italian and seafood specials along with its great views.

7

SHOPPING

Back before the malling of America, big cities were ideal for shoppers. Grand old department stores were flanked by a myriad of specialty shops where shopping was fun. When you got tired of walking, there was always a pleasant café around the corner. You didn't even need a car to find the best deals in town. That's still true in San Francisco, where you can shop in classic downtown department stores, ride through glitzy new emporiums on circular escalators, browse at quaint bookshops on quiet lanes, and, coincidentally, find some of the best deals around on everything from designer clothing to lap-top computers.

Retailing remains an art form in San Francisco, the birthplace of intriguing chains such as the Nature Company and home of the city's first major urban adaptive reuse project—a shopping, dining, and entertainment complex called Ghirardelli Square. From browsing to recreational shopping, San Francisco is a city full of surprises on the retail side. The good news is that you don't need a car to explore major shopping districts, such as Union Square, Embarcadero Center, Union Street, and Fisherman's Wharf. If you're a bargain hunter, the South of Market area is just the ticket. Recreational shoppers will be delighted to find inviting cafés and restaurants at their service in all the major shopping districts.

Downtown

Market Street, once the city's retail hub, is experiencing a renaissance of sorts. Shopping beneath the dome at the **Emporium,** 835 Market Street, is a delightful San Francisco shopping tradition. Adjacent to this vast department store is the new kid on the block, a nine-story urban mall called **San Francisco Centre.** Ride the spiral escalator up to **Nordstrom's,** the fashion specialty store so obsessed with service that it has been known to take returns on shoes brought back two years after they were purchased.

Union Square

Nearby Union Square is San Francisco's most important retail center, the home of such major department stores as **Macy's, Saks Fifth Avenue, Neiman Marcus,** and **I. Magnin.** Especially appealing when the windows are decorated for Christmas, this area is the place to shop for Asian antiques, fine jewelry, couture gowns, T-shirts (yes, T-shirts), and designer labels ranging from Lapidus to Lauren. Post Street between Union Square and Kearny is the mainline for apparel (**Polo/Ralph Lauren** at 80), leather goods (**Mark Cross** at 170), and fine arts with an Asian touch (**Gump's** at 250). Kids and teens (and even their parents) can shop for bargains on the second floor of the **Fila** fashion sportswear shop at 239 Grant Avenue. For shoes, try **Bally of Switzerland** at 238 Stockton or (for women only) **Maud Frizon** at 249 Grant Avenue. **FAO Schwarz** at 48 Stockton offers a vast selection of one-of-a-kind toys.

Just off Union Square is Maiden Lane with its mix of tea rooms, espresso bars, boutiques, and specialty stores. **Williams-Sonoma,** an excellent cookware store, is nearby at 576 Sutter Street. For a spot of New-Wave shopping, try the trendy 800 block of Post Street, just two blocks up from Union Square. **MAC** (812) is the place for avant-garde apparel favored by customers such as Madonna when she's in town. **Gimme-Shoes** (868) offers New-Wave European shoes for men and women. **Fun Display** (820) is a first-rate furniture showroom.

Nearby Sutter Street is also home to many fine clothing and accessory stores. For women, there's **Laura Ashley** (563) and **Jessica McClintock** (353). For menswear, try **Wilkes Bashford** (375) and **Ariston** (349). Continue east on Sutter past Kearny to **Crocker Galleria,** where fifty stores and restaurants are spread across three levels beneath a glass dome.

Union Square Department-Store Eating

San Francisco department-store restaurants maintain some fairly high standards, as befits a city obsessed with food. So, should hunger gnaw at your vitals while you try on a new hat, you won't have to leave the building to re-energize.

Macy's: Plum Restaurant and Bar: Light California-style food, with something to satisfy the kids.

I. Magnin: Narsai's Café and Market presents exquisite, almost precious delicatessen: upscale sandwiches, fancy breads, the richest and most decorated of French-style pastries to eat there or take-out, all complemented with good wine.

Neiman Marcus: You don't have to be a shopper to take tea at Neiman Marcus. Doctors, lawyers, and literary agents, men and women, all sit at one of the window-side tables, nibble on delicate sandwiches and fresh fruit tarts, and watch the parade below.

At the foot of the California Street cable-car line is **Embarcadero Center,** a vast office-and-hotel complex that has more than 140 shops and fine dining. (See "dim sum" under *Priorities.*) On a sunny day, this complex, with its maze of elevated walkways, pedestrian bridges, and patios, is ideal for the recreational shopper. The Hyatt Regency hotel is part of this complex. To see the city's finest antique dealers, walk over to **Jackson Square,** a one-time Barbary Coast hub bounded roughly by Jackson, Montgomery, Sansome, and Pacific streets. After visiting the antique shops on Jackson, wander over to 722 Montgomery to see attorney Melvin Belli's handsomely restored Belli Building.

Fisherman's Wharf

Fisherman's Wharf has three major shopping areas. **Pier 39** offers an eclectic mix of shops complemented by mimes, jugglers, and other performing artists. **The Cannery** is an old Del Monte landmark with a variety of shops and galleries. An outdoor patio here at street level is a good place to enjoy takeout from one of the vendors or seafood restaurants. A few blocks away is **Ghirardelli Square,** a chocolate factory turned into a popular shopping and dining complex. After browsing amidst specialty shops devoted to music boxes, kites,

Greek fashion imports, and folk art, you can have dinner at **Paprika's Fono** for an outstanding view of the bay. Also here is the **Ghirardelli Chocolate Manufactory,** where you can see displays of an old-time chocolate-making operation and sample the finished product on a hot fudge sundae. Also worth a visit in the Fisherman's Wharf area is **Cost Plus Imports,** the 2522 Taylor Street bazaar offering moderately priced imports—including clothes, cookware, rugs, furniture, and toys—from 35 nations.

Neighborhoods

San Francisco's neighborhoods offer excellent shopping possibilities. Chinatown is, of course, a good place to go for ivory, pottery, and baskets, as well as inexpensive gift items. The **Chinatown Kite Shop** at 717 Grant Avenue offers handsome creations that you'll certainly want to try out on one of the city's windy beaches. North Beach is the home of **City Lights Bookstore** at 261 Columbus Avenue. Environmentalists will definitely not want to miss the **Sierra Club Bookstore** at 730 Polk Street.

In Japan Center you'll find art galleries, the excellent **Kinokuniya Book Store** at 1581 Webster, and Tansu dynasty chests. Take a break at one of the local sushi bars, restaurants, or, if you like, the **Kabuki Hot Springs** at 1750 Geary Boulevard. The warm waters are ideal for the foot-sore shopper.

Union Street with its many galleries, boutiques, craft stores, and antique shops is a pleasant place to stroll. Among the highlights here are **Fumiki Fine Asian Arts** (1894). For an upscale experience in toyland, try **Heffalump** (1694) where European toys include hand-crafted rocking horses and dollhouses plus unusual art, music, and science toys and games. The lotions, oils, and soaps at the **Body Shop** (2072) are always popular gifts. The dark or full city roast coffees from 32 countries (including Ethiopia) from **Peet's Coffee** (2156 Chestnut in the Marina) and San Francisco sourdough bread are great ways to remember the city once you've returned home. Fillmore Street, once a run-down commercial area, has blossomed into an excellent shopping area between Sutter and Washington. You can find folk art at **Primitive** (2241) and American handicrafts at

Heartland (1801A). Don't miss **Podesta Baldocchi** (2525 California Street), the florist that sells elaborate Christmas tree ornaments during the holiday season.

Factory Outlets

If you're serious about saving money, you've come to the right place. Many of the best bargains are found South of Market. Try **Six Sixty Center** at 660 Third Street and Townsend, a factory-outlet mall offering clothes, jewelry, and accessories. The **Esprit Factory Outlet** (499 Illinois Street and 16th) offers women's clothing, shoes, and bed-and-bath items. The **Coat Factory Outlet** at 1350 Folsom between 9th and 10th specializes in women's coats and jackets. The **Raincoat Outlet** at 543 Howard, second floor, has a wide array of jackets, blazers, and sportswear including heirlooms from the fifties and sixties. For jewelry and fine watches try **Niederholzer Jewelers** at 140 Geary (fourth floor) downtown. Sally Socolich's *Bargain Hunting in the Bay Area* (Wingbow Press) is recommended reading. This monumental guide takes you to outlet stores across the entire retailing spectrum.

San Francisco is also an outstanding place to find computer bargains. Two free publications, *Computer Currents* and *Microtimes,* will tip you off to stores offering vast discounts on all sorts of hardware and software. The prices range from great to unbelievable.

Caveat emptor: Make sure you have at least a ninety-day warranty and/or exchange privileges for electronic equipment.

Residents from all over the Bay Area drive to Berkeley's 4th Street shopping area, just north of University Avenue, for the one-of-a-kind minerals and artwork at **The Nature Company,** the unusual and exquisite home-and-garden furnishings at **The Gardener,** and the valuable handmade papers at **Elica's Paper.**

8

RESTAURANTS

What do people in the San Francisco Bay Area do? They eat. And those few minutes a day when they don't eat, they talk about food. And not just the nouvellest cuisine—all food, from the latest $50 creation by this weeks's most fashionable chef, to the simplest, juiciest chicken from the mom-and-pop Italian joint around the corner. (*Grilled* in Californese, by the way, usually means barbecued over glowing coals. *Barbecued* generally means grilled and slathered with a sauce, usually red.)

San Francisco has nurtured its reputation as a restaurant capital for decades. In the early years of this century, San Franciscans were offering oysters and rather heavy French classics to the likes of Diamond Jim Brady, Lillian Russell, and Enrico Caruso. And, in the early sixties, when most of the United States was still pushing Beaver Cleaver mashed potatoes and frozen string beans around their plates, Bay Area chefs began the revolution toward fresh, locally grown food and light, real French-style techniques that soon spread throughout the country.

The highest accolade a San Franciscan can pronounce is "very San Francisco." The restaurants in this guide are all, in one way or another, very San Francisco. That is, they serve very creative (yet often unaffected) food made from fresh, usually local ingredients. We've included a full range of prices, styles, and formality, hoping you'll find a restaurant for your every mood.

French-inspired food is always a prime choice in the Bay Area, but so is American, be it dream diner food or inventive haute cuisine. And, due to the history of immigration to the area, a world of other ethnic cuisines leads to a wonderland of restaurants. Italian, Mexican (as well as most of the other Central and South American countries), Vietnamese, Cambodian, Burmese, and Thai are all represented. Savor the regional cuisines of India, Pakistan, Afghanistan, Lebanon, Ethiopia, Korea, and Japan. If there's been a war somewhere, the Bay Area has a restaurant serving the surviving specialties.

And then there's Chinese. The Bay Area has always boasted some of the finest Chinese restaurants in the country, but now that so many people are leaving Hong Kong before 1997 when China takes over (people who have enjoyed the best in Hong Kong and expect to find it here), some of the finest Hong Kong restaurants have opened branches here. Almost uniformly, these restaurants are haute Cantonese. Many Americans believe that Cantonese food is the same as chop suey or Chinese-American food. However, the Chinese people themselves consider Cantonese food to be the subtlest and most evolved of all their cuisines.

Meal prices vary with the ethnic territory. Don't expect bargains from any restaurant with marble walls. Expect to pay a bare minimum of $35–$40 per person in a temple of gastronomy, including twenty percent tip, but not including drinks or wine. However, restaurants with working-class clientele may offer real value for money. Indian dinners in many restaurants run about $9 per person, including twenty percent tip and a beer. Most restaurants, even plain, ethnic ones, accept MasterCard and Visa, but not always American Express. The following abbreviations are used: AE-American Express; CB-Carte Blanche; D-Discover; DC-Diners Club; MC-MasterCard; and V-Visa.

Dress for the best restaurants means coat and tie for men, comparable attire for women. (The last holdout against women in pants gave up only a few years ago.) The finest restaurants require reservations well in advance (occasionally three or four weeks ahead), but even the plainest restaurant is likely to be full, so it pays to call ahead if possible.

Many Bay Area cities have public no-smoking ordinances and require no-smoking sections in restaurants. In fact, before you light up, you should inquire whether any smoking is allowed at all.

The key to the right of each name refers to the neighborhood or area the restaurant's located in and, where applicable, to the appropriate page and coordinates of the color atlas at the back of the book.

☕ THE SELECTIONS

Angkor Wat Cambodian Restaurant   NEAR
PRESIDIO HEIGHTS, P. 2, B2
4217 Geary Blvd.; 221-7887
Dinner appetizers $4.95–$5.75, entrées $6.95–$11.95

The standard of comparison for all Cambodian restaurants, with an elegant setting (mitigated slightly by the noise and crowds) divided into three sections—one a smoke-filled area close to the lobby and bar, the other two make up the main dining room. From Thurs. to Sun. Cambodian classical dancers take to the stage, offering a sense of authenticity. Pictures of famous temples decorate the walls of the carpeted rooms. Somewhat dark, candles and soft lights illuminate the tables enough to view elaborate and creative food tasting like an intricate mix of Thai and Vietnamese. You can't go wrong with dishes such as: lott (springrolls); chicken salad; prawn salad; green papaya salad; beef salad; special grilled rabbit; special lamb curry; charbroiled beef roll; sliced beef in red curry; pan-fried catfish; stir-fried mixed vegetables in olive oil; jackfruit custard; and fried bananas. As in a Third World country, service is often frantic, abrupt, disengaged, and even surly. Expect to spend an hour and a half over dinner. Open Tues.–Sat. 5–10:30 P.M., Sun. 5–10 P.M. Closed Mon. Reservations essential on weekends. Full bar. AE, MC, V. Parking nearby.

John Ash & Co.   SANTA ROSA
4330 Barnes Rd. (less than half a mile west of the River Rd. exit off Hwy. 101), Santa Rosa, 50 miles north of San Francisco; (707) 527-7687
Lunch appetizers $3.50–$8.95, entrées $6.50–$9.95
Dinner appetizers $4.50–$13, entrées $13–$23.50, prix fixe four-course dinner $42.50

A few years ago, John Ash was ranked by *Food & Wine* magazine as one of America's great young chefs. Now he's established, and so is his restaurant. At the mouth of the Sonoma and Napa Valley, John Ash & Co., overlooking the vineyards, is a serious restaurant featuring his regional cuisine (a very California wine country section) based almost entirely on local ingredients of dazzling quality. The menu changes according to season and availability of ingredients, but past winners include carpaccio of fresh ahi tuna; rillette of duck; Roquefort ravioli; cold lavender-blueberry soup; boned quail; breast of muscovy duck; roast breast of chicken; rack of milk-fed veal; dry-aged loin of beef; pecan cheesecake; caramel, chocolate, and macadamia nut tart; lemon tart; fresh peach and almond tart. The dining area is large, with wide, open spaces and huge windows that offer a grand view. With a quiet atmosphere, this is a relaxing place to go after sipping on wines all afternoon or to simply enjoy the surrounding sea of vineyards. Open for lunch Tues.–Fri. 11:30 A.M.–2 P.M.; Sun. brunch 10:30 A.M.–3 P.M.; dinner Tues.–Sat. 6–10 P.M., Sun. 5:30–10 P.M. Reservations advisable. Full bar. AE, CB, DC, MC, V. Parking.

Bay Wolf   OAKLAND
3853 Piedmont Ave., Oakland; 655-6004
Lunch appetizers $3–$6, entrées $7.75–$10
Dinner appetizers $4–$7, entrées $12–$16

Rated by many locals as one of the most creative restaurants in the Eastbay, Bay Wolf offers lunches that run to familiar and unfamiliar sandwiches (house-smoked pork loin with grilled eggplant and pesto sauce), spinach salads, and grilled foods, while the inventive dinner items are much more lavish and varied than at that High Temple of Gastronomy Chez Panisse, and yet are often equally creative. The atmosphere is just as important as the food at Bay Wolf. Located in a house redesigned into a restaurant, the two dining areas are decorated with contemporary art by the owners' friends. An outdoor deck offers more room in this intimate setting. Fifteen years in the running, Bay Wolf has its own set of regulars but first-timers are made to feel welcome by the relaxed and friendly atmosphere. Service is fast but sometimes haughty. Open for lunch Mon.–Fri. 11:30 A.M.–2 P.M.; dinner Mon.–Fri. 6–9:30 P.M., Sat. and Sun. 5:30–9:30 P.M. Reservations for dinner essential. Wine and beer. MC, V. Parking nearby.

Buca Giovanni   NORTH BEACH, P. 3, D1
800 Greenwich St.; 776-7766
Dinner appetizers $4.70–$6.95, entrées $10.65–$15.40

For those of you up on your Italian, you should be able to envision this restaurant just by its name. But this is no ordinary cave. Walk down off the street and enter what slightly resembles a wine cellar—brick walls, arches, mosaic tile floor, and low ceilings. Photographs of different areas of Italy and lattice work separating the dining rooms add to the scene. Expect a casual, yet formal, atmosphere—light beige cotton tablecloths and candles offset the dark feel of la buca. While this atmosphere may be too dim for some, and the upstairs dining room too frantic, it is worth any discomfort to enjoy some of the best Northern Italian food in San Francisco. If you're lucky enough to find one of their rich, creamy polentas on the menu, order it, along with just about any simmered veal dish and whatever seafood they've found fresh in the markets that day. Open Mon.–Thurs. 5:30–10:30 P.M., Fri.–Sat. 5:30–11 P.M. Reservations suggested. Wine and beer. AE, MC, V. Parking nearby.

Butler's   MILL VALLEY
625 Redwood Hwy. (at Seminary Dr. exit off Hwy. 101), Mill Valley; 383-1900
Appetizers $3.75–$6.75, entrées $9–$16

The sunlight during the day is extraordinary. The view at dusk romantic. The glint off the black water at night coolly tranquilizing. It's Richardson Bay and, with its mirrored back walls, you own the view from just about every seat in this noisy, airy, only slightly formal waterside restaurant. Florid California cuisine prevails here, making it a great place to turn several appetizers into a full meal. The menu changes frequently, so use these recommendations as guidelines: Butler's antipasto platter; sweet corn and red-pepper fritters; goat cheese in pesto; grilled chicken breasts marinated in bourbon and lavender honey; pork scaloppine with orange ginger cream and potato leek pancakes. Service is silky smooth. Open Tues.–Thurs. 6–9 P.M., Fri.–Sat. 6–10 P.M., Sun. 6–9:30 P.M. Reservations necessary. Full bar. AE, MC, V. Parking.

Campton Place Restaurant   UNION SQUARE,
                                                P. 3, D1
340 Stockton St.; 781-5155
Breakfast entrées $9–$13
Lunch appetizers $7.50–$8.50, entrées $13.50–$16
Dinner appetizers $10–$12.50, entrées $25–$29

THE place to go for that perfect evening out featuring an array of often subtle innovations based on all-American ingredients in warm, elegant, yet comfortable surroundings. Discreet lighting, heavy carpets, and contemporary art combine to create a romantic, slightly elegant setting. Soft apricot tones, white linen tablecloths, crystal glassware, and heavy silver plates provide a classy background for the dinner items. Some favorites from past menus: briny fresh seafood platter; seared halibut with shrimp salsa; roast lamb loin with fennel ratatouille; a fantasy of homemade ice creams. At press time, founding chef Bradley Ogden's departure was quite recent, but we expect Campton Place to remain a good solid, tranquil three-star–style restaurant. Open for breakfast Mon.–Fri. 7–11 A.M., Sat. 8–11:30 A.M.; Sun. brunch 8 A.M.–2:30 P.M.; lunch Mon.–Fri. 11:30 A.M.–2:30 P.M., Sat. 12–2:30 P.M.; dinner Sun.–Thurs. 5:30–10 P.M., Fri.–Sat.

5:30–10:30 P.M. Reservations strongly suggested. Lovely, elegant full bar. AE, DC, MC, V. Valet and nearby parking.

Casa Madrona Restaurant   SAUSALITO
801 Bridgeway, Sausalito; 331-5888
Lunch appetizers $3.50–$6, entrées $7.50–$14
Dinner appetizers $3.50–$10, entrées $12–$22

Take one part waterfront, one part romantic winding brick paths, and one part Victorian inn, and you've got a lovely destination at the end of a ferry ride. Perched high on a hillside in Sausalito, Casa Madrona offers fantastic views of the San Francisco skyline and bay. A glass enclosed terrace, with a retractable roof in this mansion dating back to 1885, allows for a mixture of inside and outside dining. Fireplace, harpist, and pianist add to the romance. The menu features new American-style cuisine with selections such as roasted loin of pork with mustard glaze, grilled swordfish with pepper and walnut relish, and grilled chicken salad with watercress and apple dressing. Open for lunch Mon.–Fri. 11:30 A.M.–2:30 P.M., dinner daily 6–10 P.M., Sun. brunch 10 A.M.–2:30 P.M. Reservations suggested; no reservations taken for Sun. brunch. Wine and beer. AE, MC, V. Valet parking.

Ristorante Castellucci   NORTH BEACH, P. 3, D1
561 Columbus Ave.; 362-2774
Dinner appetizers $4.50–$6.50, entrées $8.50–$14

With wood tables and sixty seats small, this year-old restaurant conjures up memories of old-time North Beach Italian eateries: friendly, casual, homey, cheerful, noisy, and crowded. The proprietors hail from Argentina and have created simple, satisfying grilled steaks, made-to-order ravioli and other fresh pastas, warming soups, and a great Caesar salad, all very Italian but with overlays of Argentina and America. Friendly, sometimes frantic service by a few stalwarts. Open Mon.–Thurs. 5:30–10 P.M., Fri.–Sat. 5–11 P.M. Reservations suggested. Wine and beer. AE, DC, MC, V. Parking nearby.

Chevys Mexican Restaurant   SOUTH OF MARKET, P. 3, D2
150 Fourth St.; 543-8060
Lunch and dinner appetizers $4.95–$7.95, entrées $6.75–$12.95

Take the shoreline footpaths up to Chevys and enter northern Mexico—hubcaps and all. Decorated with bare bulbs and signs to test your retention of high school Spanish, this is an American version of Tijuana. Spread over the Bay Area, ten of these large, noisy, jolly restaurants serve large portions of their own all-American versions of

Bay Area Breakfasts

To breakfast as the natives do, consider the following:

Doidge's Kitchen (2217 Union Street, 921-2149). The "in" place among politicos and literary types for weekend brunch or weekday breakfast meetings. Creamy omelettes; rich, thick French toast; the freshest of squeezed juices; and fruit on every plate.

Sear's Fine Foods (439 Powell Street, 986-1160). The lightest of Swedish pancakes with fresh fruit, eggs galore, and just about anything you might crave for breakfast.

Bechelli's Restaurant (2346 Chestnut Street, 346-1801). A well-worn green-on-green diner with a thirties overlay to their fifties horseshoe-shaped counter and booths. Thick slabs of egg-custard French toast; a near-infinite variety of thin, dry omelettes; and huge gummy pancakes loaded with fresh blueberries. Go on a weekday if you don't want to wait two hours.

Sally's (300 De Haro Street, 626-6006). Great whole-grain pancakes (including generous blueberry renditions), omelettes, frittata, made-on-the-premises muffins, and coffee cakes in a Potrero Hill Industrial Arts cafeteria.

Café Fanny (1603 San Pablo Avenue, Berkeley; 524-5451). A crowded, tiny, French-inspired, zinc-topped, stand-up bar, complete with brass rail to rest your foot. The "in" crowd elbow their way into this joint for poached eggs on toast, fresh fruit crisps, buckwheat crepes, fruit upside-down cakes, muffins, caffe latte and other steamed milk and espresso drinks, and peach tea.

Oakland Grill (301 Franklin Street, Oakland; 835-1176). This no-nonsense, real American breakfast-all-day-long almost-diner in the middle of Oakland's produce district serves heartland breakfasts amid wood, hanging plants, and industrial lighting. Try the hotcakes, French toast, sirloin steak with eggs, two-egg scramlet, one-third-pound sausage patty, homefries, and fried apples.

The Half Day Café (848 College Avenue, Kentfield; 459-0291). A gloriously sunny, comfortable, and casually inviting upscale barn-like space serving fresh, California-style breakfasts including fruit plate, Belgian waffles, omelettes, tortilla scramble, and muffins—a revivifying stop-over on the way to Point Reyes, Mount Tamalpais, or the Wine Country.

And then, there are always **Bette's Oceanview Diner** (see *Berkeley Eateries*), **Campton Place**, and **Il Fornaio** (see *Restaurants*).

Tex-Mex and Mexicanesque specialties—not to mention their famous margaritas in frosted mugs. We focus on the San Francisco venue because it is about as convenient as you can get to Moscone Center. Try the beef and chicken fajitas, broiled quail, and chiles rellenos. Open Sun.–Thurs. 11 A.M.–10 P.M., Fri.–Sat. 11 A.M.–11 P.M. Reservations accepted for eight or more. Full bar. MC, V. Parking nearby.

Chez Panisse Restaurant and Café
BERKELEY
1517 Shattuck Ave., Berkeley; dinner reservations: 548-5525; Café: 548-5049
Lunch and dinner (Café upstairs) appetizers $6.50–$10, entrées $8.50–$16
Dinner (Restaurant downstairs) prix fixe $55

The forerunner of the food revolution not only in California but in the entire country, Alice Waters's Chez Panisse has evolved over the years from perfectly French traditional herb-roasted lamb in a Burgundy sauce based on a genuine (and time-consuming) recipe for lamb demiglace, to the latest nouvelle seasonal classics. The bustling, very noisy, elite Café upstairs offers long waits, fashionable salads made of organic local leaves and flowers grown especially for Chez Panisse, organic free-range chickens roasted, grilled, and dressed-up into salads, pizzas, and calzones baked in one of the first fashionable wood-burning ovens in the state. The quiet, more formal Restaurant downstairs features a single prix-fixe meal each night, served in two seatings. If you don't fancy sweetbreads or seared salmon that night, you may order a pasta from upstairs or just suffer silently. Café open Mon.–Sat. for lunch 11:30 A.M.–3 P.M.; dinner 5–11:30 P.M. Reserve dinner downstairs, especially for weekends, exactly one calendar month in advance, although it may be possible to get a reservation for Tues.–Thurs. only two weeks before. Reservations for lunch only in Café. Wine, beer, and aperitifs. AE, DC, MC, V. Parking nearby.

Circolo Restaurant and Champagneria
FINANCIAL DISTRICT, P. 3, D1
161 Sutter St.; 362-0404
Lunch and dinner appetizers $2.95–$5.95, entrées $6.95–$14

The mirror-shiny brass elevators, peach banquettes, and Medici's ransom in marble make this a high-tech/Art-Deco dream elegant enough to entertain clients, romantic enough for a special night on the town, and yet comfortable enough to go back to. Service is usually smooth and attentive, yet unintrusive. Selections include charred beef salad; linguini with scallops and sun-dried tomatoes; agnolotti; Margherita (or just about any other) pizza; calzone; grilled fish of the day; loin lamb chops; semisweet chocolate tart with pecan crust; and ricotta cheesecake. Open for lunch Mon.–Fri. 11:30 A.M.–3 P.M.; dinner Mon.–Thurs. 5–10 P.M., Fri.–Sat. 5–10:30 P.M. Closed Sun. Reservations advised. Full bar. AE, CB, DC, MC, V. Parking nearby.

The Business Lunchbox

The following restaurants meet our criteria for business lunching: efficient service; short lines or last-minute reservations honored; food and ambience that are at least excellent and often impressive. Full reviews appear earlier in this chapter.

Downtown: Circolo, Il Fornaio, Zuni, Corona Bar and Grill, Chevy's, Donatello, Yaya Cuisine.

Other San Francisco: Tortola, Café Majestic, Little City Antipasti Bar, Greens at Fort Mason, Stars.

Eastbay: Fourth Street Grill (Berkeley), Bay Wolf (Oakland), Chez Panisse Café (Berkeley), Chevys (Alameda and El Cerrito), Tourelle Café and Restaurant (Lafayette in Contra Costa County).

Marin: Butler's (Mill Valley).

Corona Bar and Grill

NEAR UNION SQUARE, P. 3, D2

88 Cyril Magnin and Ellis St.; 392-5500
Lunch appetizers $3.95–$7.25, entrées $6.50–$13.95
Dinner appetizers $3.95–$7.75, entrées $9.25–$13.95

Eight-foot palm trees mix with cacti in this predominantly Southwestern hangout. Carved masks watch you from the walls as you watch the city go by through the many windows. Dome lighting and sun-shaped glass lights in shades of pink and green emit low light. The vegetables are organic, the meat free range. Large portions of strictly upscale, trendy Mexican-ish seafood, grilled meats, tortilla creations, and fresh salads and salsas in this crowded wood-and-brass setting. One of *the* places to meet after work, before the theater, or for business. Open Mon.–Sat. 11:30 A.M.–11 P.M., Sun. 5–11 P.M. Reservations suggested. Full bar. AE, CB, D, DC, MC, V. Parking nearby.

Donatello
NEAR UNION SQUARE, P. 3, D2

501 Post St.; 441-7182
Breakfast entrées $7.50–$8.50
Lunch appetizers $5–$9, entrées $12–$15
Dinner appetizers $10–$14, entrées $23–$28

Perhaps the most elegant Italian restaurant in town, Donatello is a maze of little rooms which allows for some extra privacy for those who want to experience one of the better-known Italian restaurants in San Francisco. The elaborate decor is as rich, textured, and tastefully done as the food this ambitious place turns out: creamy, musky wild-mushroom risotto and ethereal pastas. Their strikingly reasonable lunch, considering the stately setting, features an antipasto cart with an array of appetizers and salads plus a rustic stuffed cabbage dish the critics write home about. Open for breakfast daily 7–10:30 A.M.; lunch Mon.–Fri. 11:30 A.M.–2 P.M., closed Sat. and Sun. lunch; dinner daily 6–11 P.M. Reservations essential. Full bar. AE, CB, DC, MC, V. Parking nearby.

Ebisu Restaurant
NEAR GOLDEN GATE PARK, P. 2, B2

1283 9th Ave.; 566-1770
Lunch $4.25–$7.95
Dinner $6.85–$14

Out of the way, but easily the best sushi bar in San Francisco, Ebisu is a friendly, bustling, informal restaurant with perfectly fresh, artfully arranged, meticulously prepared traditional and original—almost Art Deco—creations in generous portions. Expect a long wait during prime eating time. Best dishes include just about all fish and shellfish, such as red clam, tuna, yellowtail, salmon, oysters, katsuo tataki (slices of fish cooked outside and raw inside), pickled cod roe, amaebi (a kind of shrimp—ask them to fry the heads tempura-style), bonsai roll, soft shell crab roll, and tekka temaki (tuna in a hand-held, unsliced sushi roll). Open for lunch Mon.–Fri. 11:30 A.M.–2 P.M.; dinner Mon.–Sat. 5–10 P.M. Closed Sun. No reservations. Beer and small selection of wine. MC, V. Parking nearby.

Ernie's
FINANCIAL DISTRICT, P. 3, D1

847 Montgomery St.; 397-5969
Dinner appetizers $8.50–$12.50, entrées $22–$29.50, prix fixe dinner $38

One of the grande dames of the San Francisco restaurant scene, this 1934 establishment was given a facelift from red plush to lightly elegant in champagne colors, marble, and mirrors. The upstairs Ambrossia Room maintains the original red silks and velvets. If you prefer the lighter style, an intimate dining room is by the bar, and a larger one in the foyer. Also explore the Bacchus room in the cellar. Most of the old, heavy, long menu remains, resplendent with overworked meats in often gluey sauces (plus a lovely, classic Grand Marnier soufflé), but young, recently arrived Texas chef Craig Thomas has added his touch to the fresh foie gras, chicken liver soufflé, pasta with a ragout of seafood, squab in watercress sauce, and roast duck (most of them personal variations of California cuisine standbys). Friendly service. Expensive and expansive French and California wine list. Open daily 6:30–10:30 P.M. Reservations suggested. Full bar. AE, CB, DC, MC, V. Valet and nearby parking.

La Fiammetta Ristorante

NEAR PACIFIC HEIGHTS, P. 3, C1

1701 Octavia St.; 474-5077
Dinner appetizers $5–$13.50, entrées $9–$17

For a city with a large, historic Italian neighborhood and a whole mythology of Italianness about it, San Francisco has remarkably few really good, really Italian Italian restaurants. This is one of the newest entries on that short list. Small, bustling, friendly, yet elegant in setting, serious about its food, warm in its welcome, and with a menu that is strong on grilled fish and meats as well as homemade stuffed pastas. Do try an appetizer of grilled radicchio and mozzarella wrapped in pancetta (Italian bacon). Open Mon.–Sat. 6–10 P.M. Seatings only. Reservations essential. Wine. MC, V. Parking nearby.

Il Fornaio

NEAR FINANCIAL DISTRICT, P. 3, D1

1265 Battery St. (Levi's Plaza); 986-0100
Breakfast $4.50–$8.95
Lunch and dinner appetizers $3.50–$6.95, entrées $5–$17

Combination Italian bakery, delicatessen, and crowded, stylish restaurant, Il Fornaio has something for just about everyone. Divided into two rooms, the open kitchen is visible from both areas. Handpainted murals of hills and vineyards, and marble imported from Italy create great atmospheres in both areas. If you want a close, bustling ambience go to the delicatessen. The quieter half in the atrium is light and spacious with high ceilings and a view of the fountain in neighboring Levi's Plaza. The variety of foods is equally enticing. Breakfast on baked-on-the-premises Italian breads and pastries. Lunch on take-out meats, salads, and sandwiches, or savor grilled meats and pizzas at the counter or at either an indoor or outdoor table. Dine on pizzas, fresh pastas (the ravioli stuffed with greens and served in a walnut cream sauce is quite popular), grilled lamb and chicken, and casseroles baked in terra-cotta pots. Oddly enough, service tends to be slow and chaotic. Open for breakfast Mon.–Fri. 7–10 A.M., Sat. 8–10:30 A.M.; lunch and dinner Mon.–Thurs. 11:30 A.M.–11 P.M., Fri.–Sat. 11:30 A.M.–midnight, Sun. 9 A.M.–11 P.M. Reservations for dinner essential (expect a wait anyway). Full bar. MC, V. Parking nearby.

Fountain Court   PRESIDIO HEIGHTS, P. 2, B2
354 Clement St.; 668-1100
Lunch specials $3.25–$4.75
Lunch and dinner appetizers $3.25–$5.95, entrées $5.25–$22

One of the best of the new guard, Hong Kong–inspired Chinese restaurants, combining the friendly elegance of calm, cool, and California airy pale green walls and brass fixtures, with the best in a continually evolving, stunningly creative menu of Chinese seafood and the added fillip of Shanghainese slow-braised dishes. Soft, ample lighting. And service is so smooth, you never have to hunt for a waiter: one or another is there waiting, before you even know you need one. Try the fried shrimp in shell with scallions, juicy Shanghai steamed buns, garlic chicken, shredded pork, pickle greens and bean curd skin, dry sautéed shredded beef, scallops in garlic sauce, hot braised catfish (price varies), catfish clay pot (price varies), and Shanghai crispy duck. Open for lunch Mon.–Sat. 11 A.M.–3:30 P.M., Sun. 11 A.M.–3 P.M.; dinner daily 5–10 P.M. Reservations suggested. Wine and beer. AE, CB, DC, MC, V. Parking nearby.

Garden House   PRESIDIO HEIGHTS, P. 2, B2
133 Clement St.; 221-3655
Dinner appetizers $3.95–$5.75, entrées $5.95–$9.95

Most Vietnamese food is easy on the Western palate—a mix of Western beefiness mingled with Southeast Asian exotica—and this is one of the two best places in town to try it. (The two Golden Turtles, lumped together, make up the other one.) Head for the cool, tangy, yet rich lemon beef salad; roast Cornish hen; sizzling fish with fresh dill; broiled rack of pork with lemon grass; sautéed beef cubes; crispy fried egg noodles with pork, prawns, and vegetables. Waiters and waitresses guide and advise you through the menu. A white tablecloth setting is offset by green hanging plants and red, white, and pink flowers. Remarkably good prices for such quality. Open for dinner Mon.–Fri. 5–10 P.M., lunch and dinner Sat. and Sun. 11 A.M.–10 P.M. Reservations suggested. Wine and beer. AE, MC, V. Parking nearby.

Golden Turtle Vietnamese Restaurant

NEAR NOB HILL, P. 3, D1

2211 Van Ness Ave.; 441-4419
Lunch appetizers $5.50–$7.95, entrées $7.95–$16.50
Dinner appetizers $5.95–$7.95, entrées $8.50–$17.50

The Golden Turtle, and its branch located at 308 Fifth Ave. (221-5285), is generally acknowledged to be the grand duchess San Francisco Vietnamese restaurant. (For the heir apparent, see Garden House.) The Fifth Ave. branch's white-tablecloth service is less formal than the Van Ness venue, where the flamboyant setting features entire walls of carved-wood bas reliefs, hundreds of pin-point Christmas lights, and a carp pond at the entrance. Both, however, serve haute Vietnamese restaurant food, the sort that Saigon can now only dream about. We recommend the barbecued quail; shrimp and pork salad; fresh catfish in a clay pot; pan-fried crab (seasonal); Saigon style barbecued pork; and seven-jewel beef, a seven-course beef eaters' banquet. Open on Van Ness Ave. for lunch 11 A.M.–3 P.M.; dinner Tues.–Sun. 5–11 P.M. On Fifth Ave. open for dinner only Tues.–Sun. 5–10:30 P.M. Both closed Mon. Reservations suggested at the Van Ness location. Wine and beer. AE, MC, V. Parking nearby.

Greens at Fort Mason

NEAR FISHERMAN'S WHARF, P. 3, C1

Bldg. A (west side of Fort Mason; enter parking lot from Marina Blvd. at Buchanan St.); 771-6222
Lunch entrées $7.75–$8.75
Dinner appetizers $6–$7, entrées $9.50–$11.50

Take a cathedral-like setting and combine it with the bustle of a successful restaurant, and you have Greens— the Greens of the highest standards and the cleanest, simplest, most enticing creations. Located in a renovated army museum on a pier in the park, the place is vast. Thirty-foot ceilings leave room for the large redwood sculpture in the middle of the room. One wall holds bright abstract paintings, another more subdued art. The opposite side, about 250 feet in length, is all window. Small redwood tables, actually sculptures with flat surfaces, are scattered throughout the dining area. Interesting note— these tables don't have a nail or screw in them. Atmosphere is casual and calm, which would probably please the Zen Buddhist designers. You'll never notice this food has no meat. Service is occasionally so leisurely as to be somnolent and once in a while they even run out of food by mid-evening. But you can't beat the view of the San Francisco marina and Golden Gate Bridge. From an ever-changing seasonal menu, try the incredible home-baked

The Best Chinese Restaurants in the Entire Bay Area

These are for real connoisseurs only because (1) you have to be willing to drive to Millbrae (beyond the San Francisco Airport) and (2) you have to be Chinese enough to know that the finest Chinese food in the world is Cantonese (not chop suey or Chinese-American Cantonese, but the stuff that poets wrote aphorisms about hundreds of years ago and Hong Kong millionaires boast about today).

The **Flower Lounge** (1671 El Camino Real, Millbrae; 878-8108) and **Fook Yuen** (195 El Camino Real, Millbrae; 692-8600) sit within blocks of each other on a very plain stretch of El Camino Real. But look at the parking lots and you'll realize that the crowds of people crammed inside arrived in flotillas of Mercedes Benzes and BMWs.

It's hard to choose between the two. Both offer staggeringly large menus plus announced and unannounced specials; the freshest, most delicate shellfish; the richest fried fish slices (try the deep fried flounder at Fook Yuen); juicy barbecued pork and duck; pure, clean stir-fried and steamed vegetable dishes; dim sum; and abrupt but good English.

breads; full-bodied, bright spinach salad; baked Sonoma goat cheese; teriyaki-style grilled vegetables; smooth, rich soups; assertive, robust pizzas on fluffy yet crisp crusts; warming, thick vegetable stews; and smoky brochettes of fresh seasonal vegetables. Open Tues.–Sat. for lunch 11:30 A.M.–2:15 P.M., for dinner 6–9:30 P.M.; Sun. brunch only, 10 A.M.–2 P.M. Closed Mon. Reservations necessary. Wine and beer only. MC, V. Choice of several parking lots.

Hayes Street Grill NEAR THE CIVIC CENTER, P. 3, D2
320 Hayes St.; 863-5545
Lunch appetizers $3.25–$5.75, entrées $8–$15
Dinner appetizers $4–$7.75, entrées $9–$21

One of the places locals head for when they want the best and freshest fish simply prepared and offered with a choice of sauces. Menu changes daily, following the availability of local and imported seafood. Convenient to the Civic Center, Federal Building, opera, and symphony. Open for lunch Mon.–Fri. 11:30 A.M.–3 P.M.; dinner Mon.–Thurs. 5–10 P.M., Fri. 5–11 P.M., Sat. 6–11 P.M. Closed Sun. Reservations very strongly recommended. Wine and beer. MC, V. Parking nearby.

Julie's Supper Club   SOUTH OF MARKET, P. 3, D2
1123 Folsom St.; 861-4084
Appetizers and snacks $3.25–$6.50,   entrées
$8.50–$15.50

Located in the fashionable warehouse and trend-setting South of Market area (akin to New York's SoHo), Julie's combines a superkitschy, retro-fifties singles scene (more pink, gray, black, yellow, and green than you've ever seen together), blaring music (a mix of Frank Sinatra, the Coasters, Astrud Gilberto, and Charlie Mingus), supergenerous drinks, and habit-forming ultra-American appetizers and desserts. From their ever-changing menu, try (if available) the "crisscut" potato chips (grilled in two directions to form a pattern), jerk chicken wings, deep-fried beer-batter catfish, grilled fish of the day, roasted duckling with pecan BBQ sauce, cho cho cho (triple-chocolate) dessert, lemon tart, mango sorbet, and berry crisp. Service is surprisingly accommodating and efficient. Live entertainment every Mon., Tues., Wed. night—expect anything from rockabilly to jazz to the typical lounge act. Open for dinner Mon.–Thurs. 6–11 P.M. Fri.–Sat. 6 P.M.–midnight. Closed Sun. Reservations recommended. Full bar. AE, MC, V. Parking nearby in a marginal neighborhood.

Kincaid's Bay House   BURLINGAME
60 Bayview Place, Burlingame; 342-9844
Lunch appetizers $1.95–$2.95, entrées $6.50–$9.95
Dinner appetizers $3.95–$6.50, entrées $9.95–$18.95

Kincaid's main attraction is the bar. From the top of the ceiling it's all glass, covered in bottles of every kind of alcohol known to man. Bartenders use a library ladder to find the mixings. Best known for their malts and huge selection of local beers. If you are feeling truly eccentric try some shots, some as much as $175, and enjoy the vistas of airplanes landing and seabirds taking off. Kincaid's also offers a very large menu based on fresh, meticulously cooked fish, grilled Nebraska beef, and coffee ground fresh just before brewing. Its soaring windows opening just feet from the bay present spectacular night views. Inside, Italian tile, wood furniture, Himalayan granite table tops, and instrumental music make for a pleasant meal. Outdoor dining available in the summer. Open for lunch Mon.–Fri. 11:30 A.M.–2:30 P.M.; dinner Mon.–Thurs. 5:30–10 P.M., Fri.–Sat. 5–11 P.M., Sun. 5–10 P.M. Reservations suggested. Full bar. AE, MC, V. Parking lot.

King Charcoal Barbecue Restaurant
PRESIDIO HEIGHTS, P. 2, B2
3741 Geary Blvd.; 387-9655
Appetizers $4.95–$25, entrées $7.95–$12.95

Korean barbecue is a western meat eater's dream come true: endless slabs of grill-it-yourself beef, pork, and chicken marinated in garlic, onion, sesame, soy sauce, and, sometimes, chiles. Sort of a cross between backyard barbecue and Mexican food. This place, at the beginning of Little Asia, offers terrific food and fast, inattentive service in a crowded, smoky, rather dingy room. Good English. Try the bul ko ki (Korean teriyaki), kal bi (tender short ribs), pork bul ko ki (pork tenderloin), dark gu-i (chicken), and shrimp and vegetable tempuras. Open daily 11 A.M.–3 A.M. Asian beer and barely passable wine. MC, V. Parking nearby.

Little City Antipasti Bar
NORTH BEACH, P. 3, D1
673 Union St.; 434-2900
Lunch appetizers $4.50–$7.50, entrées $6.50–$10
Dinner appetizers $4.50–$7.50, entrées $11–$14

The quintessential old-time, friendly, bustling Italianate North Beach hangout (a dying breed) updated with an eighties California grill and some light pastas. Regulars make an entire, moderately priced meal out of several of the 17 or 18 nightly antipasti and a little good Italian wine. Entrées change every night, but fish and shellfish are usually good. Other excellent choices include pepper-spiced flank steak, grilled shrimps borrachos, Manila clams in black bean–ginger sauce, and Greek frittata. Open daily 11:30 A.M.–midnight; full lunch 11:30 A.M.–2:30 P.M.; appetizers and salads 2:30–6 P.M.; full dinner Mon.–Thurs. 6–11 P.M., Fri.–Sat. 6 P.M.–midnight; appetizers and salads daily 11 P.M.–midnight. Reservations for six or more. Full bar. AE, MC, V. Parking nearby.

Café Majestic
NEAR PACIFIC HEIGHTS, P. 3, C2
1500 Sutter St.; 776-6400
Breakfast $5–$8
Lunch appetizers $3.50–$11.50, entrées $8.50–$12.50
Dinner appetizers $3.50–$11.50, entrées $14–$22

Majestic it is—in an elegant European hotel dining room, with a marble entry, columns, plasterwork on the ceilings, and subdued salmon and gray-green decor. Take a look at the bar—a 125-year old set up from a Parisian café. Also note the butterfly collection around the mirrors. Food is a usually meticulous hybrid of French and California cuisines. No matter which seasonal menu, it will feature several varieties of freshly baked breads, elaborately blended sauces, and the most fashionable of vegetables. Service is strikingly attentive: bread plates and tea pots are refilled without reminder. The meal proceeds at the ideal pace—leisurely enough for conversation, quickly enough to keep the momentum up. Open Tues.–Sat. for breakfast 7–10:30 A.M.; Tues.–Sun. for lunch 11:30 A.M.–2:30 P.M.; dinner 6–10 P.M.; Sun. brunch 7:30 A.M.–2:30 P.M. Closed Mon. Reservations essential on weekends, strongly suggested on weekdays. Full bar. AE, MC, V. Parking nearby.

Masa's
NEAR UNION SQUARE, P. 3, D1
648 Bush St.; 989-7154
Dinner appetizers $10.50–$18.50, entrées $29–$38.50

This is San Francisco's only four-star restaurant. Chef Julian Serrano applies his virtuosity and passion to French techniques and the finest of California's fish, fowl, and produce, plus some imports, such as *rouget* (a fish flown in from France), and the most exquisite of caviars. His masterpieces over the past few years have included duck livers, crisped on the outside, almost runny inside (nearly, dare we say it, like a toasted marshmallow); creamy, exquisite sweetbreads; and such rebellious culinary puns as seafood sausages *(boudin des trois poissons)*, salmon aiguillettes (salmon strips cut up duck breast style), and lamb sashimi. He also creates silken, rounded, perfectly shaped sauces and delicate dessert pastries, although mousses tend toward the waxy. There is also a staggeringly impressive wine list and service that matches the food nuance for nuance. Open Tues.–Sat. 6–10 P.M. Reservations essential, sometimes several weeks in advance. Small full bar. AE, DC, MC, V. Valet and nearby parking.

Mustards Grill
YOUNTVILLE
Two miles north of Yountville on Hwy. 29; (707) 944-2424
Lunch and dinner appetizers $2.95–$8.50, entrées $8.95–$15

Created by the group that went on to create, among other jewels, Tra Vigne, also in the Napa Valley. You don't have to know that Mustards boasts about its condiments rather than its sauces in order to enjoy its classically crisp onion rings or fried potatoes with homemade catsup, or its liver with caramelized onions and bacon. Or its grilled then braised lamb chops with onion and mint. Or its baby-back ribs, or smoked ducks and chickens. Desserts such as creamy, fluffy bread pudding with apples and caramel sauce, or chocolate pecan cake with chocolate sauce will break the most confirmed dieter's resolve. Great selection of beers and local wines. Often slapdash but kindly service. Open daily 11:30 A.M.–10 P.M. Reservations suggested during peak hours. Full bar. MC, V. Parking lot.

Pierre at Le Meridien   SOUTH OF MARKET, P. 3, D2
50 Third St. (in the Le Meridien Hotel); 974-1030
Dinner appetizers $7.50–$18, entrées $22–$26, prix fixe five-course dinner $53

If you're looking for an impressive restaurant near downtown or the convention center to conduct a business dinner, Pierre's sleek, formal service and living-room-like setting should be ideal. The food tends toward elaborate presentation and sauces. Favorites from past seasonal menus: salads with fresh foie gras; thin grilled or sautéed salmon filets and slices; melanges of fresh fish and summer vegetables; sautéed sweetbreads with white port wine sauce; roasted breast and leg of pheasant; lamb chops; veal medallions with onion confit. Open Tues.–Sun. 6–11 P.M. Closed Mon. Reservations suggested. Full bar. AE, CB, D, DC, MC, V. Parking in hotel.

Postrio   NEAR UNION SQUARE, P. 3, D1
545 Post St.; 776-7825
Lunch appetizers $5.50–$9.50, entrées $11–$15
Dinner appetizers $7.50–$12, entrées $16.50–$22

An immensely fashionable, contemporary American-Italian-Chinese brasserie recently opened by the darling of L.A. café society, Wolfgang Puck. Gold and dark colors wrap the walls, creating a warm, partially formal feel that is enhanced by jazz music in the background. The menu features such creations as Cantonese-style roast duck and spicy mango sauce on arugula leaves and new onions; barbecued Chinese sausage with sweet-and-sour cabbage; grilled quail with spinach and soft egg ravioli; marinated tuna with avocado, sweet onions, and lime-ginger vinaigrette; and crisply sautéed sweetbreads with arugula. Open daily for lunch 11:30 A.M.–2:30 P.M.; dinner 5:30–10:30 P.M. Reservations highly advised. Full bar. AE, MC, V. Parking nearby.

Rosalie's   NOB HILL, P. 3, D1
1415 Van Ness Blvd.; 928-7188
Dinner appetizers $5.50–$9.50, entrées $13–$23

A fun, noisy, popular adventure in off-the-wall decor and food. The multileveled area is a decorator's playhouse. Theatrical projectors toss shadows onto the walls, adding to the already dramatic lighting. Vanilla leather banquettes blend with terra-cotta platters. Stacked in one corner are large heavily stuccoed blocks of different colors. Resist the urge to climb. Pianists play show tunes during the dinner hour, turning to more upbeat selections later on. All of this competes for your attention with food that ranges from flailing experiments to artful originals. We suggest the charred tuna appetizer, stuffed squash blossoms, prawn tamal, shellfish pan roast, duck burrito with pork and hominy stew, and fried chicken and mashed potatoes. Open Sun.–Thurs. 5:30–10:30 P.M., Fri.–Sat. 5:30–11:30 P.M. Full bar. AE, CB, D, DC, MC, V. Valet parking and parking nearby.

Ruth's CHRIS Steak House   PACIFIC HEIGHTS, P. 3, D1
1700 California St.; 673-0557
Dinner appetizers $2.50–$8.50, entrées $14–$25

This seventeenth franchise of the Louisiana chain serves up he-man portions of real midwestern prime (yes, prime) steaks and chops although the meat isn't aged enough for the true, deep, red-wine flavor of the finest steaks. (Not as good as home if you're from Omaha or Chicago. But some of the best steaks in San Francisco unless you get one of the occasional overcooked ones.) Then they heap on whooeeee portions of au gratin potatoes; four shapes and thicknesses of golden and greaseless French fries made from real potatoes (!); a few vegetables; watery, thin salads; and a few rather dull, gluey all-American desserts just to fill in the cracks. Everything is à la carte, so the bill can mount up. Best to stick with these favorites: 14-ounce filet; 8-ounce petite filet; beefy and juicy 16-ounce veal chops; thick, mild, and well-nigh perfect lamb chops (market price); boneless grilled chicken breasts with a lemon marinade; any of the four shapes of French fries. Like many franchises, Ruth's CHRIS hasn't been able to develop its own personality. Instead of a colorful, burly steakhouse feel, the management has kept with the clean, streamlined, oh-so-contemporary look of white and gray. Don't feel intimidated about eating a sizzling, rare steak on white linen; everyone else in this gigantic four-room corral has to as well. Open Sun.–Thurs. 5–10 P.M., Fri.–Sat. 5–10:30 P.M. Reservations suggested. Full bar. AE, MC, V. Parking nearby.

Stars   CIVIC CENTER, P. 3, D2
150 Redwood Alley; 861-7827
Lunch appetizers $6–$8, entrées $9.50–$12
Dinner appetizers $6.25–$11, entrées $19–$26

Talk about fashionable! Celebrity chef Jeremiah Tower has the publicist's gift of keeping his Hollywood-style bistro in the columns. As a place to be seen, it's popular with show-biz types and politicos alike. Dishes range from thick, juicy steaks and poached salmon to crusty snapper (fish) hash; grilled peppers stuffed with crabmeat; steamed mussels with marinated tomatoes and rosemary cream; and even tuna carpaccio (raw slices) with sesame cucumbers, ginger cream sauce, and golden caviar. Great (and fun) before or after the nearby opera or symphony. **Stars** is open for lunch Mon.–Fri. 11:30 A.M.–2:30 P.M.; dinner 5:30–10:30 P.M. daily. Reservations for Stars strongly suggested. Full bar. AE, CB, DC, MC, V. Valet or nearby parking.

The tiny **Stars Café** next door **(555 Golden Gate)** boasts large sandwiches; tapas (Spanish bar food); light, imaginative entrées; and juicy, crusty fish and chips from Starfish, Tower's takeout venture. Open Mon.–Fri. 7:30 A.M.–10 P.M., Sat.–Sun. 10 A.M.–10 P.M.

Tokyo Sukiyaki   FISHERMAN'S WHARF, P. 3, D1
225 Jefferson St.; 775-9030
Lunch appetizers $3.50–$8, entrées $7.50–$17
Dinner appetizers $4.50–$12, entrées $12–$50

Despite its Fisherman's Wharf location, which should suggest tourist schlock, this is *the* restaurant visiting Japanese diplomatic and corporate dignitaries return to again and again. The tourist dinners are sad, lean affairs, but the small dishes and entrées from the Japanese menu, available in an English translation upon request, are some of the most delicate, most satisfying, most evocative Japanese food in California. Depending on the season, try the soft-shell crab, deep-fried oysters, beef teriyaki, salt-broiled flounder, chawan mushi (savory custard), nasu dengaku (eggplant), assorted sashimi, yakitori, and beef tataki. English is very good. Open Mon.–Fri. 4–11 P.M., Sat.–Sun. 11:30 A.M.–11 P.M. Reservations suggested. Full bar. AE, CB, DC, MC, V. Parking nearby.

Tortola Restaurant   PRESIDIO HEIGHTS, P. 2, C1
3640 Sacramento St.; 929-8181
Lunch appetizers $2.25–$6.95, entrées $7.50–$9.75
Dinner appetizers $2.25–$6.95, entrées $8.50–$15.50

Resembling a long brick box on the outside, Tortola's is an airy, skylit haven of wooden tables and chairs, and pastel walls. Canvases hang from the high ceilings, adding some contour and swallowing the echoes. Potted cacti contribute to the Southwestern theme at this reincarnation of a very old San Francisco tradition featuring grilled and California-Southwestern-nouvelle dishes that are both interesting and emotionally satisfying— genuinely good food. The original Tortola's Early Califor-

Japantown

Best tempura: **Isuzu Japanese Seafood Restaurant** (1581 Webster Street, 922-2290). Light, tender, lacy, often shatteringly crisp vegetable and shrimp tempura—an easy eight unless it's greasy. Also at Isuzu: a well-appointed sushi bar with Japanese soap operas playing in the corner (most of the clientele speak Japanese) and a broad, thoroughly Japanese menu offering everything from chicken miso yaki to fried pork cutlet, but the emphasis is on seafood. Try their tender, mild clams steamed in fish stock and sake with a tart soy sauce and citron vinegar dipping sauce.

Vying for first place with Isuzu is **Sanppo** (1702 Post Street, 346-3486). Probably the oldest full-spectrum restaurant in Japantown, this crowded, noisy, underlit restaurant with the long lines and the lightning-fast service boasts a large menu with a staggering array of top-notch choices, from Japanese clichés to Japanese soul foods. Try the *nizakana,* an improvement on teriyaki: your choice of fish in season is grilled until firm yet moist in soy sauce and sake, much less sweet than teriyaki, and served with big chunks of tofu and fried eggplant, also doused in sauce. Tempura, oysters teriyaki, sukiyaki, nuta (a Japanese squid and cucumber salad) . . . they're all first-rate.

Best plastic food models, with food to match: **Iroha** (1728 Buchanan Street Mall, 922-0321). Iroha's downstairs window display of twenty-odd bowls and plates of scrupulously accurate custom-made plastic noodles, yakitori, tempura, salads, and soups gives you a good idea of what you can choose from upstairs. Our favorites include chewy homemade ramen (noodles) immersed in a robust white miso broth and accompanied by bracken fern and various other seasonal vegetables (miso sansei ramen), and a combination yakitori of skewered shrimp, chicken, and vegetables in sweet marinades of varying intensity.

Best place to take the kids for sushi: **Isobune Sushi** (1737 Post Street inside the Japan Center, 563-1030). A river runs through a channel in a horseshoe-shaped counter. Small wooden boats carry pairs of sushi around and around the course—white-water sushi-ing. You never have to wait; something's always coming around the bend, although it may not be what you want (the best things are snatched up by the people at the headwaters) and what you do take may be tired from riding the rapids more than a few times.

Best nibbles, especially with beer: **Echigo-Ya** (1740 Buchanan Street Mall, 567-3852). Small, crisp fritters of

> marinated chicken tatsuta age (batter-fried); delicate deep-fried soft shell crab; and *nishime,* the vegetable assortment they misleadingly describe as a stew because the tender eggplant, tofu, squash, and other vegetables have been briefly simmered before being dabbed each with its own sauce. Not the place for main dishes, however: they're all far too sweet.

nia tacos, enchiladas, and tamales are uniformly bland, better suited to Maine than California, but the California-style entrées draw their inspiration from Tortola's Mexican roots. From an ever-changing menu we recommend guacamole, quesadillas, corn cakes, grilled meats and fish, and just about anything else that isn't called "early California." Open Tues.–Fri. for lunch 11:30 A.M.–2 P.M., dinner 5–10 P.M.; Sat. 11:30 A.M.–10 P.M.; Sun. 5–9 P.M. Reservations suggested. Wine and beer. MC, V. Parking nearby.

Tourelle Café and Restaurant LAFAYETTE
3565 Mt. Diablo Blvd.; Lafayette; 284-3565
Lunch appetizers $4.50–$7.50, entrées $4.50–$16.50
Dinner appetizers $4.50–$7.50, entrées $11.50–$17.50

A combination of Parisian elegance and suburban comfort, Tourelle aims high. The movers, shakers, and deal makers of Contra Costa County lunch on light, moist grilled chicken sandwiches, grilled fish, or extravagant salads in an open, sunny setting reminiscent of a French chateau. At dinner, they return for elegance, festivity, and a good wine list. The restaurant is located in a rustic old brick and wood building encompassing a small plaza with a fountain. The dining room inside is elegant with chandeliers and fabric chairs comfortable enough to sink into at the end of the meal. Open Tues.–Sat. 11 A.M.–11 P.M., Sun. 10 A.M.–10 P.M. Reservations suggested. Full bar. AE, MC, V. Parking lot.

Tra Vigne ST. HELENA
1050 Charter Oak (at Hwy. 29), St. Helena; (707) 963-4444
Lunch appetizers $2.95–$5.50, entrées $6.60–$11.95
Dinner appetizers $2.95–$5.50, entrées $10–$13

You've been to a diner. You've been to a bar and grill. You've been to a tony pastel restaurant. But you've never been to a Tra Vigne. This restaurant presents an original and independent vision, from its striking setting (a greenish-gray dream of a warm, pristine Italian castle) to its startlingly intense, lusty, marvelously creative Tuscan-inspired (yet very Napa Valley) specialties. Patios and high ceilings add to the impression you've been whisked back to ancient Italy. Old stone-like walls and marble contribute to the austerity. Renovated to create one large space, Tra Vigne now also has a bar where food can be ordered and an open kitchen where skilled hands create quite a show. Service is abundant, eager, and thorough; the list of Italian and California wines is most impressive. Winners from the frequently changing seasonal menu: plump, cool green-lipped New Zealand mussels perfumed with fresh fennel and Sambuca liqueur; braised artichoke bottoms with home-grown basil and thyme; Tuscan white beans in a garlic prosciutto broth; juicy strips of veal flank steak impregnated with Barolo wine and rosemary; pizza rustica, with a thin, crisp, almost nutty dough and filled with fresh mozzarella, garlicky sautéed red chard, pancetta (unsmoked bacon), roasted red peppers, and Parmesan; moist, firm, and cheesy polenta with pesto and an intense topping of cheeses and herbs. Open daily noon–10 P.M. Reservations strongly suggested. Full bar. MC, V. Parking lot.

Tutto Bene   NOB HILL, P. 3, D1
2080 Van Ness Ave.; 673-3500
Dinner appetizers $1.90–$5.70, entrées $9.25–$14.25

An Italianate theme restaurant, this bustling, glittering place offers small portions of antipasti, pastas, and meat plates so you can nosh your way through dinner Italian-style. The refrigarator cases of cheeses, vegetables, and hams right at the entrance will get the mouth watering. Head straight to the double bar where shelves of Italian groceries hang overhead. Grab a drink and some appetizers here while you wait for a table, enjoying the outside view of Van Ness Ave. Our favorites include gioielli del vagabondo (raw beef slices wrapped around celery and cheese), trittico di bruschetta (toast covered with mozzarella and fresh tomato sauce), marinated eggplant, rotolino ai quattro formaggi (sliced mozzarella rolled around pesto, dried tomatoes, pine nuts, and cheese), gnocchi al coniglio (potato pasta in rabbit sauce), tortelloni dell'orto, and rabbit with eggplant. The dining room is up above—a design which allows for optimum people watching. Open Sun.–Thurs. 5–11 P.M., Fri.–Sat. 5 P.M.–midnight. Reservations essential. Full bar. AE, DC, MC, V. Valet parking; other parking nearby.

Yaya Cuisine   SOUTH OF MARKET, P. 3, D2
397 Eighth St.; 255-0909
Lunch appetizers $3.25–$5.75, entrées $5.50–$9
Dinner appetizers $3.75–$5.75, entrées $10–$13

Light pink walls, white tables, black chairs, and an art display that changes every six weeks make this a typical SoMa eatery. Despite the common atmosphere, Yaya's has an original twist. Small, with 46 seats, the atmosphere is casual and friendly. Yaya will cook up everything on the mesquite grill, letting you observe and comment on the preparations. The specialties here are endless. Take the salads, fragrances, and light touches of Middle Eastern cooking, knead in a strong dose of California cuisine, and you've got some of the jazziest, most creative, and reasonable food in town. The critics gush over the wondrous textures and flavors of their entrées fashioned from ground meats, not to mention the grilled chicken rolls, moistened with a sun-dried lime-and-caper sauce, and set inside a nest made of a ten-vegetable medley. Open for lunch Mon.–Fri. 11:30 A.M.–2:30 P.M.; dinner Mon.–Thurs. 5:30–10 P.M., Fri.–Sat. 5–10:30 P.M. Reservations recommended. AE, MC, V. Limited parking on the premises, ample parking nearby.

Zola's
CIVIC CENTER, P. 3, D2

395 Hayes St.; 775-3311
Lunch appetizers $3–$5, entrées $7–$15
Dinner appetizers $5–$8, entrées $16–$19

A small, serene, intimate Frencher-than-French hideaway, only slightly formal, serving country French food quietly and elegantly. The room is well lit with hanging fixtures and sconces. One entire wall serves as a canvas for artist Penelope Fried. Very intelligent wine list. Offerings on the changeable menu include roasted rack of lamb with thyme-scented jus, fresh shellfish stews, cassoulets, and homemade desserts. Open for lunch Mon.–Fri. 11:30 A.M.–2:30 P.M.; dinner Mon.–Sat. 5:30–11 P.M. Closed Sun. Reservations advised. Full bar. AE, CB, DC, MC, V. Parking nearby.

Zuni Café and Grill
MARKET STREET, P. 3, D2

1658 Market St.; 552-2522
Breakfast $2.25–$4.25
Lunch appetizers $4.50–$7, entrées $5.50–$15.50
Dinner appetizers $4.75–$8, entrées $12.50–$22

This wildly successful, cramped, wedge-shaped restaurant is almost unclassifiable. The closest we can get is Mediterranean by way of California and France with Mexican touches and a New Orleans-cum-Parisian oyster bar thrown in for good measure. Zuni's started out small and has gradually expanded into a popular place to go for a meal or to just unwind. With a European café philosophy, they let you sit and relax. The place is always friendly and cozy. Go for imaginative breakfasts, exciting lunches, and luscious dinners before or after the theater. (Don't go for a business lunch—Zuni is too crowded and the wait's too long.) Anything deep-fried is particularly crisp and grease-less. Anything sweet and baked is a sure-fire winner. Past successes include warm quail confit with spiced prunes and arugula; polenta with mascarpone; roast suckling pig with white beans and wild mushrooms; and the best hamburgers and fried onion rings this side of Orion. Open Tues.–Sat. 7:30 A.M.–midnight, Sun. 7:30 A.M.–11 P.M. Closed Mon. Reservations advised. Full bar. AE, MC, V. Parking nearby.

Dim Sum

When we speak of Chinatown, we mean the original one, once clustered around Grant Avenue but now spreading far into Italian North Beach. (Little Chinatown lies *north* in "the avenues," clustered between Geary and Clement streets.)

Once Chinatown was Cantonese, reflecting the origins of its inhabitants. Now it's a mix of most of the regions of China, with Hong Kong, Taiwan, and the ethnic Chinese from Vietnam mixed in. But it still reigns as the U.S. capital of dim sum, that breakfast-brunch-lunch meal of snacks developed in Canton and perfected in Hong Kong.

So it's only fitting that the best place to go for dim sum in Chinatown is **Hong Kong Tea House** (835 Pacific Avenue, 391-6365). Try to get there before 11:30 A.M. on weekdays, or expect to wait 15 to sixty minutes for your number to be called in Cantonese and English. (On weekends, there's no way to avoid the crowds. Take your number, ask how long, then go for a walk and return a few minutes before your allotted time.) When the waiter seats you, he or she will yell "What kind of tea?" Answer "chrysanthemum" for a cooling delicate beverage, *"po nay"* for a strong, cutting digestive. Then just point as cart after cart of goodies wheels past. You don't have to know what things are. Everything is so inexpensive and in such small portions that if you don't like something, just leave it and try something else from off the carts. Fill your table with goodies all at one time or choose each plate as it rolls by. The waiter touts up your bill by counting the plates.

Second choice for dim sum: **Ocean City** (640 Broadway, second floor; 982-2328). The variety is as lavish, the setting a bit quieter (although far from tranquil), but the workmanship is occasionally a little careless.

For truly elegant dim sum, you'll have to leave Chinatown and take a short taxi ride to **Harbor Village** (Four Embarcadero Center, 781-8833) for adventures in taste in a room set with antiques and art.

9

ENTERTAINMENT

With violinists in the BART station, tenors singing Verdi arias in front of Macy's, and bowling-ball jugglers hard at work on Fisherman's Wharf's Pier 39, it's obviously not difficult to find live entertainment in San Francisco. From the clubs of North Beach to the Top o' lounges crowning Nob Hill, it's easy to find shows that span the gamut from ragtime to heavy metal. A town that knows how to have a good time, San Francisco is an easy place to see live acts, hear jazz or classical music, see both "Broadway" and experimental theater, go dancing, or watch a major-league game. Prices are moderate and, in many cases, reservations are no problem. Unlike many major cities, San Francisco's cultural life does not, with the exception of legitimate theaters, cluster around downtown. Major first-run movies play at theaters along Van Ness Avenue, near Fisherman's Wharf, and in the Marina District. The club scene spreads out into some of the city's most interesting neighborhoods such as the Mission and North Beach, while the city's major classical music, dance, and opera performances are found around the Civic Center complex. To get an overview of current performances, pick up a copy of the *San Francisco Examiner/Chronicle's Sunday Datebook* or the *Oakland Tribune's Calendar.* Another good source of entertainment listings is a free weekly, the *San Francisco Bay Guardian.*

PERFORMING ARTS

CLUBS

No trip to San Francisco is complete without a club visit. From **Club Fugazi** (see *Priorities*) to North Beach's **Caffé Trieste** (601 Vallejo, 392-6739), a restaurant where the staff performs an opera every Saturday afternoon, the city serves every taste and budget. For comedy try **Cobb's Comedy Club** (2801 Leavenworth, 928-4320), **The Punch Line** (above 444 Battery, 397-7573), **Improv** (401 Mason, 441-7787), or the **Holy City Zoo** (408 Clement, 386-4242) where Robin Williams got his start.

A more traditional kind of entertainment is found at the Top o' clubs—lounges atop the city's fine hotels. There's music at **Sherlock Holmes Esquire** at the Holiday Inn Union Square (398-8900) and the **Top of the Mark** (Mark Hopkins hotel, 392-3434). Or dance at **Oz** (397-7000) atop the St. Francis.

The Bay Area has one of the nation's best jazz stations, **KJAZ** (92.7 FM), which offers callers a listing of current jazz shows (769-4818). For live performances, check out **Kimball's** (300 Grove, 861-5555), **Jazz Workshop** (473 Broadway, 398-9700), and **Pasand Lounge** (1875 Union, 922-4498) which offers Brazilian jazz Monday and Thursday. Definitely worth the quick trip to Oakland is **Yoshi's** (6030 Claremont, 652-9200).

San Francisco's music clubs range from the **Venetian Room** (775-5226), the Nob Hill supper club in the Fairmont Hotel featuring the likes of Lena Horne and Tony Bennett, to the **I-Beam** (1748 Haight, 668-6006), a Haight-Ashbury New-Wave venue in a disco environment that is big on laser lights and videos. The legendary **Fillmore Auditorium,** which boomed in the sixties, still brings in great bands of the past as well as current rock celebrities. A wider range of rock, jazz, and blues performers is found at the **Great American Music Hall** (859 O'Farrell, 885-0750). At **Slim's** (333 11th, 621-3330), you can enjoy the best of American roots music ranging from the World Saxophone Quartet to blues acts.

Besides Oz there are many other dance clubs in town such as **Club DV8** (540 Howard Street, 957-1730), a South of Market rock palace where iguanas are displayed for those who don't have time for a trip down to Puerto Vallarta. At the **Oasis** (11th and Folsom, 621-8119), you can dance to hits played by bands or disk jockeys all on a plexiglass floor laid atop a pool of water. For a Latin scene, try **Cesar's Latin Palace** (3140 Mission, 648-6611). If you'd prefer to dance to the nostalgic pop music of Don Neely's Royal Society Sextet, try the **New Orleans Room** (772-5259) at the Fairmont.

THEATER

From Sam Shepard dramas to Shakespearean repertory, the San Francisco area offers an eclectic mix of productions. Gilbert and Sullivan, black and Latin drama, avant garde, cabaret, musicals, and touring companies make the city a kind of ongoing theater festival. Prices are reasonable and Tuesday through Saturday you can often get half-price day-of-performance seats at the STBS outlet on the Stockton Street side of Union Square (433-STBS).

The **American Conservatory Theatre (ACT),** the city's excellent repertory company, offers everything from Ibsen and Shaw to recent Broadway hits. Call 749-2228 for information. The **Berkeley Repertory Theatre** (2025 Addison, 845-4700) is conveniently reached by BART and offers new dramas as well as old favorites. Among the city's smaller theater companies, consider the **Magic Theatre** at Fort Mason (441-8822) or the Mission's **Eureka Theatre** (2730 16th, 558-9898). For Gilbert and Sullivan, try **The Lamplighters** (361 Dolores, 752-7755). The summertime **Berkeley Shakespeare Festival** at John Hinkle Park in Berkeley (548-3422) is highly recommended.

Major road shows generally come to the **Orpheum** (1192 Market, 474-3800), **Curran** (445 Geary, 474-3800), and **Golden Gate** (Market at Taylor, 474-3800). **Theatre on the Square** (450 Post, 433-9500) and the **Marines Memorial** (609 Sutter, 771-6900) offer smaller touring comedies and musicals and sometimes stage their own shows.

MUSIC AND DANCE

Civic Center, home of the War Memorial Opera House, Davies Symphony Hall, and Herbst Theatre, is San Francisco's major performing-arts center. But the Bay Area is also rich in chamber music, special events such as the Midsummer Mozart Festival, the free Stern Grove concerts (see *Priorities*), jazz-dance companies, and such outstanding regional companies as the Oakland Ballet. In addition, Fort Mason Center (at Buchanan Street and Marina Boulevard) frequently showcases ethnic events such as the Asian American Dance Collective.

The **San Francisco Opera** (864-3330) offers a three-month fall season at the city's grand War Memorial Opera House, located at 301 Van Ness. With tickets at a premium, and major performances sold out, you might prefer to see the less expensive, but very worthwhile, **Pocket Opera** (101 Embarcadero, 398-2220). The **San Francisco Symphony** performs at Davies Symphony Hall (Grove and Van Ness, 431-5400) and the **Oakland Symphony** can be heard at the Paramount Theatre (2025 Broadway in Oakland), one of California's great Art-Deco palaces. **Old First Concerts** at the Old First Presbyterian Church (Van Ness and Sacramento, 474-1608) offers everything from swing to Vivaldi.

The **San Francisco Ballet** is another good reason to visit the War Memorial Opera House (621-3838). Equally worthwhile is the **Oakland Ballet** at the Paramount (452-9288).

SPORTS

TO WATCH

Football: The National Football League's **49ers** play at Candlestick Park (468-2249), eight miles south of downtown off Highway 101. Often windy, sometimes foggy, it's a good idea to bring a jacket to the 65,700-seat stadium.

Baseball: The National League's **San Francisco Giants** also play at Candlestick, which was recently in the news as the site of the 1989 World Series that was interrupted by the largest quake in the area since 1906. Call 467-8000 for tickets. For a sunnier experience, watch the American League's **Oakland Athletics,** winners of the 1989 World Series, at the Oakland Coliseum (638-0500). Easily reached by BART, this 54,500-seat stadium is also the setting for major rock concerts.

Basketball: Adjacent to the Coliseum's stadium is the 14,200-seat arena, home of the National Basketball Association's **Golden State Warriors** (638-6000). Circuses, concerts, the Ice Capades, and many other special events are staged here.

Horse Racing is year-round in the Bay Area. The two major racetracks are **Bay Meadows** (574-7223) in San Mateo and **Golden Gate Fields** (526-3020) in Albany. Racing at Bay Meadows begins in August and continues to the end of January. On Sunday, fans can sit in the infield. This program is immediately followed by racing at Golden Gate Fields, which runs through the end of June. From late June to August, there are country fairs in Pleasanton, Vallejo, Santa Rosa, and Stockton. If you're not feeling ambitious, there is satellite wagering for other tracks at Bay Meadows, Golden Gate Fields, and several of the fair facilities. Races are broadcast on closed-circuit television. Consult local sports pages for details. Food service is mediocre at the tracks; bring your own picnic.

Also: The two major college sports programs in the Bay Area are at **UC Berkeley** (642-5150) and **Stanford** (723-1021). Each November football teams from these two universities play the "Big Game" in Palo Alto or Berkeley. The winner traditionally keeps the coveted axe until the following year's game.

TO PLAY

Tennis: The San Francisco Recreation and Parks Department (558-4532) manages over one hundred tennis courts at parks across town. A small fee is charged for 21 courts in Golden Gate Park; the rest are free.

Golf: There are four public courses in the city. **Lincoln Park** (221-9911) in the Richmond District charges $10 weekdays, $14 weekends. **Harding Park** (664-4690), in the Ingleside, offers two courses. There is also a nine-hole course in **Golden Gate Park** (751-8987) charging $4 weekdays and $7 weekends. **McLaren Park** (558-4655), located near the Cow Palace on the south side of the city, also has a nine-hole course.

Hiking and biking: With trails winding through Golden Gate Park, along the northern waterfront, and up and down the nearby Marin Headlands, there is no shortage of promising footpaths in the San Francisco area. **Point Reyes, Angel Island** (*Priorities*), Marin County's **Mount Tamalpais,** and the Eastbay's **Tilden Park** are also recommended. In town, the San Francisco Convention and Visitors Bureau publishes and distributes *Union Square* and *Chinatown Walking Tour* guides. Marked scenic bike trails take you through Golden Gate Park to Lake Merced or over the Golden Gate Bridge to Marin County. You'll find bike rental shops on Stanyan Street at the entrance to Golden Gate Park.

Silver Screen by the Bay

San Francisco and the Bay Area have played a role in many movies. These movies were shot partially or entirely by the Bay.

Casualties of War	*On the Beach*
Presidio	*Vertigo*
Tucker	*Pal Joey*
Star Trek IV	*The Glenn Miller Story*
Howard The Duck	*The Time of Your Life*
A View to a Kill	*I Remember Mama*
The Right Stuff	*Dark Passage*
Cujo	*The Maltese Falcon*
Invasion of the Body Snatchers	*San Francisco*
High Anxiety	*The Jazz Singer*
Towering Inferno	*True Believer*
The Conversation	*Dead Pool*
Play It Again Sam	*Inner Space*
Dirty Harry	*Burglar*
The Candidate	*Jagged Edge*
Harold and Maude	*Woman in Red*
THX-1138	*Shoot the Moon*
Take the Money and Run	*48 Hours*
Bullitt	*Tell Me A Riddle*
Guess Who's Coming to Dinner	*Greed*
Flower Drum Song	*Fog Over Frisco*
Days of Wine and Roses	*Lady From Shanghai*
The Birds	*Hell on Frisco Bay*
Birdman of Alcatraz	

10

EXCURSIONS

Oakland and Berkeley

Who was it who said all of Oakland is on the wrong side of the tracks? Certainly not Jack London, who was born in this city, or Earl Warren, who got his first big political break here. You won't hear any loose talk like that from Oakland A's bash brothers Jose Canseco or Mark McGwire. Top-40 rapper M.C. Hammer is proud of his Oakland heritage. Why, even Al Davis is talking about bringing his Los Angeles Raiders home. Could it be that Gertrude Stein had tried one too many of those kinky Alice B. Toklas brownies when she summed up her hometown by saying, "There's no there there."

This city of 350,000 offers a chance to stay in a castle-like resort hotel, visit the finest museum of Californiana in the state, explore redwood parks, and enjoy some of the best views in the Bay Area. Blessed with sunnier weather than nearby San Francisco, Oakland has an urban gem in Lake Merritt, which is adorned with a necklace of lights in the evening. There's good waterfront dining on Jack London Square and across the estuary in Alameda. The city has some of California's best Asian restaurants, as well as high-quality oyster bars, rib joints, and ice cream parlors. Just minutes away, in Berkeley, is the birthplace of California cuisine, Chez Panisse. And the jazz scene thrives in the University of California neighborhood.

The smart place to begin a visit is the **Oakland Museum** (see *Priorities*) at 1000 Oak Street, just twenty minutes by BART from downtown San Francisco. (Take the Lake Merritt Exit and walk west on Oak Street).

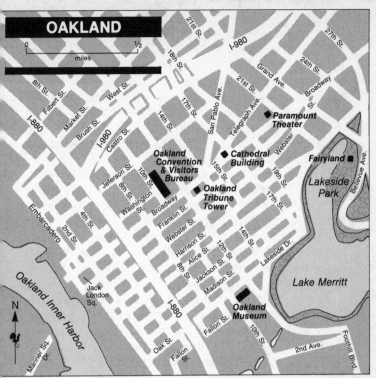

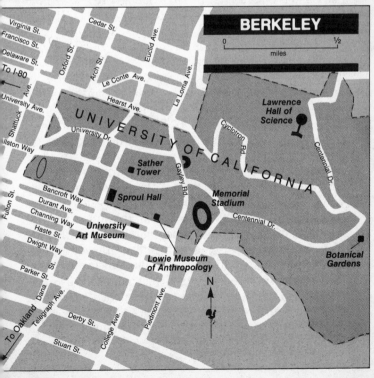

Built on three levels with a beautiful sculpture garden, this museum covers all aspects of the state's heritage. From Native American through the Spanish period to modern times, this collection offers a panoramic look at the California story. Along the way you'll find many legendary characters like the Big Four railroad barons (Stanford, Huntington, Hopkins, and Crocker) who made Oakland the terminus of the transcontinental railroad in 1868.

From Gold Rush era entrepreneur John C. Fremont—who once exclaimed, "When I came to California I hadn't a cent. Now I owe two million dollars."—to Richard M. Nixon, you'll learn about the people who helped turned this modest pre-Gold Rush land into one of our largest states. The Oakland Museum is open Wednesday through Saturday, from 10 A.M. to 5 P.M., on Sunday from noon to 7 P.M. (273-3401).

One block east of the museum is **Lake Merritt,** surrounded by one of the finest urban parks in the San Francisco area. Kids will love **Fairyland,** a charming park located across the lake at Grand and Bellevue avenues with play areas designed around fairy-tale themes. Fairyland is open Friday through Sunday, 10 A.M. to 4:30 P.M. during winter; Wednesday through Sunday, 10 A.M. to 4:30 P.M. in spring; and daily 10 A.M. to 4:30 P.M. during summer. Admission is $2 for adults, $1.50 for children 1–12, and free for children under 1. Call 832–3609 for information. On weekends you can enjoy a tour of the lake abroad the *Merritt Queen,* a small paddlewheeler that delights families. Call 444–3807 for information.

Ten minutes from the lake is the Broadway corridor, home to a number of the city's most important architectural landmarks. Among them is the **Paramount Theatre** at 2025 Broadway, an Art Deco showcase where you can see the Oakland Ballet (465-6400) and Oakland Symphony (446-1992). A blend of Byzantine figures, fountains of light, and bas-relief murals, the Paramount is probably the most elegant theater in the Bay Area.

Also in the downtown area are the **Oakland Floral Depot,** a handsome blue-tiled building at 19th Street and Telegraph Avenue, and two landmark buildings crowned with French château style roofs—the **Cathedral Building,** on Broadway at Telegraph, and the **Oakland Tribune Tower,** on 13th Street and Franklin. A good vantage point to view many of these buildings is the City Square plaza at Broadway and 13th Street.

If you're ready to take a break, the tables here are ideal for outdoor dining on a sunny day. There are many take-out restaurants in the area as well as **Crogan's** at 505 14th St. (464–3698), a sit-down establishment offering seafood, salads, chicken, and hamburgers. The bar here is a popular gathering spot.

Oakland is a good restaurant town. If you arrive early in the day, stop in at **La Creme de la Creme** (420–8822) at 5362 College Ave. for early American breakfasts featuring such classics as biscuits and gravy. In the downtown area you can choose between Burmese cuisine at **Nan Yang,** 301 Eighth St. (465-6924), **Jade Villa,** serving dim sum at 800 Broadway (839–1688), Vietnamese dishes at **Le Cheval,** 1414 Jefferson St. (763-8495), and **Saigon Deli,** 1600 San Pablo Ave. (465-4545). The **Gulf Coast Oyster Bar and Restaurant** on Washington St. (839-6950) serves wonderful seafood. Ten minutes away is a branch of **Chevys** (see *Restaurants)*, at 2400 Mariner Square Dr. (521-3768) on the Alameda Estuary. Take a table outside and enjoy the sailboats cruising by. For pork ribs consider **Flint's** at 6609 Shattuck Ave. (653-0593).

Oakland's preeminent dessert spot is **Fenton's Creamery,** 4226 Piedmont Ave. (658-7000), which offers sundaes and banana splits in vast portions.

Any visit here should include the **Oakland Hills** and Skyline Boulevard. Besides offering excellent views of the Bay Area, this neighborhood is convenient to **Redwood Regional Park,** part of an open-space network that extends more than fifty miles along the Eastbay hills. Drive north on Skyline Boulevard to Claremont Boulevard and head down the hill into Berkeley.

On the way, you'll pass the castle-like **Claremont Resort Hotel** at 41 Tunnel Rd. (843-3000). Situated on 20 acres, the Claremont Resort is a Victorian style hotel whose facilities include a spa, tennis courts, and large swimming pool. Singles are $145; doubles, $165; suites, $210–$700.

Berkeley is home to one of the nation's most prestigious universities—the University of California at Berkeley.

The school is noted for its scientific research as well as its student political activity. (U.C. Berkeley was the site of the famous Free Speech Movement protests of 1964.) The observation deck of Sather Tower sports a fascinating view of Berkeley, the bay, and San Francisco. The tower was modeled after Saint Mark's campanile in Venice.

One of the best spots in the Bay Area, unfortunately missed by most visitors, is the **University of California Botanical Gardens.** More than eight thousand plants are found in this thirty-acre Strawberry Canyon glen. The gardens are open daily from 9 A.M. to 5 P.M. (642-3343). Admission is free.

Take Centennial Drive east from the U.C. Berkeley football stadium and you'll come to the **Lawrence Hall of Science** (642-5132), a museum with excellent exhibits on nuclear science, astronomy, earthquakes, natural history, computers, chemistry, and physics. The hands-on exhibits make this a great place to take the kids. Open Monday to Friday from 10 A.M. to 4:30 P.M., Saturday from 10 A.M. to 5 P.M., and Sunday from 11 A.M. to 5 P.M. Admission $3.50 for adults, $2.50 for seniors and students over seven. Children six and under enter free.

Also on the University of California campus you can visit the western and oriental art collections at the **University Art Museum,** 2626 Bancroft Way (642-0808). Open from Wednesday through Sunday, 11 A.M. to 5 P.M. Admission is $3 adults, $2 seniors and students. Across the street in Kroeber Hall is the **Lowie Museum of Anthropology** (642-3681) where exhibits range from prehistoric artifacts to art collected in the Pacific Islands. Open Tuesday through Friday from 10 A.M. to 4:30 P.M., and weekends from noon to 4:30 P.M. Admission is $1.50 adults, $.50 seniors, $.25 children.

A few blocks away at 2476 Telegraph Avenue is **Moe's** (849-2087), an outstanding used bookstore. Next door is one of the Bay Area's largest bookstores, **Cody's** (845-7852). Also in Berkeley, at 1400 Shattuck, is **Easy Going** (843-3533), a travel bookstore.

At 1517 Shattuck Ave. is the Eastbay's most famous restaurant, **Chez Panisse** (see *Restaurants*).

There are a number of good restaurants on University Ave. For southwestern cuisine in a converted railroad station, try the **Santa Fe Bar and Grill** at 1310 University

Ave. (841-4740). Lunch is served 11:30 A.M.–2 P.M. daily, dinner 5:30–10 P.M. nightly. Farther up the ave. is a traditional Italian restaurant—complete with red, green, and white decor. **Ristorante Venezia** at 1902 University (644-3093) remains a favorite spot; reservations are essential. Another outstanding restaurant that's been around awhile, **Plearn Thai Cuisine** at 2050 University Ave. (841-2148) is noted for its excellent but inexpensive Oriental food.

The **Sedona Bar and Grill** at 2086 Allston Way (841-3848) serves innovative southwestern cuisine. Lunch Mon.–Fri., 11:30 A.M.–2:30 P.M., dinner Tues.–Sat., 5:30–9:30 P.M., Sun. brunch 10 A.M.–2 P.M.

A little farther afield, but worth the short jaunt to nearby Albany, **Lalime's Café** (527-9838) serves French food with Middle Eastern touches. Reservations are a must here. A prix fixe meal is $25, Tues.–Thurs., 5:30–10:30 P.M., and Fri. and Sat. at 6 P.M. and 9 P.M. (two seatings only). Entrées are about $8 Tues.–Thurs. Take the Albany exit from I-80 to 1410 Solano Ave. in Albany.

Among the many pleasant neighborhoods worth strolling through in Berkeley is the Elmwood district about a mile south of the university campus. As you walk down College Avenue, beginning at Russell Street, you'll find the old soda fountain at the **Elmwood Pharmacy** (number 2900, tel. 843-1300), **Avenue Books** (number 2904, tel. 549-3532), and **Ethnic Arts** (number 2937, tel. 549-3781), offering jewelry, textiles, sculptures, and artifacts that run the gamut from African masks to Haitian voodoo flags. After a short hiatus, the College shopping district continues a few blocks south at Alcatraz Avenue. Over the next mile and a half to Broadway there are dozens of shops, restaurants, bars, antique stores, and other specialty shops such as **Katrina Rozelle Pastries and Desserts** at 5940 College Avenue (655-3209), and **Yoshi's** at 6030 Claremont Boulevard near College (652-9200), which serves up jazz and Japanese cuisine.

Oliveto Café and Restaurant, at 5655 College Ave. (547-5356), serves northern Italian dishes.

Many visitors to the Eastbay find **Oakland International Airport** a convenient alternative to the San

Francisco terminal (see *Transportation*). The **Oakland Convention and Visitors Bureau** is located at 1000 Broadway (839-9000).

Area Eateries

A good part of the revolution in American tastes and food culture started at Chez Panisse in Berkeley, and the new traditions are still going strong. In addition to Chez Panisse (see *Restaurants*) and the Bay Wolf, Berkeley and the nearby stretches of Oakland boast some of the most exciting, creative restaurants in the United States as well as an abundance of ethnic adventures and good, solid, value-for-money eateries.

The so-called Gourmet Ghetto covers Shattuck Avenue between, say, Virginia and Rose streets. Here you'll find **Chez Panisse Poulet** (1685 Shattuck Avenue, 845-5932), a delicatessen and restaurant devoted primarily to, yes, chicken; **The Cheese Board** (1504 Shattuck Avenue, 549-3183) for French-style picnics of homemade breads and more than a hundred prime cheeses; the hole-in-the-wall **Juice Bar Collective** (2114 Vine Street, 548-8473) for the freshest of juice concoctions and healthy snacks; and **Saul's Restaurant and Delicatessen** (1475 Shattuck Avenue, 848-3354) offering chopped liver, fish platters, and kishke as close as what you can find in Chicago or New York on the West Coast.

When sightseeing around the University of California campus or shopping among the street merchants on Telegraph Avenue, try **Cody's Café** (2460 Telegraph Avenue, 841-6344) right in the midst of Cody's, the largest, most remarkable bookstore west of the Mississippi.

The café offers exotic salads (curried chicken, Greek, turkey), imaginative sandwiches, great homemade pies and baked puddings, and espresso drinks. And, of course, there's always the **campus cafeteria** across from Sproul Hall, and the **Bear's Lair coffeeshop** (843-0373) in the basement of the student union.

For soul-satisfying food try Bette's and the Fourth Street Grill. **Bette's Oceanview Diner** (1807A Fourth Street, 644-3230) serves breakfasts of dreamy pancakes and omelettes; lunches of such idealized diner food as black-bean chili, the juiciest of hamburgers, the crispest of French fries, and real homemade berry, banana cream, or whatever-else-is-in-season pies. No dinners. The take-out store next door offers many of the same items to go for those who don't like to wait in line. **Fourth Street Grill** (1820 Fourth Street, 849-0526) offers exciting pastas, perfect grilled steaks and chops, even better fried potatoes, a terrific wine list, and a long wait for both lunch and dinner.

If the lines at Bette's and Fourth Street are too long, continue your drive up University to **Bombay Cuisine** (inexpensive, complexly fragrant specialties; 2006 Ninth Street, 843-9601) in Berkeley's Little India, or try **Plearn Thai Cuisine No. 2** (Thai food with a light California touch; 2050 University, 841-2148).

Marin County

One of the great joys of the Bay Area is the close proximity of city to country. Less than half an hour from the breakneck pace of the Financial District are romantic headlands, isolated valleys, lagoons teeming with waterfowl, and coves that are home to seals and fascinating tide pools. This is Marin County, the city's back-door retreat famous for its hot tubs and "mellowspeak." The very name Marin conjures up an image of a landscape deep in Mercedes-Benzes and Nautilus machines. While you can find plenty of trendy boutiques and restaurants, and quaint inns, Marin County is also an ideal escape with mountain trails, redwood groves, bike paths, and rural villages.

The county's best-known destination, accessible via the Golden Gate Bridge or ferry, is **Sausalito.** Bridgeway Street, located near the waterfront, has many shops and restaurants and is a visitor's primary destination. The **Village Fair** (800 Bridgeway) has four levels with over thirty shops. On the first level, the **Sausalito Country Store** (332-7890) sells handcrafted American folk art by local artists. Also on the first level, **Quest** (332-6832) is an artisans' gallery where you can buy every kind of applied art ranging from clothes to jewelry. There are also upscale boutiques where European and American designers display avant garde fashions. At 34 Princess, right off of Bridgeway, **The Kite Shop** (332-8944) sells every kind of kite imaginable. You can find everything for the gourmet from cookware to specialty items such as rare olive oils and mustards at **Venice,** an old European store located at 625 Bridgeway (332-3544). **Timber Land** at 668 Bridgeway (332-1096) sells hunting, hiking, fishing, and sailing clothes as well as leather jackets and bags.

🍵 If you should happen to get hungry or thirsty, you're in luck because there are all types of eateries here. The **No Name Bar** at 757 (332-1392) is one of the more famous establishments in Sausalito. Noted for its intellectual crowd, particularly writers, No Name also offers live music Thurs.–Sat. nights.

If you want something substantial look no farther than the awning **Hamburgers** at 737 (332-9471). It serves 2-inch-thick char-grilled patties with just about anything from blue cheese to bacon on top for $4. **Angelino** at 621 Bridgeway (331-5225) has outstanding Italian food served up with views of San Francisco and the bay. Open 11:30 A.M.–10 P.M. daily. You can lunch on sandwiches and salads or enjoy fish and steaks in addition to the classic pasta specials for $7–$18.

On the north end of town, **Zacks By The Bay** (332-9779) serves fabulous sandwiches and entrées at indoor/outdoor tables.

The restaurant at the **Casa Madrona** Hotel, 801 Bridgeway (331-5888), is a special treat. Sit outside and enjoy views of the water while lunching on baked eggplant sandwiches, cheesesteak with mushrooms and white cheddar, or a grilled prawn sandwich, each about $8. Dinner entrées run from $12 for lasagna with shellfish and sweetpeppers to $22 for roast leg of lamb or roast pork tenderloin.

🧳 The **Casa Madrona Hotel** has a variety of romantic old rooms ranging from $90 for a drawing room to $145 for a room with king-size bed, deep bath, and lace-curtains. Suites are $300. Call 332-0502 for reservations.

Off Bridgeway at 16 El Portal, the **Sausalito Hotel** (332-4155) built in 1915 and recently redone, is a favorite haunt of actors and writers (including Sterling Hayden, who lived here while finishing *The Voyage*). The hotel has also served as a backdrop for "Serial" and "Partners in Crime." Rooms start at $65 for a double with no bath, running to $150 for a room furnished with General Grant's fixtures. Suites are $195. Call 332-4153 for reservations.

Not far from the center of town is Sausalito's houseboat colony. Walk north on Bridgeway to the Waldo Point Harbor and Gate 6 Road. Turn in here and you'll see some of the three hundred houseboats that drop anchor in the area. Nearby, at 2100 Bridgeway, is the **Bay Model** (332-3870), an excellent introduction to the inner workings of San Francisco Bay and the adjacent river deltas. Simulations of local tidal power make this model a big hit with kids. The Army Corps of Engineers uses this project to do research on the bay. The model is open from Tuesday to Saturday from 9 A.M. to 4 P.M. Not far away, on 400 Gate 5 Road, is **Heath Ceramics** (332-3732), where you can pick up excellent pottery or stoneware.

Sausalito is also a gateway to the Golden Gate National Recreation Area (556-0560), extending from San Francisco north along the Marin Coast. The world's largest urban park, with 114 square miles, it encompasses Marin's sandy beaches, lagoons, marshes, redwoods, ranchlands, rugged promontories, streams, and wildlife sanctuaries.

Near Sausalito a number of former military sites has been converted to community use. In the Marin Headlands near the Golden Gate Bridge is **Fort Cronkhite,** a one-time Nike missile site, now the home of the California Marine Mammal Center (331-7327) which helps treat injured sea mammals so they can return to their natural habitats. An easy trail leads up to an old Nike site where you'll get a great view of the headlands. Another popular trail starts at the end of Tennessee Valley Road. It's reached via Shoreline Highway north of Sausalito and Marin City. This four-mile hike leads to coastal Tennessee Cove.

Continue north on Shoreline Highway toward Mill Valley and you can pick up the road to **Muir Woods National Monument** (388-2595). Named for naturalist and Sierra Club founder John Muir, this redwood grove was the site of the United Nations charter signing in 1945. The only important source of lumber in the Bay Area, the giant redwoods here were first cut in large numbers during the Gold Rush and used for construction of many buildings in San Francisco. Fortunately this isolated box canyon was spared and now is one of the area's most popular nature preserves. John Muir called it "the best tree-lover's monument that could be found in all of the forests of the world." While most visitors confine themselves to the main path along Redwood Creek, there are 27 miles of trails to explore, accessible by foot, tour bus, or car. You can proceed on from this popular redwood grove up Panoramic Highway and the Pan Toll Road to the top of **Mount Tamalpais State Park** (388-2070).

The mountain is also known as the Sleeping Lady; view it from a distance and you'll see why. At the park you'll find walk-in camps, and a hillside amphitheater where plays and musicals are staged in May and June. Fifty miles of hiking trails make it easy to explore this Marin landmark. Alternatively, hikers can walk from Muir Woods up Mount Tamalpais via the Bootjack Trail. If you have the time, take the Steep Ravine Trail from Mount Tamalpais to **Stinson Beach.** Be aware that northern California's beaches are often cool and foggy, making them better for beachcombers than sun bathers. You can also drive down Stinson Beach Highway to the coast where Highway 1 leads north to the **Audubon Canyon Ranch** (383-1644). Hiking trails in this thousand-acre bird sanctuary offer close encounters with egrets and great blue herons. The ranch is open on weekends and holidays March through early July. If you're interested in visiting the nearby artists colony of **Bolinas,** ask the Audubon Ranch people for directions. It seems the Bolinas residents, in the interest of privacy, have removed road signs pointing the way. One of the best reasons to visit Bolinas is for the great view of the ocean and to examine the abundant marine life at the tide pools at **Duxberry Reef.**

Continue on Highway 1 north to the **Point Reyes National Seashore** (663-1092), a 64,000-acre peninsula that includes the ocean beaches where Sir Francis Drake landed the *Golden Hind* in 1579. Begin your visit at the Visitors Center. Adjacent to the headquarters is an earthquake trail that dramatically points out the fact that Point Reyes is a geologic island separated from the mainland by the San Andreas Fault. A reconstructed **Miwok Indian Village** here provides a look into the daily lives of some of the first inhabitants. You can drive out through the woodlands to **Limantour Beach,** a beautiful spot for a picnic. Or if you prefer, enjoy lunch in **Inverness,** a small community with a number of bed-and-breakfast lodges for those who want to stay overnight. Manka's Inverness Lodge at 30 Calendar Way (669-1034), also includes a restaurant that serves Czech food. Another spot worth visiting is the **Tomales Bay**

State Park, with its beautiful beach at **Heart's Desire Cove.** The road out to the coast leads to the **Point Reyes Lighthouse** (669-1534), an excellent whale-watching spot in the winter months. Visitors descend 312 steps to reach the lighthouse station.

A good way to return from Point Reyes to urban Marin County is Lucas Valley Road. Take U.S. 101 south to San Rafael, home of the **Marin Civic Center** (499-6104), Frank Lloyd Wright's last commission. With its arches, spire, and dome, this building is one of the Bay Area's most intriguing architectural landmarks. You can dine upstairs in the public cafeteria or picnic outside by the fountain. Be sure to see the indoor gardens of native plants and trees. Self-guiding tours are available Monday through Friday from 9 A.M. to 5 P.M. (499-6014). In Marin County east of San Rafael on San Pablo Bay, is **China Camp State Park,** a bayfront spot ideal for a picnic. (China Camp was a 19th century Chinese fishing village.) To the south is **Tiburon,** a wealthy peninsula community. This town is home to the **Richardson Bay Audubon Center** at 376 Greenwood Beach Road off Tiburon Boulevard (388-2524). Visit between October and March and you'll find all manner of gulls, egrets, ducks, and great blue heron.

Santa Cruz

San Francisco and Marin County's beaches are inviting spots, with dramatic coastlines, wildlife, and parks. But for the classic beach scene complete with boardwalks, cotton candy, roller coasters, and an active surfing scene, you need to drive ninety miles down the coast to Santa Cruz.

The most popular route via U.S. 101 to Highway 17 takes about two hours from San Francisco. Another route follows U.S. 280 south to 92 west into Half Moon Bay and picks up Highway 1 South. This coastal route leads past a string of state beaches as well as the Pescadero Marsh Nature Preserve (take Pescadero Road exit off of Highway 1) where ranger-led hikes on weekends make it easy to see migratory loons and grebes, mallards, American coots, snowy egrets, and great blue heron. The preserve is open daylight hours. Call 879-0832 for further information. Late fall and early spring are ideal times for bird watching. A few miles inland is

Pescadero, an old dairy-farming community that has been handsomely restored.

Fifty-five miles south of San Francisco on Highway 1 is **Ano Nuevo State Reserve** (879-0227), a major breeding ground for elephant seals and stellar sea lions. Although you can see some of these marine mammals just about any time of year, the big attraction is the winter breeding season which runs from December through March. During these months your tour must be led by a docent. Allow about three hours for the three-mile walk. Tour reservations can be made by calling Ticketron at 392-7469. During the rest of the year pick up a free permit to visit Ano Nuevo at the entrance station.

Twenty-five miles south of Ano Nuevo is Santa Cruz. On the way into town you can stop off at the **Lighthouse Surfing Museum** on West Cliff Drive at Lighthouse Point (408-429-3429). In 1912, Hawaii's Duke Kahanamoku helped popularize surfing in California by giving demonstrations on the local beaches. The museum collection showcases everything from 13-foot, 120-pound redwood boards to high-tech fiberglass models. The museum is open daily in summer from 11 A.M. to 4 P.M. Call for hours at other times of year.

Of course the primary reason for a Santa Cruz visit is the beach. The **Natural Bridges State Park,** about a mile north of the surfing museum (408-423-4609) is one of the city's best. To the south is **Santa Cruz Beach,** the **Municipal Wharf** (408-429-3628), and the **Santa Cruz Beach Boardwalk** (408-423-5590). While it may lack some of the high-tech attractions found at more modern theme parks, the Boardwalk is the only place in California where you can find a classic wooden roller coaster. Now in its 64th year, the Giant Dipper is the main attraction at this old-fashioned park. Skeeball fanatics can have a field day here while their children are out riding on Cap'n Jack's Pirate Ship or on the high-speed Wave Jammer. The Boardwalk also offers Big Band dancing on weekends.

In the hills above town is the **University of California at Santa Cruz** at 1156 High Street (408-459-0111). With its redwood groves, open meadows, and great marine views, the campus adds another dimension to a traditional college education. Built on the old Cowell ranch, the grounds include old farm buildings and stone ruins; there's even an organic farm that supplies fresh fare for the dining halls. Among the specialized tours of the area is a visit to the **Arboretum** (408-427-2998) with its native plants and species from Africa, Australia, and New Zealand. You can also visit the **Lick Observatory** and **Long Marine Laboratory.** The Long Marine Laboratory (408-459-4087) features maritime exhibits that include a whale skeleton and a hands-on display of tide pool life, such as starfish. The observatory is home of the world's second-largest reflector telescope. The observatory (408-459-2513) was originally built with funds donated by James Lick, a piano tuner who turned to real estate and made a killing. Lick, who also has a major San Francisco freeway named in his memory, is buried directly under the 120-inch telescope.

In the spring months the **Santa Cruz Museum Association** at 1305 East Cliff Drive (408-429-3773) offers wildflower walks. Also worth a visit is the Santa Cruz County Historical Trust's **Octagon Museum** at 118 Cooper Street (408-425-2540). Here you'll find exhibits of county memorabilia. The Octagon museum is open Monday through Saturday from noon to 5 P.M. Admission is free. The **Santa Cruz City Museum,** at 1305 East Cliff Drive (408-429-3773), is a good place to learn about Native Americans, see displays of fossils and animals, or lay your hands on a tide-pool tank. The museum is open Tuesday through Saturday from 10 A.M. to 5 P.M. and Sunday, noon to 5 P.M.

Santa Cruz also has a number of excellent self-guiding walking tours. You can pick up a route map at the **Santa Cruz County Conference and Visitors Council** office at 701 Front Street (408-425-1234). One 25-minute walk, the **Mission Hill Tour,** begins at the Gothic revival Holy Cross Roman Catholic Church and continues past adobes, stick villas, and an 1872 saloon that doubled as the residence of the town jailer. The 35-minute **Laurel Area Tour** leads past 19th-century row houses, Italianates, Queen Annes and Eastlake style cottages.

For an offbeat experience visit the **Mystery Spot** at 1953 North Branciforte Drive (408-423-8897), where the laws of gravity are obviously defied as balls roll uphill and visitors walk about tilted at precarious angles. It's open daily from 9:30 A.M. to 4:30 P.M. Another worthwhile excursion is to the Roaring Camp and Big Trees Narrow Gauge Railroad. You can depart from the Boardwalk area and head up the San Lorenzo River. Or, if you prefer, drive on Graham Hill Road six miles north to Felton. At **Roaring Camp** (408-335-4400), a re-created 1880s logging town, you can board a train up Bear Mountain. Adjacent to Roaring Camp is **Henry Cowell Redwoods State Park** (408-335-4598) where trees tower as high as 285 feet. You can hike along the self-guiding trails.

A good choice for lunch is one of the pleasant cafés along the downtown Santa Cruz Mall. Among them is **India Joze's** at 1001 Center St. (408-427-3554). On the garden patio you can choose between Continental, Spanish, Italian, Brazilian, and American cuisine. The **Greenhouse** restaurant at the Farm, 5555 Soquel Dr. (408-476-5613) in nearby Soquel, is another good choice for outdoor dining.

Palo Alto

Drive south from San Francisco via U.S. 101 to explore the peninsula, home of the beautiful Stanford University campus. You can also take CalTrain from the station at 4th and Townsend south of downtown. A pleasant day trip begins at the Palo Alto Station where you can walk over to the **Stanford University** campus. Opened in 1891 by Leland Stanford to commemorate his son, who died at age 15, the university offers free tours at 11 A.M. and 2:15 P.M. (723-2560), as well as maps for self-guiding visits. Start at the Main Quadrangle. Ride up to the top of Hoover Tower for a good overview of the campus, which was designed by Frederick Law Olmsted, who did New York's Central Park. The tower is part of the **Hoover Institution on War, Revolution and Peace,** one of the world's leading conservative think tanks.

While on campus you'll want to visit some of the other sandstone buildings such as the **Stanford Art Museum** (723-3469). Open Tuesday through Friday, from 10 A.M. to 5 P.M., Saturday and Sunday from 1 to 5 P.M.; closed in August. Among the collection's highlights is the golden spike driven by rail baron Stanford at the junction of the Union Pacific and Central Pacific railroads in Promontory Point, Utah. The museum collection is strong on Asian, Egyptian, and Native American art, plus there's a Rodin sculpture garden and memorabilia from the Stanford family. You can also visit the old Stanford Stables.

On the campus's north side (180 El Camino Real) is the **Stanford shopping center.** This well-designed center is reason enough for a trip to Palo Alto. Among the department stores here are Nordstrom, Neiman Marcus and I. Magnin. Specialty shops range from the Nature Company to the Phileas Fogg Travel bookstore.

If you get hungry from running from store to store, the **California Café** in the Old Stanford barn on Quarry Rd. (408-325-2233) offers California cuisine.

Near the campus you can take a ninety-minute tour of the two-mile long **Stanford Linear Accelerator** (854-3300), which is used to study small atomic particles. After your physics lesson head across the El Camino Real into downtown Palo Alto. Along University Avenue you can explore the shops, galleries, bookstores and sidewalk cafés. A number of wall murals (including one depicting a nun shooting off a windup plane) at 436 University Avenue are worth a look.

If you came down the peninsula by car, consider making the short drive north to visit the headquarters of **Sunset Magazine** at Middlefield and Willow roads in Menlo Park. This western publication (focusing on travel, food, gardening, and home remodeling) offers tours Monday though Friday from 10:30 A.M. to 3 P.M. You'll get a look at the adobe style buildings, handsomely furnished with Native-American and Mission-style pieces. The gardens are great. Call 321-3600 for reservations.

Julia Morgan, one of the Bay Area's most celebrated and prolific architects, designed over eight hundred buildings including William Randolph Hearst's San Simeon. But only one of them has become a dining establishment. It's a home created for Menlo Park's Camp Fremont. The building was moved to 27 University Ave. in Palo Alto where it has become **MacArthur Park restaurant** (321-9990). The menu features fish and ribs.

Monterey

About two and a half hours south of the Bay Area are some of the touchstones of the California experience.

Cannery Row, Pebble Beach, the Carmel Mission, and Big Sur coast are all good reasons to visit the Monterey County area. While there's plenty to do at the new Monterey Bay Aquarium, on the Path of History, or along the 17-mile drive, it's also possible to have a good time by simply kicking back at one of the Carmel Valley resorts.

The easiest way to reach the **Monterey Peninsula** is to take U.S. 101 south to Highway 156 west and then pick up Highway 1 south to Monterey. Stop off at the **Monterey Peninsula Chamber of Commerce** at 380 Alvarado Street (408-649-1770) to pick up a map to the three-mile-long Path of History. Along the way you'll want to visit some of the landmarks of this community that has been the capital of Spanish, Mexican, and American California.

In the pre-Gold Rush era, when San Francisco was still a sleepy hamlet, Monterey was a flourishing port, a capital city with beautiful adobes, the state's first theater, and a presidio. Walk the **Path of History** and you'll see dozens of historic adobes, the Custom House, and Colton Hall, site of the state's first constitutional convention. One of the most popular old buildings here is the **Robert Louis Stevenson House** on Houston Street. Tours of the house are available daily 10 A.M. to 5 P.M. during summer, and 10 A.M. to 4 P.M. in the winter. For further information call (408) 649-2905.

A short walk from the Path of History is **Cannery Row,** subject of John Steinbeck's famous novel. The sardine business has dried up and the canneries are now recreational shopping centers, restaurants, and museums. The number-one attraction is the **Monterey Bay Aquarium** at 886 Cannery Row (408-375-3333). This vast aquarium features sea otters, kelp forests, large sharks, aviary, and coastal slough. The new "Living Treasures of the Pacific" exhibit showcases the poisonous lionfish, exotic weedy sea dragon, sweetlips, and surgeonfish. The visit begins at the listing hull of a South Seas shipwreck and continues on to a western coral reef. Admission: adults $8, students and seniors $5.75, children $3.50. Open from 10 A.M. to 6 P.M. daily.

☕ For seafood try **Domenico's,** at no. 1 Fisherman's Wharf (408–372–3655). A moderate alternative is **McA-**

bee Beach Cafe at 700 Cannery Row (408-372-5114). Hamburgers and sushi are among the favorites here.

Casa Munras at 700 Munras Ave. in Monterey (408-375-2411) offers rooms starting at $70. At the **Victorian Inn,** 487 Foam St., near Cannery Row (408-373-8000) rooms start around $80.

Just beyond Monterey is **Pacific Grove,** home of the butterfly trees that each winter attract vast numbers of monarch butterflies from all over this region. (Take Lighthouse Avenue westbound from Historic Monterey and Cannery Row to Pacific Grove.) Heading past this city's notable Victorian buildings, you'll reach **Point Piños,** where Juan Rodriguez Cabrillo first landed in 1542. From this point you can drive along the beach and loop back through Pacific Grove, past the historic **Monterey Presidio** and on down to Carmel. Or you can take the private 17-mile drive through scenic **Pebble Beach,** one of the state's most exclusive residential areas. Probably best known for the AT&T Pebble Beach Pro-Am, this area abounds in golf courses, country clubs, private schools, and riding trails. Visitors are charged $5 to drive through Pebble Beach.

The **Tap Room** at the Lodge at Pebble Beach (408-624-3811) is a good lunch choice for burgers, sandwiches, and steaks while you continue on the 17-mile drive.

No matter which way you choose to reach **Carmel,** you'll probably be impressed by the tight zoning that has allowed this small residential community to gracefully accommodate over two hundred shops, restaurants, galleries, and inns. On Ocean Avenue, the village's main drive, you'll be able to shop or dine at Carmel Plaza.

The **Hog's Breath Inn** on San Carlos St. at Fifth St. (408-625-1044) is partially owned by actor and former mayor Clint Eastwood. Here you can enjoy a drink and a Dirty Harry Burger.

Try the **Clam Box Restaurant** on Mission St. near Fifth Ave. (408-624-8597) for moderately priced fish specialties. The **Thunderbird Bookshop and Restaurant** in the Barnyard shopping center complex (408-624-1803) offering a solarium patio on which to enjoy sandwiches, salad bar, and burgers, is good. For expensive Continental cuisine, try **The Covey at Quail**

Lodge, 8205 Valley Greens Dr. (408-624-1581) in Carmel Valley.

📖 For lodging in Carmel, **Mission Ranch** at 26720 Dolores St. (408-624-6436) has rooms starting around $60. At **La Playa Hotel,** Camino Real and 8th Ave. in Carmel (408-624-6476), rooms begin around $90.

At the end of Ocean Avenue is cypress-shaded **Ocean Beach,** a great place for a picnic or a stroll. South of town on Carmel Point is poet Robinson Jeffers's **Tor House** (408-624-1813). Open for tours on Fridays and Saturdays by reservation only from 10 A.M. to 3 P.M., the house has a forty-foot-high tower that includes stones from the Great Wall of China. At the north end of town, off Scenic Road, is **Carmel River State Beach,** one of the prettiest spots on the northern California coast. With its sand dunes, marshes, and views of the coastal range, this is a great spot for photos. Three miles south of town (take Highway 1 South one mile from Carmel to the entrance of the **Point Lobos State Reserve**) is a 1,276-acre park where you can often watch sea otters and sea lions from the headlands. The reserve is open daily 9 A.M. to 5 P.M.; till 7 P.M. in summer. Admission is $3 per car. Call (408) 624-4909 for further park information.

Carmel Valley just east of Carmel Village is an excellent spot to escape the city, particularly when fog cools off the coast. Often warm, this is a wonderful place to golf, play tennis, swim, bike, or hike along the base of the Santa Lucia Mountains. Within a matter of minutes you can be off in remote areas such as **Robinson Canyon,** ideal for hiking and birdwatching, or make your way into the **Los Padres National Forest** wilderness for backpacking, rock collecting, swimming, and surf fishing. For more information concerning Los Padres, call (408) 385-5434. If you're feeling really ambitious make the forty-mile drive (take G-16 East from Highway 1 to Arroyo Seco Road) to **Arroyo Seco Recreation Area** and enjoy the secluded swimming holes on the river that can easily keep a family entertained all day. Another possibility is to head down Route G-16 to Cachagua Road (about thirty miles south of Monterey) which leads to **Los Padres Dam,** a trailhead for the **Los Padres National Forest.** Stretching south along the county's mountainous backbone, the forest includes the Ventana wilderness, Hastings Natural History Reservation, and an extensive network of hiking trails that extends inland from the Big Sur coast.

Of course you don't have to go this far to find great hiking in Carmel Valley. **Garland Ranch Regional Park,** just eight miles east down G-16 from Highway 1, has a number of worthwhile hiking trails ranging from the easy Lupine Loop to the Garzas Canyon Trail. Ambitious hikers who head up the oak-covered slopes will reach a grassland mesa in the Santa Lucias where there's a splendid view of the valley. There's also steelhead fishing here in the winter. (You can obtain a fishing permit at sporting goods stores.) Especially recommended is the Buckeye Nature Trail where you're likely to spot blacktail deer and, if you're lucky, a bobcat or two. At the trail's end is Indian Rock, where the Costanoan Indians ground acorns in holes that served as stone mortars. The ranch is open daily dawn to dusk. Call (408) 659-4488 for information.

About a mile beyond the ranch is **Los Laureles Lodge** (408-659-2233) where visitors can use the adults-only pool for $3 per day. Continuing west you'll come to the **Hidden Valley Music Center** on Carmel Valley Road—the site of concerts, opera, and dance performances year-round. Call (408) 659-3115. There are, of course, many other possibilities in Carmel Valley. Naturally, there's a winery close at hand in **Château Julien** at 8940 Carmel Valley Road (408-624-2600). And if Pebble Beach is fogged in, why not try **Rancho Canada Golf Course** located on Carmel Valley Road one mile west of Highway 1 (408) 624-0111.

South of Carmel, the **Big Sur coast** is best seen in springtime when wildflowers dominate the coastal mountains. If it's not too wet the Old Coast Road off of Highway 1 makes a good side trip through wooded canyons and provides easy access to a number of creeks that are hard to reach from the main highway. This old route cuts off the highway near Bixby Creek Bridge, largest of the many graceful spans found in Big Sur country. In a state notorious for its wretched highway-construction excesses, these bridges provide a notable example of intelligent design that helps minimize the main road's intrusion on the coastal landscape.

Heading past the **Point Sur lighthouse,** the road leads away from the coast along **Andrew Molera State Park** (a 4,800-acre park that includes three miles of beach, over a dozen hiking trails, and a walk-in campgrounds; tel. 408-667-2315) and into the modest Big Sur settlement. There is no town here per se, since local residents live in homes scattered over this forested locale. But there is a variety of lodges as well as the **Pfeiffer-Big Sur State Park** (reserve a site by calling 800-444-7275) where you can camp, take day hikes through the redwoods, or head off into the adjacent Ventana Wilderness.

💼 **Big Sur Lodge** at Pfeiffer-Big Sur State Park (408-667-2171) charges around $70. **Ventana,** the Big Sur resort, has rooms beginning at $175 (408-667-2331).

Although ocean access is somewhat limited by steep rugged cliffs, you can reach **Pfeiffer Beach** via a two-mile road that cuts off Highway 1 at Sycamore Canyon. (Get directions from a park ranger.) Travel the entire California coast and you probably won't find a better place to watch the sun set. Continuing down Highway 1 you'll come to the **Henry Miller Memorial Library** (408-667-2574) where you view exhibits commemorating the author who lived in Big Sur from 1944 to 1962. The library is open daily 10 A.M. to 6 P.M. Farther south is **Julia Pfeiffer Burns State Park** (408-667-2315) where a hike out to the headlands will frequently yield a view of sea otters. The Big Sur coast continues south for another two hours. This beautiful drive ends in San Luis Obispo County where you can visit Hearst San Simeon State Park.

💼 For additional lodging suggestions try the **Monterey Peninsula Chamber of Commerce** (408-649-3200) or Monterey Peninsula Reservations (800-822-8822).

Napa Valley—Wine Country

Within an hour's drive north of San Francisco you will find the heart of the California wine country. Well worth the price of a rental car and a day of your trip, a visit to the Napa Valley is a great way to escape the city, as so many San Francisco locals do. The easiest way to get here from San Francisco is to take U.S. 101 north to SR 37 east and then pick up SR 29 north. Highway 29 runs straight through the heart of the valley, past many wineries you'll want to visit.

WINE TASTING

A tour of the wine country unlocks the mystery of the age-old tradition of wine making. A stop at one of the two hundred-plus wineries in the valley is a great way to shed the mystique associated with wines and wine tasting. You'll find familiar labels and countless others of which you may never have heard. Well known or not, the wines will generally be of high quality and, certainly, less expensive than at home. In addition, you can sample them prior to purchase. Of course, this is what everyone wants to do, and the traffic along the highway can make Los Angeles jams look minimal. To avoid these tie-ups try to plan your trip to the Napa Valley on a weekday when lines are shorter and you can enjoy a leisurely pace. One thing you won't want to do is rush through this beautiful rural area.

Many wineries offer daily tours and tastings, though some are by prearranged appointment only. In any case, it is best to call for hours, as small wineries often have sporadic opening times. If you don't want to join the gaggle of drunken tourists on Highway 29, you can leave your car in Napa and board the refurbished, turn-of-the-century pullman **Napa Valley Wine Train.** You can enjoy lunch or dinner on the twenty-mile trip from Napa to St. Helena. The round-trip route takes three hours and passes a panorama of famous wineries and vineyards. The lunch service departs from 1275 McKinstry Street in Napa at 11:30 A.M. from Tuesday to Friday, at 12:30 P.M. on Saturday and Sunday. The fare is $25 and lunch is $20. Dinner service departs from the same place at 6:30 P.M. on Tuesday through Saturday, at 6 P.M. on Sunday. Fare is $12.50 and dinner is $45. Of course, there is an extensive wine list. Credit cards are accepted. Call (707) 253-2111 or (800) 522-4142 for reservations.

Below is our choice of wineries and tasting rooms to visit. Some are more impressive for their architecture and tours than for their wine, but all are worth your time.

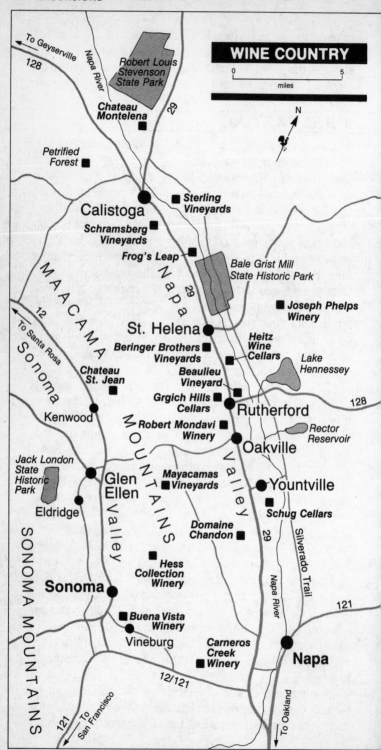

WINE COUNTRY

0   5
miles

N

To Geyserville
128

Napa River

Robert Louis
Stevenson
State Park

Chateau
Montelena

29

Petrified
Forest

Sterling
Vineyards

Calistoga

Schramsberg
Vineyards

Frog's Leap

Bale Grist Mill
State Historic Park

29

Joseph Phelps
Winery

M A A C A M A

Napa

St. Helena

Beringer Brothers
Vineyards

Heitz
Wine
Cellars

Lake
Hennessey

12

Sonoma

To Santa Rosa

Chateau
St. Jean

Beaulieu
Vineyard

Grgich Hills
Cellars

Rutherford

128

Kenwood

Robert Mondavi
Winery

Rector
Reservoir

M O U N T A I N S

Oakville

Jack London
State
Historic
Park

Glen
Ellen

Mayacamas
Vineyards

Yountville

Eldridge

V A L L E Y

Schug Cellars

Domaine
Chandon

29

Napa River

Silverado Trail

Hess
Collection
Winery

S O N O M A

Sonoma

121

Buena Vista
Winery

Vineburg

Carneros
Creek
Winery

Napa

M O U N T A I N S

12/121

121   To
San Francisco

To
Oakland

Beaulieu Vineyard, 1960 St. Helena Highway, Rutherford; (707) 963-2411. Open daily 10 A.M. to 4 P.M. Just what you had in mind when you set out to tour the Napa Valley—an ivy-covered winery set in the midst of a hillside vineyard. The tour here is a good way to learn about the wine maker's art. Beaulieu is known for its Cabernets.

Beringer Brothers Vineyards, 2000 Main Street, St. Helena; (707) 963-7115. Open daily 9:30 A.M. to 4 P.M. The main attraction here is the Rhine House, a century-old mansion that was brought over piece by piece from Germany. The tour takes you into the stone caves cut into the hillside where fermentation takes place.

Carneros Creek Winery, 1285 Dealy Lane, Napa; (707) 253-9463. Open Wednesday through Sunday, 9 A.M. to 5 P.M. Away from the madding crowd, this smaller winery has a pleasant picnic area.

Château Montelena, 1429 Tubbs Lane, Calistoga; (707) 942-5105. Open daily 10 A.M. to 4 P.M. for tasting and sales. Tours by appointment only. Here's a chance to go wine tasting in a castle adjacent to a pretty little lake with oriental-style pavilions. Try the Chardonnays and Cabernets.

Château St. Jean, 8555 Sonoma Highway, Kenwood; (707) 833-4134. Open daily 10 A.M. to 4:30 P.M. Just 17 years old, relatively young by valley standards, Château St. Jean sells excellent varietals. The tour is first rate.

Domaine Chandon, California Drive, Yountville; (707) 944-2280. Open daily 11 A.M. to 5:30 P.M., May through October; Wednesday through Sunday, 11 A.M. to 5:30 P.M., November through April. This champagne-producing winery owned by France's Moet & Chandon is settled in the vineyard-covered hills near Yountville. The tour is free, but tasting is not.

Frog's Leap Winery, 3358 St. Helena Highway, St. Helena; (707) 963-4704. Tours by appointment only. Named for a former business of raising frogs (for gastronomical purposes) in a nearby creek, Frog's Leap is small, but rich in atmosphere. An old livery stable now houses the winery. The adjacent farmhouse is a private residence and owner's office. The facilities can be toured during the day, at which time wines may be tasted and purchased.

Grgich Hills Cellars, 1829 St. Helena Highway, Rutherford; (707) 963-2784. Open daily 9:30 A.M. to 4:30 P.M. for tasting and sales. Tours by appointment only. The union of these two entrepreneurs, Mike Grgich and Austin Hills, created a large, successful winery that has received much acclaim. All the wine-making and storage occurs in a single concrete building. The nearby 1885 Victorian house, now Grgich's private residence, balances the scale of old and new.

Heitz Wine Cellars, 436 St. Helena Highway South, St. Helena; (707) 963-3542. Open daily 11 A.M. to 4:30 P.M. A premium small winery known for its Cabernets.

Hess Collection Winery, 4411 Redwood Road, Napa; (707) 255-1144. Open daily 10 A.M. to 4 P.M. Former site of the Christian Brothers Mount La Salle Vineyards in the redwoods eight miles northwest of Napa, this spot is well worth a visit. The Hess wines are complemented by a good modern-art collection.

Joseph Phelps Winery, 200 Taplin Road, St. Helena; (707) 963-2745. Open daily 10 A.M. to 4 P.M. for tasting and sales. Tours by appointment. Tucked away in Spring Valley, this 350-acre vineyard produces a variety of wines. The winery itself is a conglomeration of wooden cellars, steel fermentors, oak barrels, and the recently added visitor's center.

Mayacamas Vineyards, 1155 Lokoya Road, Napa; (707) 224-4030. Tours by appointment only. This winery, built in 1899, has a beautiful mountain setting. Try the Chardonnay and Cabernets.

Robert Mondavi Winery, 7801 St. Helena Highway, Oakville; (707) 963-9611. Open daily from 9 A.M. to 5 P.M. from May to October, 10 A.M. to 4:30 P.M. from November to April. Call for reservations. One of the valley's largest wineries offers an excellent tour of the vintner's art. Try the Chardonnay, Fume Blanc, and Chenin Blanc. There's an art gallery here and concerts are scheduled during the summer. If you plan to be in the area from June to August, call for tickets to this event that often begins with a picnic on the lawn at noon and extends to midnight under the stars.

Schramsberg Vineyards, Schramsberg Road, Calistoga; (707) 942-4558. Tours by appointment only.

The valley's preeminent champagne cellar was founded in 1862 by Jacob Schram, who aged his wines in limestone tunnels dug out by coolies. Ironically, this is the brand Richard Nixon took along when he made his first visit to see Chairman Mao. Heads of state continue to serve it to honored guests. Although these champagne cellars are now a state historic landmark, it's not easy to get inside. Be prepared to be convincing on the phone. Because champagne is produced in limited quantities, tasting is not allowed. But be polite and you'll be allowed to purchase some of this premium product to take home.

Schug Cellars, 6204 St. Helena Highway, Yountville; (707) 963-3169. Tours by appointment only. Walter Schug, previously the winemaker for Château Montelena and Joseph Phelps Winery, has opened his own small winery south of Yountville. While a tour may not be possible, make an effort to sample one of the Schug's fine wines.

Sterling Vineyards, 1111 Dunaweal Lane, Calistoga; (707) 942-5151. Open daily from 10:30 A.M. to 4:30 P.M. A $5 ticket buys you a ride on the tram running up to this Moorish winery. That fee can be applied to the purchase of any vintage wine you buy but, really, the view of the entire valley from this white monastery is more than worth the price. The winery's tour is perhaps more educational and more interesting than many, as it is self-guided with descriptions of machinery and processes along the way.

THE VALLEY

While winery hopping is many visitors' favorite sport, you could have a splendid time here without ever uncorking a bottle. Its beautiful setting makes Napa Valley a great place to enjoy many outdoor activities—biking, horseback riding, and hiking, to name a few. You can also relax overlooking the vineyards by balloon or soaking in a mud bath at the hot springs.

A river town with roots in leather tanning, stone masonry, cattle ranching, farming, and viticulture, Napa was reached in pioneer days by steamer. While visitors come today to sample more intoxicating beverages, it was Napa's mineral waters that originally brought tourists in. The valley's first spa, White Sulphur Springs re-

Wine Tasting for Everyone

With so many labels and varieties, it's easy to get confused or intimidated. Don't let this bother you. The important thing to remember is what you like about wines. Combine this with an open mind and you're sure to discover a taste you enjoy. To help you through the tangle of tasting-room terminology, here is a brief listing of terms often used to describe wines.

Dry: A dry wine is one in which all the sugar from the grapes has been converted to alcohol. Typical dry wines include Chardonnay, Cabernet, Zinfandel, and Merlot. If you like dry wines, it is probably the crisp, clean feeling of the acidity you enjoy.

Fruity: This term refers to the flavor of the grape berry in a wine. Contrary to popular belief, a wine does not have to be sweet to show fruitiness. Many dry wines, such as Chardonnay, show nice berry flavors. Another fruity wine to try is Pinot Noir.

Balance: You may hear someone describe a wine as well balanced. This refers to the balance of fruit flavor and the acids that enhance a wine's crisp feeling in the mouth. Without good acid, a wine will taste flabby, as if it were clinging to the tongue, as opposed to clean and refreshing. After a few sips it will become boring. This is especially important with dessert wines because of their sweetness.

Oak: Many wines are fermented and/or aged in small oak barrels. These give off the flavor of oak wood to the wine. Some find the taste pleasant, with a vanilla character in the aroma. Others object to the rough feeling left in the mouth by tannin, which comes from the wood. The use of oak adds a new dimension to dry wines that might otherwise be thin and watery, giving them many pleasing characteristics.

Bouquet: This is the wine's aroma. A good bouquet will give you an idea of what the wine will taste like. Try to detect the fruit, oak, and any other aromas you can imagine. A wine that smells good to you will probably taste good. A vinegar or cork smell will alert you to possible problems with the wine.

Texture: A wine's texture refers to how it feels in your mouth. What does it do in your mouth? Do you feel the roughness of tannins? How about the smooth viscosity of honey? Does the acidity make your mouth pucker? A wine with complexity will offer many of these traits as it passes from lips to throat. As with balance, if a wine feels soapy or clingy in texture, it probably does not have good acid.

Color: A wine's color is an important indicator of its balance. A wine that looks thin and watery will probably not have a very rich taste. Color can also show imperfections such as oxidation or off flavors. A brown tinge often means the wine is too low in acid. Look for a rich, true color for an equally pleasing taste.

Temperature: The temperature at which a wine should be served is a good indicator of its quality. A wine that is well balanced with good acid will have a clean, refreshing taste at room temperature. Wines that are lacking in character must be well chilled to be equally satisfying.

Use these terms for your overall evaluation of the wine. Then forget about everything else and just decide for yourself—do I like this wine? After all, that's what matters.

—Axel Schug

sort near St. Helena, opened in 1852. Palatial hotels and an opera house sprang up as San Francisco millionaire Sam Brannan began working to turn Calistoga into a spa town like New York's Saratoga, after which it was supposed to be named. The speaker, however, got tongue tied and pronounced the town the "Calistoga of Sarafornia." It stuck. While tourists flocked to the springs, Napa remained an agricultural center with a large Chinese community.

Begin your tour of Napa at the **Napa County Historical Society's** headquarters located in the Goodman Building downtown. It's open Tuesday and Thursday from noon to 4 P.M. (707-224-1739). This is a good place to prime yourself on the local spa history before visiting one yourself. You can also pick up architectural-walking-tour brochures to the downtown area. The city is rich in landmark buildings such as the Italianate **Napa Opera House** at 1018 Main Street, the classical revival **American Savings Building** at 903 Main Street, and the Art-Deco **Main Street Bar and Grill.** At the **County Courthouse,** west of Main Street between

Second and Third streets, you can explore a hall of history that will help orient you to the valley's communities.

☕ While in the neighborhood you may want to stop for cappuccino at the popular **Napa Valley Coffee Roasting Company** in the century-old Winship-Smernes Building at First and Main sts. (707-224-2233).

If you're in the mood for nineties diner cuisine with fifties jukebox accompaniment, head for the nearby **Blue Plate Diner** at 811 Coombs St. (707-226-2583).

While there is much architectural grandeur in Napa, it would be a mistake to overlook a small utilitarian stone building at Clinton and Main streets. Known since the twenties as the **Sam Kee Laundry,** this is the oldest stone commercial building in town. Constructed as the Pfeiffer Brewery with an Italianate false front, it later served as a saloon and became a laundry during Prohibition. Other landmarks worth visiting include the **Juarez Adobe,** now the Old Adobe Bar and Grille, at 376 Soscol (707-255-4310), and the **Veterans Home of California** perched on a hillside west of Yountville.

☕ **The Diner,** 6476 Washington St., Yountville; (707) 944-2626, serves fabulous American breakfasts and Mexican dinners. Enjoy its great coffee on the patio while you wait for a table. **Mustards Grill,** 7399 St. Helena Hwy., Yountville; (707) 944-2424, is a popular spot for California cuisine.

For more upscale dining in Yountville, **Mama Nina's,** 6772 Washington St.; (707) 944-2112, serves northern Italian cuisine in an ivy-covered stone building. The **French Laundry,** Washington and Creek sts.; (707) 944-2380, will probably be booked a year from now but the French country food at this tiny place is worth planning for well in advance.

A favorite of locals, **Piatti Ristorante,** 6480 Washington St.; (707) 944-2070, serves coal-oven pizzas and calzones plus fine pastas and other Italian dishes.

Five miles east of Napa, up a steep grade, is **Wild Horse Valley.** This horse ranch is heaven for equestrians. With its splendid hilltop setting the ranch is an ideal location for a Sunday barbecue-breakfast trail ride. Morning and afternoon horseback trips are also offered. Views of the valley below are outstanding. In addition the public is welcome to watch horse trials or schooling shows. Call (707) 224-0727 for information.

Many of the region's treasures are found in the St. Helena area. **The Silverado Museum,** located at 1490 Library Lane (707-963-3757), focuses on the life and career of Robert Louis Stevenson, whose words "and the wine is bottled poetry," greet you as you enter the valley. The famed author honeymooned near St. Helena in 1880 and wrote about the region in his book *The Silverado Squatters.* Nearly eight thousand items—Stevenson manuscripts, books, letters, paintings, and other memorabilia—are found here. The museum is open Tuesday through Sunday, from noon to 4 P.M.

St. Helena is also a splendid spot for a picnic thanks to the **Napa Valley Olive Oil Manufacturing Company.** Located in a white barn on Charter Road just off of McCorkle Avenue (707-963-4173), this company also operates a deli counter where customers can select cheese and lunch meats to make their own sandwiches. Patrons are welcome to enjoy their lunch at one of the picnic tables shaded by olive trees.

Located at the heart of the valley, the small town of St. Helena has many fine restaurants offering a variety of cuisines. **Green Valley,** 1310 Main St.; (707) 963-7088, is owned by the restaurateurs of San Francisco's Café Sport in North Beach. Enjoy Italian food at the counter and small tables in this former diner. **Miramonte Restaurant,** 1327 Railroad Ave.; (707) 963-3970, serves fine French food. Reservations are essentials. For a break from the European, try **La Placita,** 1304 Main St.; (707) 963-8082, for outstanding Mexican food. The chicken salad and soup of the day are favorites here. The restaurant has no liquor license at present, but it will happily uncork anything.

For the ultimate in French food (and in prices) **Auberge du Soleil,** 180 Rutherford Hill Rd., Rutherford; (707) 963-1211, is the place to go. This hillside restaurant deserves its place in wine-country lore. Make reservations well in advance.

Continue into the hills to find some lesser-known treasures. Among them is the rustic **White Sulphur Springs** resort five miles west of St. Helena (707-963-8588). It is now being restored by Seward and Betty Foote, the 23rd owners of this 1840s property. Guests can stay in comfortable cottages and bathe in a small mineral-water spa. Smaller hotel rooms are currently being upgraded into suites. Although the main pool is closed, guests can wade in Sulphur Creek and hike the wooded trails up to small falls.

Dedicated to preserving the resort's heritage, the owners have created a small museum with many artifacts that trace the evolution of Napa Valley's pioneer resort. A kind of cultural timeline, White Sulphur Springs has, under various owners, sported names as diverse as Bob's Steak House and Sun Valley. Clearly, there's an ecumenical spirit here in the fir and madrone forest. Prior to the Footes' arrival, the springs were operated by the Methodist Church Conference, Hadassah, and Santana Dharma Foundation. You can spend the night here or enjoy the facilities on a day-use basis (707-963-8588).

North of St. Helena are the **Bale Grist Mill State Historic Park** (707-963-2236) where you can view an 1846 water-wheel mill that used to grind corn and **Bothe-Napa Valley State Park** (707-942-4575) where you can cool off in the warm months at a swimming pool. Continue on Highway 29 to the spa town of Calistoga. Eight resorts offer mineral pools plus mud and sulphur baths. Among them are **Calistoga Spa Hot Springs** at 1006 Washington Street (707-942-6269) and **Dr. Wilkinson's Hot Springs** at 1507 Lincoln Avenue (707-942-4102). Two miles north of town at 1299 Tubbs Lane is the "Old Faithful" geyser that erupts about once every fifty minutes. It's open daily 9 A.M. to 6 P.M. in the summer months and 9 A.M. to 5 P.M. during winter.

The town of Calistoga, created by millionaire Sam Brannan, centers around the handsome commercial buildings of Lincoln Avenue. To learn more about the region's history and the career of Robert Louis Stevenson, visit the **Sharpsteen Museum** at 1311 Washington Street (707-942-5911). North of town via Highway 29 is **Robert Louis Stevenson State Park.** Six miles northwest of Calistoga is the **Petrified Forest** (707-942-6667). It's open daily from 10 A.M. to 5 P.M. Admission adults $3, children $1.

Half an hour east of Napa Valley, via Deer Park and Howell Mountain roads, is Angwin, home of the Seventh Day Adventist's **Pacific Union College** (707-965-

Sunrise, Sunset

If you're not satisfied with a view from one of the local peaks, by all means go aloft with one of the half-dozen ballooning companies that charge about $150 for the sunrise ride over the valley and champagne brunch. Among them are Calistoga's **Once in a Lifetime Balloon Co.** (707-942-5641) and Napa's **Balloon Aviation of Napa Valley** (707-252-7067). The **Calistoga Soaring Center** (707-942-5592) offers glider rides across the valley.

6311). In a small shopping center directly across from the college, is a community store offering vegetarian sandwiches, fresh bread, and pastries. Keep in mind that the store and college facilities shut down on Saturday. Continue east on Howell Mountain Road to Pope Valley. Three miles north of this hamlet via Pope Valley Road is California State Historic Landmark number 939, the late Litto Damonte's **Hubcap Ranch.** Damonte left behind a kind of chrome Stonehenge, one that's easy to find, thanks to the more than two thousand shiny hubcaps that dominate the fences, homes, barns, and pastures. Hubcaps here have been artfully arranged and in some places appear to be mushrooms from the fields. No shrinking violet, Litto even went to the trouble of slapping his name on the barn—in hubcabs, naturally.

If you'd like to prolong your visit, or just thoroughly relax, consider staying overnight here. It's a good idea to book ahead however, particularly on weekends. If price is no object, the $200 and up per night at **Auberge du Soleil** at 180 Rutherford Rd. in Rutherford (707-963-1211) is an excellent choice. If you'd like to try one of the valley's many bed-and-breakfast inns, the **Beazley House,** 1910 First St., Napa (707-257-1649), offers a convenient location. Rooms run $80–$150. **Brannan Cottage Inn** (707-942-4200) at 109 Wapoo Ave., Calistoga, offers rooms in the small home that once belonged to the community's founder, Sam Brannan. Rooms runs $55–$100. Also in Calistoga, **Mount View Hotel,** 1475 Lincoln Ave. (707-942-6877), is located in the heart of town at a comfortable walking distance from the spas. Rooms run $60–$135.

For a recreational stay, the **Silverado Country Club,** 1600 Atlas Peak Rd. (800-532-0500 or 707-257-

0200), has two 18-hole golf courses, as well as twenty tennis courts and eight swimming pools. Rooms and cottages run $130–$470.

Additional lodging suggestions are available from the **Napa Chamber of Commerce** (707–226–7455), 1900 Jefferson Street, Napa and the **Wine Country Bed and Breakfast** service, P.O. Box 5059, Napa 94581-0059 (707-257-7757).

Sonoma Valley

Located 46 miles north of San Francisco on Highway 12, the town of Sonoma played an important role in California's early history. Mission San Francisco Solano, the last mission in a system designed to convert the local Indians to Christianity, was founded in 1823. In 1834 Mexican General Mariano Guadalupe Vallejo was sent to secularize the mission. He laid out the town of Sonoma around an eight-acre plaza which is now the central town square. The first California flag, made from a muslin petticoat and displaying both a star and a bear, was raised here in 1846 signifying the "Bear Flag Revolt" which made California an independent nation for three weeks.

Today Sonoma has a population of eight thousand. As part of the Sonoma Valley, also known as the Valley of the Moon, it is a popular destination for visitors; tree-lined streets around the central plaza have many shops, restaurants, hotels, and historical buildings.

The Legend of the Name

There are two stories surrounding this valley's mysterious second name. The first is perhaps more likely, if less romantic. According to locals, Sonoma means Valley of the Moon in Indian. The other story claims that, as General Vallejo rode over the hills on a moonlit night, he saw the moon rise anew each time he ascended a peak. He later named the spot the Valley of the Moon.

The plaza itself is like a huge park with footpaths, a duck pond, and a playground. In the center is the **City Hall.** The area around the plaza is a pleasant place to stroll.

On the northside of the plaza **The Sonoma Cheese Factory,** (707) 996-1000, has every kind of cheese, meat, and salad, as well as gift packs. You can watch the cheese being made while waiting for your order to be filled.

At 110 W. Spain is the **Sonoma Hotel** (707-996-2996), a fine dining and lodging establishment built in 1872. Rooms run $58–$98 based on double occupancy.

On the west side of the plaza is the site of the **El Dorado Hotel,** which is soon to be converted into the Sonoma Valley branch of Piatti Ristorante in Yountville.

Just off the square, on Broadway, **Finet's** (707-996-3397) sells sandwiches and picnic fixings. On the east side of the plaza at 420 1st St. E., is **Gino's** (707-996-4466), a landmark Italian restaurant known for its varying specials, pastas, and hamburgers.

Along the east side you'll find the **Sebastiani Theater** (707-996-2020), an ornate two-story movie theater owned by one of the Sebastiani Winery brothers. Next door to the theater, the **Arts Guild of Sonoma** (707-996-3115) displays and sells local pottery, paintings, and weaving.

One reason to visit this historic old town is the **Mission San Francisco Solano.** Reached via U.S. 101 north to Highway 37 east and Highway 12 north, this mission is part of Sonoma State Historic Park (707-938-1578). Founded in 1823, Mission San Francisco Solano was proposed by Franciscan Padre Jose Altamira who was at Mission Dolores in San Francisco. Due to poor conditions at Dolores, he proposed starting a new one in the fertile Sonoma Valley. The original church building has been replaced by a chapel built by Mexican General Mariano Vallejo. Prior to its restoration in 1903, the mission (named for a Peruvian saint) once served as a winery and barn. Open daily 10 A.M. to 5 P.M.

While not in the center of the Wine Country, California's oldest winery, **Buena Vista Winery,** is located here at 18000 Old Winery Road, (707) 938-1266. The winery is open daily from 10 A.M. to 5 P.M. The setting here is perfect and you can taste the wines in the beautiful stone cellar. There are concerts in the summer. Perfect for picnics.

As you leave Sonoma, take Highway 12 back through Glen Ellen, and stop at the **Glen Ellen Inn,** 13670 Arnold Dr. (Hwy. 12); (707) 996-6409. This tiny restaurant seats only a dozen for the fine French-nouvelle dinners. A delightful way to prepare for your drive back into the city.

11

CITY LISTINGS

Following is a comprehensive list of San Francisco's sights. It can be used as a supplement to the *Priorities* section or as a quick reference of those places described in the *Neighborhoods* chapter. Because schedules are subject to change, it's always a good idea to call first to confirm hours for the attractions listed here. Many are closed on holidays and some have extended hours during the summer season. A number of art museums add supplemental charges for special exhibits.

Sights are keyed into the appropriate page number and map coordinates of the color atlas in the back of the book.

MUSEUMS

American Carousel Museum   FISHERMAN'S WHARF, P. 3, D1

633 Beach St.; tel. 928-0550; daily 10 A.M.–6 P.M. Admission: $2 adults, $1 seniors and students 13–17, children 12 and under free.

Asian Art Museum   GOLDEN GATE PARK, P. 2, B2

Golden Gate Park; tel. 668-8921; Wed.–Sun., 10 A.M.–5 P.M. Admission: $4 seniors and youths, $2 children under 12 free. Admission ticket also good at M.H. de Young and California Palace of the Legion of Honor museums on the same day.

Cable Car Museum   NOB HILL, P. 3, D1

1201 Mason St.; tel. 474-1887; daily 10 A.M.–6 P.M. daily. Free.

California Academy of Sciences   GOLDEN GATE PARK, P. 2, B2

Golden Gate Park; tel. 221-5100; daily 10 A.M.–5 P.M., summer till 7 P.M. Includes the Steinhart Aquarium and the Morrison Planetarium. Admission: $4 adults, $2 seniors and youths 12–17, $1 children age 6–11. See *Priorities*.

California Historical Society (Whittier Mansion)   PACIFIC HEIGHTS, P. 3, C1

2090 Jackson St. at Laguna; tel. 567-1848; Tues.–Fri. tour at 1:30 P.M., Sat. and Sun. at 1:30 and 3 P.M. Admission: $3 adults, $1 students and seniors.

California Palace of the Legion Of Honor   NEAR GOLDEN GATE PARK, P. 2, B2

Lincoln Park; tel. 750-3600; Wed.–Sun. 10 A.M.–5 P.M. Admission: $4 adults, $2 for seniors and students age 12–18, under 12 free. Ticket also good same day at M.H. de Young and Asian Art museums.

Cartoon Art Museum   SOUTH OF MARKET, P. 3, D2

665 Third St., fifth floor; tel. 546-3922; Wed.–Fri. 11 A.M.–5 P.M., Sat. 10 A.M.–5 P.M. Admission: $2.50 adults, $1 children under 12.

Chinese Cultural Center   CHINATOWN, P. 3, D1

750 Kearny St., Holiday Inn, third floor; tel. 986–1822; Tues.–Sat. 10 A.M.–5:30 P.M. Free.

Chinese Historical Society of America   CHINATOWN, P. 3, D1

650 Commercial; tel. 391-1188; Wed.–Sun. noon–4 P.M. Donation.

Exploratorium   MARINA, P. 2, C1

Palace of Fine Arts, 3601 Lyon St.; tel. 563-7337 (531-0362 for Tactile Dome); Wed. 10 A.M.–9:30 P.M., Thurs.–Sun. 10 A.M.–5 P.M. Admission: $5 adults, $2.50 seniors, $1 youths age 6–17. See *Priorities*.

Hyde St. Pier/Maritime Museum   FISHERMAN'S WHARF, P. 3, D1

Hyde St. Pier, Fisherman's Wharf; tel. 556-6435; 10 A.M.–5 P.M. daily, till 6 P.M. in summer. Admission: $2 for visitors 16–62, seniors and under 16 free. The museum, located at the foot of Polk St., is open Wed.–Sun. 10 A.M.–5 P.M.

Jeremiah O'Brien   FISHERMAN'S WHARF, P. 3, C1

Fort Mason, Landmark Bldg. A, Pier 3 East, Marina Blvd. and Laguna St.; tel. 441-3101; 9:30 A.M.–3:30 P.M. daily. Admission $2, seniors and children $1. See "Fort Mason" under *Priorities*.

Jewish Community Museum   SOUTH OF MARKET, P. 3, E1

121 Steuart St.; tel. 543-8880; Tues., Wed., Fri., and Sun. 10 A.M.–4 P.M., Thurs. 10 A.M.–8 P.M. Free; charge for some special exhibits.

Joseph Dee Museum of Photography   FINANCIAL DISTRICT, P. 3, D1

45 Kearny St., second floor; tel. 392-1900; Mon.–Fri. 9 A.M.–5 P.M. Free.

M.H. de Young Memorial Museum   GOLDEN GATE PARK, P. 2, B2

Golden Gate Park; tel. 750-3600; Wed.–Sun. 10 A.M.–5 P.M. Admission: $4 adults, $2 seniors and students 12–18, under 12 free. Ticket also good same day at Asian Art and California Palace of the Legion of Honor museums.

Masonic Museum   NOB HILL, P. 3, D1
  1111 California St.; tel. 776-4917; Mon.–Fri. 8:30–4:30. Free.

Mexican Museum   MARINA, P. 3, C1
  Fort Mason, Laguna St. and Marina Blvd., Building D; tel. 441-
0404; Wed.–Sun. noon–5 P.M. Admission: $2 adults, $1 students and
seniors.

Musée Mécanique   NEAR GOLDEN GATE PARK, P. 2, A2
  1090 Point Lobos; tel. 386-1170; Mon.–Fri. 11 A.M.–7 P.M.,
Sat.–Sun. 10 A.M.–8 P.M. Free.

Museo Italo Americano   MARINA, P. 3, C1
  Fort Mason, Laguna St. and Marina Blvd., Building C; tel. 673-
2200; Wed.–Sun. noon–5 P.M. Free.

Museum of Russian Culture   NEAR PRESIDIO HEIGHTS,
                                              P. 3, C2
  2450 Sutter St.; tel. 921-4082; Wed. and Sat. 11 A.M.–3 P.M. Free.

North Beach Museum   NORTH BEACH, P. 3, D1
  1435 Stockton St.; tel. 626-7070; Mon.–Thu. 10 A.M.–4 P.M., Fri.
10 A.M.–5:30 P.M., Sat. 10 A.M.–noon. Free.

Oakland Museum   OAKLAND
  1000 Oak St., Oakland; tel. 273-3401; Wed.–Sat. 10 A.M.–5 P.M.,
Sun. noon–7 P.M. Free; charges for some special exhibits. See *Priorities.*

Old Mint   SOUTH OF MARKET, P. 3, D2
  88 Fifth St.; tel. 744-6830; Mon.–Fri. 10 A.M.–4 P.M. Free.

Pacific Heritage Museum   FINANCIAL DISTRICT, P. 3, D1
  608 Commercial St., Bank of Canton; tel. 362-4100 ext. 715;
Mon.–Fri. 10 A.M.–4 P.M. Free.

Presidio Army Museum   NEAR MARINA, P. 2, C1
  Lincoln Blvd. and Funston Ave., Bldg. 2; tel. 561-4115; Tues.–Sun.
10 A.M.–4 P.M. Free.

Randall Museum   HAIGHT-ASHBURY, P. 2, C2
  199 Museum Way off Roosevelt Way; tel. 554-9600; Tues.–Sat.
10 A.M.–5 P.M. Free.

**San Francisco African-American Historical and Cultural
Society**   MARINA, P. 3, C1
  Fort Mason, Marina Blvd. and Laguna St., Building C; tel. 441-
0640; Wed.–Sun. noon–5 P.M. Donation.

San Francisco Art Institute   RUSSIAN HILL, P. 3, D1
  800 Chestnut St.; tel. 771-7020; Tues.–Sat. 10 A.M.–5 P.M. Free.

San Francisco Craft and Folk Art Museum   FISHERMAN'S
                                              WHARF, P. 3, C1
  Fort Mason Center; tel. 775-0990; Tues.–Sun. 11 A.M.–5 P.M., Sat.
10 A.M.–5 P.M. Admission: $1 adults, $.50 seniors and youths.

San Francisco International Toy Museum   FISHERMAN'S
                                              WHARF, P. 3, D1
  The Cannery, 2801 Leavenworth; tel. 441-TOYS; Tues.–Sat. 10
A.M.–5 P.M., Sun. 11 A.M.–5 P.M. Admission: $1.

San Francisco Museum of Modern Art   **NEAR SOUTH OF MARKET, P. 3, D2**
Veterans' Building, 401 Van Ness Ave., Civic Center; tel. 863-8800; Tues., Wed., Fri. 10 A.M.–5 P.M., Thurs. 10 A.M.–9 P.M., Sat. and Sun. 11 A.M.–5 P.M. Admission: $3.50 adults, $1.50 seniors and children under 16, children under 5 free. Free on Tues.

Tattoo Art Museum   **SOUTH OF MARKET, P. 3, D2**
30 7th St.; tel. 864-9798; daily noon–midnight. Free.

Telecommunication Museum   **SOUTH OF MARKET, P. 3, D2**
140 New Montgomery St.; tel. 542-0182; Mon.–Fri. 10 A.M.–2 P.M. Free.

Wells Fargo Bank History Room   **FINANCIAL DISTRICT, P. 3, D1**
420 Montgomery St.; tel. 396-2619; Mon.–Fri. 9 A.M.–5 P.M. except bank holidays. Free. See *Priorities*.

HISTORICAL SIGHTS

Alcatraz   **FISHERMAN'S WHARF, P. 3, D1**
Red and White ferry departs from Pier 41; tel. 546-2896 or (800) 445-8880. See *Priorities*.

Angel Island   **FISHERMAN'S WHARF, P. 3, D1**
Red and White ferry from Pier 43½; tel. 546-2896; 8 A.M.–sunset. See *Priorities*.

Filoli   **WOODSIDE**
Cañada Rd., Woodside; tel. 364-2880; open mid-Feb. to mid-Nov.; reserved tours only. Book at least one month in advance for tour of the "Dynasty" mansion. House and garden tour $6. No children under 12 allowed.

Fort Mason   **FISHERMAN'S WHARF, P. 3, C1**
Marina Blvd. and Laguna St.; tel. 441-5705; Wed.–Sat. noon–5 P.M. daily. Admission varies $1–$3 depending on museum. See *Priorities*.

Fort Point   **P. 2, B1**
Marine Drive via Lincoln Blvd. north exit off U.S. 101; tel. 556-2857; 10 A.M.–5 P.M. daily. Free. See *Priorities*.

Golden Gate Bridge   **P. 2, B1**
U.S. 101 North. Toll $2 southbound; free northbound. See *Priorities*.

Haas-Lilienthal House   **PACIFIC HEIGHTS, P. 3, D1**
2007 Franklin St. at Washington; tel. 441-3004; Wed. noon–4 P.M., Sun. 11 A.M.–4:30 P.M. Admission: $4 adults, $2 children under 12 and seniors.

Mission Dolores   **MISSION, P. 3, C2**
16th and Dolores sts.; tel. 621-8203; 9 A.M.–4 P.M. daily. Admission: $1 adults, children under 12 free.

Mission Murals   **MISSION, P. 3, D3**
24th St. from Mission to York. Free. See *Priorities*.

OUTDOOR ACTIVITIES

Coit Tower   **P. 3, D1**
Telegraph Hill Blvd.

Golden Gate National Recreation Area (headquarters)
NEAR FISHERMAN'S WHARF, P. 3, C1
Fort Mason, Building 201; tel. 556-0560. Free.

Golden Gate Park   **P. 2, B1**
Bounded by the Great Hwy., Fulton St., Stanyan Blvd., and Lincoln Wy.; tel. 666-7200.

Great America   **SANTA CLARA**
Great America Pkwy., Santa Clara; tel. (408) 988-1800; hours vary depending on season. Admission: $18.95 adults, $11.95 seniors, $9.45 children 3–6, under 3 free.

Marine World Africa USA   **VALLEJO**
Marine World Pkwy., Vallejo; tel. (707) 644-4000; Wed.–Sun. 9:30 A.M.–5 P.M., summer till 6 P.M. Admission: $18.95 adults, $14.95 seniors, $13.95 children 4–12.

San Francisco Zoo   **SUNSET, P. 2, A4**
45th Ave. at Sloat Blvd.; tel. 753–7083; 10 A.M.–5 P.M. daily. Admission: $5 adults, $2 children 12–15 and seniors, children under 12 free with adult.

Stern Grove   **SUNSET, P. 2, B3**
Sloat Blvd. and 19th Ave. Free. See *Priorities.*

12

TRAVELER'S INFORMATION

For Information . . .

The San Francisco Convention and Visitors Bureau offers booklets and brochures on vacation travel and lodging in the city. Its Visitor Information Center is on the lower level of Hallidie Plaza, 900 Market St., near the intersection of Powell and Market sts., adjacent to the Powell BART station; (415) 391-2000. The office is open 9 A.M.–5:30 P.M. Mon.–Sat. and 10 A.M.–2 P.M. Sun. Or write to the San Francisco Visitor Information Center, P.O. Box 6977, San Francisco 94101. Enclose $1 to receive *The San Francisco Book,* which offers up-to-date entertainment listings and other background.

The National Park Service offers information on the Golden Gate National Recreation Area including San Francisco, Marin County, and Alcatraz. It has a public-information office at its Fort Mason headquarters on Bay and Franklin sts. Call 556-0560 for program information as well as maps. Background on California's National Parks is also available here.

Travelers Aid Society can help if you've lost an airline ticket, are having hotel problems, or are missing a companion. Downtown at 1049 Market St., 5th fl., its office is open weekdays 9 A.M.–12 P.M. and 1–4 P.M. Call 255-2252.

The Seasons

Cooled by fog, San Francisco has a mild climate. There is little rain from May to Oct. and snowfall is unheard of in the city. Temperatures generally stay above 40° F and below 75° F. It's always a good idea to bring a sweater and jacket as evenings can get chilly. Remember, this is not Los Angeles. Standing in a brisk summer breeze on Fisherman's Wharf or Alcatraz, you'll want medium-weight clothes, not shorts and a T-shirt.

Fall: Early fall is often the warmest season in San Francisco. Indian-summer days can make Sept. and even early Oct. a delight. The rains typically begin in Nov., but you can still count on plenty of sunshine.

Winter: While this is San Francisco's rainy season, the temperatures are typically in the 40s to low 60s. Since the city doesn't get all that much rain, there will probably be plenty of sunny days. There's much less fog in the winter months than summer. Christmas, when many special events are staged, is an ideal time to visit. Many hotels offer outstanding holiday bargain rates. The Chinese New Year's Parade each Feb. is a San Francisco classic.

Spring: This season begins early with reddish pink plum tree blossoms in Feb. and cherry blossoms in Apr. This is California at its greenest, a wonderful time for the visitor interested in hiking, biking, and outdoor recreation. Crowds are moderate at most major tourist destinations, making this an excellent time to visit.

Summer: San Francisco gets busy in summertime. You're well advised to come as early as you can. Fog is common during summer mornings, particularly on the west side of the city. It often burns off and then rolls back in during the evening this time of year. Even when the city's foggy, it's usually easy to find the sun by heading over to the warmer climates of Marin County, Napa Valley, the Eastbay, or the Peninsula. If you come in late summer, the way to beat the lines is to get an early start each day.

1990 EVENTS

January

San Francisco International Boat Show, Jan. 1–7, Moscone Center (521-2558). Major exhibition of pleasure, power, and sail boats.

San Francisco Sport and Boat Show, Jan. 12–21, Cow Palace (469-6000). Power, sail, and water-related recreational vehicles.

Martin Luther King Birthday Celebration, Jan. 15, Civic Auditorium (771-6300).

Shrine East West All Star Football Classic and Pageant, Jan. 21, Stanford Stadium (723-1021). Located on the Stanford University campus in Palo Alto. Take University Ave. off Hwy. 101 south to the stadium.

San Francisco Ballet, Jan. 27–May 6, War Memorial Opera House (621-3838). Performances include *Sleeping Beauty, Forgotten Land, Le Sylphides, Rodeo, Harvest Moon, The Comfort Zone,* and *Symphony in C.*

February
Early American Photography Exhibit: The First Fifty Years, Feb. 2–Apr. 4, Palace of the Legion of Honor (750-3614).

Chinese New Year Celebration, Feb. 3–10 (982-3000). This celebration includes a Miss Chinatown pageant, outdoor festivities, cultural programs, and Golden Dragon parade complete with lion dancers.

1990 San Francisco International Motorcycle Show and Budweiser Indoor Motorcross Championship, Feb. 9–11, Cow Palace (469-6000).

March
San Francisco Chronicle Great Outdoors Adventure Fair, Mar. 2–4, Moscone Center, Concourse Exhibition Center (777-1111). Outdoor related exhibits.

St. Patrick's Day Celebration and Parade. Music, dancing, food and cultural events. The parade is staged downtown. Market St. is the recommended vantage point.

San Francisco International Film Festival, Mar. 8–9, Mar. 23–Apr. 1, AMC Kabuki 8 Cinemas at 1881 Post St., and Pacific Film Archive in Berkeley (931-FILM). Showcase of new films by major directors.

National Championship Cat Show, Mar. 24–25, Cow Palace (469-6000).

Golden Gate Park's **Japanese Tea Garden cherry trees** should be in bloom during the last week of Mar. (387-6787).

April
Baseball season begins (Apr.–Sept.). The **San Francisco Giants** are at Candlestick Park (467-8000). The **Oakland Athletics** play at the Oakland Coliseum (638-0500).

Junior Grand National Horse Show and Livestock Expo, Apr. 5–15, Cow Palace (469-6000). Kids will love this event featuring young competitors from all over the country.

Macy's Easter Flower Show, Apr. 9–15, Stockton and O'Farrell sts. (397-3333).

Cherry Blossom Festival and Parade, Apr. 20–22, Apr. 27–29, Japantown and Japan Center (922-6776). Dancing, food booths, and art exhibits. Parade on Apr. 29. Over two thousand Californians of Japanese descent, as well as performers from Japan, participate.

Friends of Recreation and Parks' Fifth Annual Landscape Garden Show, Apr. 25–29, Piers 2 and 3, Ft. Mason (221-1310). The largest garden show on the West Coast with exhibits and displays from nationally known landscape architects. Vendors sell the latest technology.

May

Cinco de Mayo Celebration and Parade, May 4–6, Mission District (826-1401). This wonderful Latin extravaganza includes crowning of a fiesta queen, plus two days of outdoor cultural festivities and live entertainment.

200th Anniversary Celebration of the U.S. Coast Guard, tentative dates Mar. 11–13 (437-3319). Parade, band performers, and tours of Coast Guard cutters and other ships.

San Francisco Examiner Bay to Breakers, May 20 (777-7770). Over 100,000 participants in the city's biggest footrace and a zany celebration from San Francisco Bay to the ocean that attracts costumed performers and deadly serious runners from all over the country.

Carnaval '90 Celebration and Parade, May 25–27, Mission District (821-1401). Parade, street festival, dancing and masquerade costume contest.

June

Stern Grove Midsummer Music Festival, Sundays Jun.–Sept., Stern Grove (398-6551). Classical, jazz, and opera performances in the park. One of the city's best free events.

Ethnic Dance Festival, Jun. 1, 2, 8, 9, 15, 16, Palace of Fine Arts (474-3914). Performances by community and professional ethnic dance troops.

Union St. Spring Festival of Arts and Crafts, Jun. 2–3 (346-4446). Major crafts show.

LEAP Sandcastle Contest for Architects, tentative date Jun. 3, Aquatic Park, Fisherman's Wharf (775-5327). Sand sculptures produced by 20 architectural firms (approx. 350 participants).

"Amish, The Art of the Quilt," Jun. 9–Sept. 3, M.H. de Young Museum (750-3600).

Fantasy Auction 1990, tentative date Jun. 9 (552-8000). Fundraiser for the San Francisco Symphony.

Haight St. Fair, Jun. 9, Haight St. between Masonic Ave. and Stanyan St. (346-4446). Food booths, arts and crafts exhibits, and live entertainment on three stages.

Juneteenth Celebration and Parade, Jun. 16–17, Western Addition (921-7976). Celebrating emancipation from slavery. Parade, food, arts and crafts booths, a special children's play area, African dancing, jazz, blues, and comedy.

New North Beach Fair, Jun. 16–17, upper Grant Ave. (346-4446). Arts and crafts exhibits, food booths, and entertainment.

Kitemakers 18th Annual Father's Day Kite Festival, Jun. 17, Marina Green (956-3181). Exhibits, demonstrations, and contests.

Festival of Performing Arts, tentative dates Jun. 23, 30; Jul. 7, 14, 21, 28; Aug. 2, 9, 16, 23, 30; Sept. 6, 13, 20, 27; Golden Gate Park music concourse (474-3914). Take a trip around the world without leaving the park. Multicultural dance and musical performances by community and professional groups. No admission fee.

Lesbian-Gay Freedom Day Parade, Jun. 24 (864-3733). Major lesbian-gay event with speeches and participants dressing up and parading through the city.

July

San Francisco Marathon, Jul. 1 (681-2323). The scenic 26.2 mile course begins at Golden Gate Bridge, winds through city streets, and ends at Golden Gate Park.

Fourth of July Celebration and Fireworks, Jul. 4, Crissy Field (556-0560). All-day celebration and fireworks show. Bring plenty of food and warm clothes for the evening. Crissy Field is located off Hwy. 101 in the Presidio.

Midsummer Mozart Festival, Jul. 11–Aug. 5, Davies Symphony Hall (431-5400) and Herbst Theatre (552-3656).

Comedy Celebration Day, tentative date Jul. 29, Golden Gate Park polo field (777-7120). The Bay Area's newest and best comics perform in an all-day comedy marathon.

August

San Francisco 49ers 1990 football season, Aug.–Dec., Candlestick Park (468-2249).

Pacific States Craft Fair, Aug. 8–12, Fort Mason (896-5060). Exhibits by craftspeople throughout the region.

San Francisco Fair Flower Show, Aug. 23–26, San Francisco County Fair Building, Golden Gate Park (558-3623).

September

Renaissance Pleasure Faire, Sept. 1–Oct. 7, Blackpointe Forest, Novato (892-0937). Medieval festival with games, dancing, entertainment, and food. Come dressed up in your best medieval costume.

Fourth Annual Reggae Explosion, Sept.1–3, Fort Mason, Pier 3 (921-8030). Features top reggae musicians and performers.

Sixth Annual à la Carte in the Park, Sept.1–3, Golden Gate Park (383-9378). Chefs and restaurants from all over the area offer their specialties. A taster's delight.

Fourth Annual West Coast National Stunt Kite Championship, Sept. 1–3, Marina Green (652-4003). Kite flying demonstrations and contests on the bay.

Sausalito Art Festival, Sept. 1–3, Sausalito in Marin County (332-0505). Arts and crafts show featuring local artists.

Fifth Annual Race to Preserve the Historic Ships, Sept. 4–9, Pier 39 (981-8030). Boat races and displays. The city's major historic fleet fundraiser.

San Francisco Opera Season, Sept. 7–Dec. 9, War Memorial Opera House (864-3330). World famous stars in major productions.

San Francisco Symphony, Sept.–May, Davies Symphony Hall (431-5400).

San Francisco Blues Festival, Sept. 8–9, Great Meadow, Fort Mason (862-1401). Great outdoor entertainment for those blues fans who want to get funky.

Festival de las Americas, Sept. 15, Mission District (826-1401). Latin-American food and arts festival.

Ninth Annual KQED Old-Fashioned Ice Cream Social Tasting, Sept. 29, Concourse Exhibition Center (553-2200). Great way to support the public television station and treat your taste buds at the same time.

October

The **Columbus Day Celebration,** tentatively scheduled for early Oct., is staged at North Beach and Fisherman's Wharf. Commemorates Columbus's discovery with Queen Isabella's coronation, civic ceremonies, landing pageant, and Sun. parade. The procession of the Madonna del Lume and blessing of the fishing fleet perpetuate centuries-old Sicilian folk rites venerating the patroness of fishermen. Religious service at Sts. Peter and Paul church (434-1492).

Festa Italiana, Oct. 5–7, Pier 45, Fisherman's Wharf (673-3782). Food, entertainment, arts and crafts all rooted in the Italian culture and language.

Castro Street Fair, Oct. 7, Castro St. (467-3354).

Fleet Week, Oct. 7–12 (765-6056). Naval vessels and support ships open to the public. Blue Angels precision flight team performs aerial maneuvers over the city.

Festival 2000, Oct. 7–28 (864-4237). Arts and crafts festivals at various San Francisco locations.

Sixth Annual California Mile, tentative date Oct. 14 (383-0314). One mile run up the California St. hill, ending in front of the Mark Hopkins Hotel. Divisions for all ages and classes, including world class Olympians and mountain bikers. The event benefits local high school sports programs.

Tenth Annual International Street Performers Festival, Oct. 20–21, Entrance Plaza of Pier 39 (981-8030). Performances by street musicians, comedians, jugglers, mime, and rap groups from around the Bay Area and the world.

Halloween and Pumpkin Festival, Oct. 20–21, Clement St. between 3rd and 8th aves. (346-4446). Features food and arts and crafts made from pumpkins.

Grand National Livestock Expo Rodeo and Horse Show, Oct. 26–Nov. 4, Cow Palace (469-6000). Similar to the Apr. event, this one gives the grown-ups a chance to compete.

San Francisco Bay Area Book Festival, Oct. 28–Nov. 5, various sites in the Bay Area (626-8220). Local authors and publishers show their latest works.

November

Twelfth Annual KQED Wine and Food Festival, Nov. 17, Concourse Exhibition Center (553-2230). Sample California varietals and fancy foods.

Twelfth Annual Christmas Tree Lighting Ceremony, Nov. 21, Pier 39 Entrance Plaza (981-8030).

Run to the Far Side, Nov. 23, Golden Gate Park (750-7142). This 10-k and 5-k race, with famed cartoonist Gary Larson, also welcomes physically limited participants.

December
Eight Annual Christmas Carol Sing–Along, early Dec., Davies Symphony Hall (431-5400).

Folk Art International Exhibition and Sale, Conference Center, Building A, Fort Mason (441-6100).

A Christmas Carol, American Conservatory Theatre, tentative dates early Dec.–late Dec. (749-2228).

Nutcracker, San Francisco Ballet, tentative dates mid-Dec.–late Dec., War Memorial Opera House (621-3838).

"A Night in Old Vienna," tentative date late Dec., Davies Symphony Hall (431-5400). San Francisco Symphony New Year's Eve Gala.

For Foreign Visitors

Valid passports and U.S. visas are required for entry. The visas are available at U.S. embassies around the world. No vaccinations are required for entry into the country. Passport information: (415) 974-7972.

Customs: Those over 21 can take into the United States two hundred cigarettes, fifty cigars, or three pounds of tobacco; one liter of alcohol; and duty-free gifts of up to $100 in value. No meats or plants, seeds, fruits, or, of course, narcotics. Customs information: (415) 556-4440.

Foreign currency is not always warmly received in the United States. Central branches of the city's major banks do not automatically accept foreign money. You'll have to inquire since few if any signs indicate the availability of this service. **Bank of America** does offer foreign-currency services at its 345 Montgomery St. office (622-2451) and at the **San Francisco International Airport's** central terminal, international building (876-7055). Private agencies also providing this service include **Foreign Exchange Ltd.,** 415 Stockton St. (397-4000); **Deak International,** 100 Grant Ave. (362-3452); and **Heng Loong Foreign Exchange,** 626 Jackson St. (362-8718).

Money Matters

While most places accept credit cards and/or traveler's checks, be certain to inquire in advance. Policies change, shops may not accept the particular card you had in mind, etc. Some of the major chains accept checks with proper identification.

Automated teller machines, usually attached to a bank, which will dispense cash at any hour of the day or night if you possess but one of a myriad of acceptable cards, are never more than a few blocks away from almost anywhere in San Francisco. Just take extra precautions if you need to use them in questionable areas, or at night.

Sales tax in San Francisco is 6.5 percent. Sales tax in Alameda and Contra Costa counties is 7 percent, 6 percent in Marin.

A standard tip in San Francisco—of a waiter, hotel employee, or other similar service person—is usually no less than 15 percent, unless you intend to transmit your dissatisfaction. Lesser tips are acceptable to taxi drivers and parking-garage attendants.

Tours

One of the best ways to see San Francisco is to join a tour. Besides giving first-time visitors an overview, these guided visits help you set priorities for the days ahead. In addition to general-interest trips, the city has a number of special-interest tours featuring San Francisco's architecture, history, ethnic neighborhoods, parks, and cafés. Many tours also cover popular one-day destinations such as the Napa Valley and Muir Woods. Below is a listing of organized tours, followed by our own suggestions for special-interest self-guided touring. (See also the *Priorities* chapter for a list of must-see stops.)

ORGANIZED TOURING

BY LAND, SEA, OR AIR

For an overview, here are three easy tours to get you started.

LAND: Our first choice is the **City Guides** walking tours operated by Friends of the San Francisco Public Library. These ninety-minute trips include such landmarks as Coit

Tower, Pacific Heights, North Beach, and Civic Center. Special trips to such destinations as the Mission Murals, Pacific Heights mansions, and Japantown are often added on weekends. There's no charge and no need for reservations. Call 558-3981.

SEA: Both the **Red and White Fleet** at Pier 41 (546-2896) and the **Blue and Gold Fleet,** Pier 39 (781-7877), offer short get-acquainted bay cruises. On the Blue and Gold's 75-minute trip you'll sail under both the Golden Gate and Bay bridges. Red and White trips last 45 minutes. At press time, Red and White was in the process of merging with Blue and Gold. Call for updated information.

AIR: **Commodore Helicopters,** 240 Redwood Hwy., Hwy. 101, Mill Valley (332-4482), has 15-minute flights over Sausalito, Alcatraz, the Bay Bridge, and Angel Island for $60 per person.

Many companies also operate **bus tours** to popular San Francisco and Bay Area destinations.

   Gray Line offers twenty different tours including three city excursions. One is combinable with a trip to Alcatraz while another includes a ninety-minute bay cruise. A popular all-day trip covers San Francisco, Muir Woods, and Sausalito. Other day trips visit the Wine Country or the Monterey area. The company also offers nightclub tours. Call 558-9400. **Golden Gate Tours** (788-5775) covers many of the same routes. **AMI Tours** (474-8888) heads for many of those destinations, Berkeley and Oakland, and the Marin coast. Custom itineraries are available.

SPECIALIZED TOURS

Golden Gate Park—Friends of Recreation and Parks guides walk you through this fascinating landscape May–Oct., Sat. and Sun. at 11 A.M. This is a wonderful introduction to one of America's most famous urban parks. Trips leave from McLaren Lodge, and Stanyan and Fell sts. Call 221-1311.

Café Walks—Much of the city's neighborhood life focuses around cafés. You'll see local favorites that tourists often miss on Judith Kahn's 2½-hour walk through such districts as North Beach, Haight-Ashbury, and Pacific Heights. Call 751-4286 for details.

Chinatown—Walk through wok country, visit a fortune-cookie factory, and see busy markets on this food-oriented tour of the Chinese community. Along the way you'll visit a Buddhist temple and explore the neighbor-

byways. Morning and afternoon trips take two
ind you can include an optional Chinese luncheon.
anette's Walking Tours of Chinatown at 982-8839.
Chinese Cultural Heritage Foundation also offers
two-hour tours on Sat. Phone 986-1822.

Shopping—San Francisco Bay Area Shopping Tours
takes you to eight or more of the city's wholesale jewelry
showrooms, discount shops, antique stores, and factory
outlets. Call 788-5940.

Cycling—Bike your way along the bay, across the Golden Gate, and into Marin County. All equipment and
guides provided by Scenic Cycling Adventours. Call 453-0676.

Sam Spade—For a look at the city's literary heritage,
join Don Herron for his Dashiell Hammett tour that looks
at landmarks made famous in the Sam Spade novels.
Phone 564-7021 for details.

Near Escapes offers a wide array of offbeat and special-interest tours in and around San Francisco. They include breweries, cemeteries, and the University of
California's Lawrence Berkeley Lab. There are even
horsedrawn tours of the Wine Country and one of hideouts used by heiress/kidnap victim/bankrobber Patty
Hearst during her 1974–75 disappearance. To get the latest schedule, call 921-1392.

TOURING ON YOUR OWN

One of the best ways to tour San Francisco and the Bay
Area is to create your own itinerary. From architecture to
literary landmarks, it's easy to build a tour around unique
features of this region. Here are a few suggestions to get
you started.

LITERARY SAN FRANCISCO

City Lights bookstore, at 261 Columbus near Broadway,
founded by poet Lawrence Ferlinghetti is a must for devotees of Jack Kerouac, Allen Ginsberg, and the rest of the
Beats. You're welcome to read to your heart's content at
the basement tables.

Portsmouth Square at Kearny and Clay was home to
Robert Louis Stevenson, who lived in the city during
1879–80. You can also visit the **Stevenson House** in
Monterey and a state park named in his honor near Calistoga, about two hours north of San Francisco on Hwy. 29.

Hike up to the site where Stevenson honeymooned with his bride Fanny Osbourne.

The **Washington Square Bar and Grill** at 1707 Powell St. in North Beach is the city's best-known literary hangout.

In nearby Oakland, **Jack London Square** commemorates the famed writer. But to get the full story, travel up to **Jack London State Historic Park** at Glen Ellen, about ninety minutes north of San Francisco via Hwy. 101 and Hwy. 12. Besides a museum here you can visit London's farm and the ruins of his dream domicile, the Wolf House.

While Monterey's **Cannery Row** has been turned into a major tourist attraction, Steinbeck devotees will want to make the short drive over to Salinas where they can see the novelist's birthplace and many landmarks that found their way into his novels.

Just south of Big Sur, the **Henry Miller Library** serves as a living memorial to the author who lived in this region from 1944 to 1962. Visitors are welcome. Phone (408) 667-2574.

The **Tao House** in Danville, about an hour east of San Francisco, is part of the Eugene O'Neill National Historic Site. Tours are available by reservation. Call 838-0249.

Outside New York, you'd be hard pressed to find a better group of bookstores than those clustered just south of the UC Berkeley campus along Telegraph Ave. and on Bancroft Way. From new books at **Cody's,** to the remarkable used-book emporium that is **Moe's,** this area is heaven for serious bibliophiles. Also in the area are a **University Press Bookstore,** major chains, and **Shambhala,** a metaphysical/New-Age book dealer.

ARCHITECTURAL LANDMARKS

450 Sutter Building—Timothy Pflueger, who also designed Oakland's classic Paramount Theatre, created this downtown Art Deco landmark.

Hallidie Building, 130 Sutter St. near Kearny. America's building with a glass curtain-wall facade, this building is also home of the San Francisco chapter of the American Institute of Architects. Changing exhibits at the AIA's sixth-floor office showcase the city's architectural heritage. 362-7397.

Haas-Lilienthal House, 2007 Franklin St. Open Wed. noon–4 P.M., Sun. 11 A.M.–4:30 P.M. This 24-room Pacific

Heights mansion is a Victorian classic with Tiffany art glass and Eastlake furniture. 441-3004.

Palace of the Legion of Honor, Clement St. at 34th. Perhaps the most majestically sited art museum in northern California, this 1924 landmark was modeled after a similar landmark in Paris. 221-4811.

Pacific Telephone Building, 130 New Montgomery near Market, downtown. Another classic from the Pflueger office, a lovely tower with a grand modern lobby and ceiling in an Asian motif.

Paramount Theatre, 2025 Broadway, Oakland (19th St. BART station). Oakland's Art Deco palace with giant Byzantine figures and fountain of light. Call 893-2300 for tour information.

Whittier Mansion, 2090 Jackson St. is open for tours 1–5 P.M. Wed., Sat., Sun. Beautiful 19th-century antiques appointed with Belgian crystal plus hand-carved woodwork grace the Pacific headquarters of the California Historical Society. Don't miss the Turkish Lounging Room.

Special Note: In Berkeley you'll find some of California's most outstanding architecture including Bernard Maybeck's masterwork, the **First Church of Christian Science** at Dwight Way and Bowditch. Julia Morgan's **Berkeley City Club** (2315 Durant Ave.) and **St. John's Presbyterian Church** (College Ave. at Derby), now called the Julia Morgan Center, are among the many classics here. Contact the Berkeley Architectural Heritage Association at 841-2242 for details.

Business Brief

If you're doing business in San Francisco, here are a few suggestions that will enhance your efforts.

- Aquaint yourself with some of the special aspects of the California market by reading up before you come. A book on the Pacific Rim, a San Francisco business publication, and, of course, financial sections of the local dailies may provide excellent background.

- The population of the Bay Area actually makes up several different markets, each with its own distinct personality. With its large minority population and mix of chic urban suburbs, university towns, and resort areas, this region is complex and unpredictable. Listen carefully as you make the rounds and avoid snap judgments.

- Because California is a very entrepreneurial economy, businesses aren't all arranged top-down. Many of the best ideas come from junior staff people and their input is often crucial. Cultivate friends at all levels of the companies you visit. Given the rapid rate of upward mobility in this fast-growing economy, this year's sales assistant could be next year's marketing manager.

- Informality and the rise of very young managers in certain Bay Area industries, such as high-tech, make it easy to misjudge the staff. Do not assume that the young person in the elevator next to you who is casually dressed and has on running shoes is a minor functionary. He or she could be a big shot.

- It is very easy to misjudge the size of the Bay Area. In addition, traffic can be very heavy especially during rush hour. If you are arriving at San Francisco airport during rush hour, allow a minimum of two, preferably three hours, to get to your first appointment. If you plan to drive around the bay, give yourself plenty of travel time to avoid being late. BART is a reliable alternative to driving when it's convenient to your destination.

- Arrange your appointments geographically so that you don't have to do a lot of doubling back that could mean getting stuck in traffic. You may find the Oakland or San Jose airports more convenient for your schedule than San Francisco International.

- Plan at least one day longer for your visit to San Francisco than you think you're going to need. These additional hours will give you a chance to do necessary followup, tie together loose ends, and perhaps become more familiar with your contacts here. You'll be more relaxed knowing everything doesn't have to be accomplished on a tight schedule.

- San Francisco may have the largest homosexual population of any city in America, or even the world. Jokes or prejudiced comments about gays are a mistake anywhere. In San Francisco they are not taken kindly in business settings or anywhere else.

- If there's a joke about the laid-back California life-style, everyone you'll meet has heard it many times. Don't be a bore on this subject.

- Do not assume that it is alright to light up at will. Ask first. Some people do mind and will let you know. Smoking is not allowed in some offices. Restaurants also have varying rules about smoking. Inquire first to avoid unpleasantness.

- It's easy to mix business and pleasure in the salubrious Bay Area. Your business contacts will be delighted, probably even flattered, to suggest restaurants, leisure opportunities, wineries, and so on. Take their advice and let them know how right they were.

CULTURAL TIMELINE

1542 Juan Rodriguez Cabrillo of Portugal discovers Farallon Islands outside the Golden Gate.

1579 Sir Francis Drake of England lands in Marin County. Claims it for Elizabeth I and calls his discovery New Albion.

1769 Expedition of Gaspar de Portola discovers San Francisco Bay.

1775 Capt. Juan Manuel de Ayala of Spain brings first ship into bay.

1776 Capt. Juan Bautista de Anza of Spain comes with settlers from Mexico. Selects sites for Presidio (army base) and Mission Dolores.

1792 Capt. George Vancouver of Britain sails into bay.

1803 First American ship enters bay.

1806 Russians arrive to purchase supplies for settlement in Alaska.

1834 Mission San Francisco de Asis (Mission Dolores) is secularized under decree of Mexican Congress.

1835 Capt. William Richardson erects first building in town of Yerba Buena (name first given to San Francisco).

1847 Yerba Buena renamed San Francisco. First newspaper published.

1848 Gold discovered at the base of the Sierra Nevadas.

1850 Population grows rapidly while there is a building boom. San Francisco becomes a city and California is admitted to the Union.

1860 First Pony Express rider arrives.

1862 First telegraph linkup between San Francisco and New York.

1869 First transcontinental train passengers arrive in Bay Area on the Central Pacific Railroad.

1873 Construction begins on first cable street railway.

1877 Riot gives vent to anti-Chinese sentiment.

1894 California Midwinter International Exposition opens in Golden Gate Park.

1906	Earthquake and the resulting fire destroy much of the city.
1913	Raker Act permits damming of Hetch Hetchy Valley in Yosemite to provide water for city; writer/environmentalist John Muir's heart is broken.
1915	Panama-Pacific International Exposition opens in what is now the Marina District.
1916	Preparedness Day bombing. Two labor leaders, Mooney and Billings, are sent to jail for 22 years.
1923	President Warren G. Harding dies at the Palace Hotel.
1934	Longshoremen's strike leads to first general strike in area.
1936	San Francisco–Oakland Bay Bridge opens.
1937	Golden Gate Bridge opens.
1939	Golden Gate International Exposition on what is now Treasure Island Naval Base.
1945	Charter of the United Nations is drafted in San Francisco.
1953	House Un-American Activities Committee hearings held in San Francisco.
1956	Republican National Convention held at Cow Palace. Eisenhower nominated for second term.
1963	Alcatraz Prison closes.
1964	Free Speech Movement student strike at University of California at Berkeley.
1967	Vietnam peace march from downtown to Golden Gate Park. Hippies create Summer of Love in Haight-Ashbury.
1968	San Francisco State University student strike. S.I. Hayakawa becomes university president (later elected U.S. senator).
1969	Indians seize Alcatraz.
1971	Fort Point under the Golden Gate Bridge is named first National Park site in city.
1973	BART opens Transbay service. Alcatraz open to the public.
1975	Sara Jane Moore attempts to assassinate President Ford outside St. Francis Hotel.
1978	Mayor George Moscone and City Supervisor Harvey Milk shot to death in City Hall by former city Supervisor Dan White. Dianne Feinstein succeeds Moscone, becoming the city's first female mayor.
1982	Cable-car system shut down for complete overhaul.
1984	Democratic National Convention in San Francisco chooses Walter Mondale and Geraldine Ferraro,

first woman vice-presidential nominee. Cable cars resume service.

1988 San Francisco 49ers win third Super Bowl of the decade and are proclaimed NFL team of the eighties.

1989 Largest earthquake since 1906, measuring 8.1 at the epicenter near San Jose, destroys many homes in the Marina. The Oakland A's win the World Series.

The City That Was

The old San Francisco is dead. The gayest, lightest hearted, most pleasure loving city of the western continent, and in many ways the most interesting and romantic, is a horde of refugees living among ruins. It may rebuild; it probably will; but those who have known that peculiar city by the Golden Gate, have caught its flavor of the Arabian Nights, feel that it can never be the same. It is as though a pretty, frivolous woman had passed through a great tragedy. She survives, but she is sobered and different. If it rises out of the ashes it must be a modern city, much like other cities and without its old atmosphere.

Over by the ocean and surrounded by cemeteries in which there are no more burials, there is an eminence which is topped by two peaks and which the Spanish of the early days named after the breasts of a woman. The unpoetic Americans had renamed it Twin Peaks. At its foot was Mission Dolores, in the last mission planted by the Spanish padres in their march up the coast, and from these hills the Spanish looked for the first time upon the golden bay.

Many years ago someone set up at the summit of this peak a sixty foot cross of timber. Once a high wind blew it down, and the women of the Fair family then had it restored so firmly that it would resist anything. It has risen for fifty years above the gay, careless, luxuriant and lovable city, in full view from every eminence and from every valley. It stands tonight, above the desolation of ruins.

—Will Irwin
The Western Gate, 1906

Area codes

415 in San Francisco, 408 in the San Jose area. Directory information for the metropolitan area: 411

Emergencies

Police, fire, and ambulance (emergency): 911

Poison Control Center: 476-6600

Rape Crisis Line: 647-7273

Suicide Prevention: 221-1423

TTY/TDD Deaf Emergency: 911 and press space bar until someone answers

Important Numbers

AAA Emergency Road Service: 863-3432

American Express Traveler's Cheques (lost or stolen information): 800-221-7282

Animal bites: 554-2840

Better Business Bureau: 243-9999

Citicorp Traveler's Checks (lost or stolen information): 800-645-6556

Dental referral service: 421-1435

Disabled visitor info: 673-MUNI for accessible bus route information, 554-6318 for the Mayor's Council on Disability Concerns

Doctor-referral service: 567-6230

Event info (National Park Service): 556-0560

Event info, San Francisco Visitor's Information Center: 391-2000 or 391-2001 (daily recording)

International Visitors Information Service: French, 391-2003; German, 391-2004; Spanish, 391-2122; Japanese, 391-2101

Police, fire, first-aid nonemergency calls: 553-0123 (police); 861-8000 (fire)

Time of day: 767-8900

Tourist information, recorded: 391-2001

Travelers Aid Society: 255-2252

U.S. Passport Office: 974-9941 or 974-7972 (recorded)

Visa Traveler's Cheques (lost or stolen information): 800-227-6811

Visa information call passport office above for referral.

Weather forecast: 936-1212

Consulates

Australia, 360 Post St.; 362-6160

Canada, 50 Fremont St.; 495-6021

Great Britain, 1 Sansome St.; 981-3030

Ireland, 655 Montgomery St.; 392-4214

Index

LANGUAGE / 30

For the International Traveler

32 languages! A basic language course on 2 audiocassettes and a phrase book Only $14.95 each + shipping

Nothing flatters people more than to hear visitors try to speak their language and LANGUAGE / 30, used by thousands of satisfied travelers, has you speaking the basics quickly and easily. Each LANGUAGE / 30 course offers:

- approximately 1½ hours of guided practice in greetings, asking questions and general conversation
- proven effective method

Order yours today.

Arabic	Greek	Korean	Spanish
Chinese (Mandarin)	Hebrew	Latin	Swahili
Czech	Hindi	Norwegian	Swedish
Danish	Hungarian	Persian (Farsi)	Tagalog (Pilipino)
Dutch	Indonesian	Polish	Thai
Finnish	Irish	Portuguese	Turkish
French	Italian	Russian	Vietnamese
German	Japanese	Serbo-Croatian	Yiddish

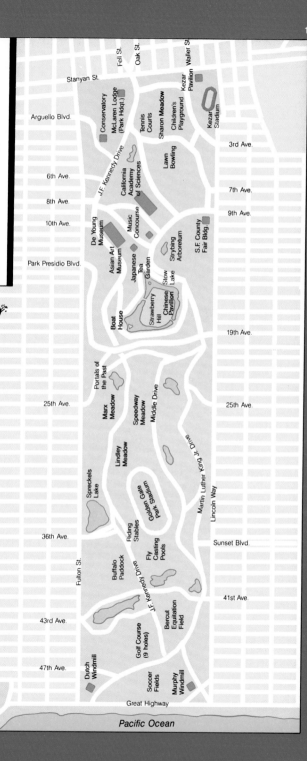

GOLDEN GATE PARK

miles

kilometers

0 .5 1

Fell St.

Oak St.

Waller St.

Stanyan St.

Kezar Pavilion

Arguello Blvd.

Conservatory

McLaren Lodge (Park Hdqt.)

Tennis Courts

Sharon Meadow

Children's Playground

Kezar Stadium

3rd Ave.

J.F. Kennedy Drive

California Academy of Sciences

Lawn Bowling

6th Ave.

7th Ave.

8th Ave.

9th Ave.

10th Ave.

De Young Museum

Music Concourse

Asian Art Museum

Strybing Arboretum

S.F. County Fair Bldg.

Park Presidio Blvd.

Japanese Tea Garden

Stow Lake

Strawberry Hill

Chinese Pavilion

Boat House

19th Ave.

Portals of the Past

Speedway Meadow

Marx Meadow

Middle Drive

25th Ave.

25th Ave.

Lindley Meadow

Martin Luther King Jr. Drive

Spreckels Lake

Golden Gate Park Stadium

Lincoln Way

Riding Stables

36th Ave.

Fly Casting Pools

Sunset Blvd.

Fulton St.

Buffalo Paddock

J.F. Kennedy Drive

41st Ave.

Bercut Equitation Field

43rd Ave.

Golf Course (9 holes)

Dutch Windmill

47th Ave.

Soccer Fields

Murphy Windmill

Great Highway

Pacific Ocean

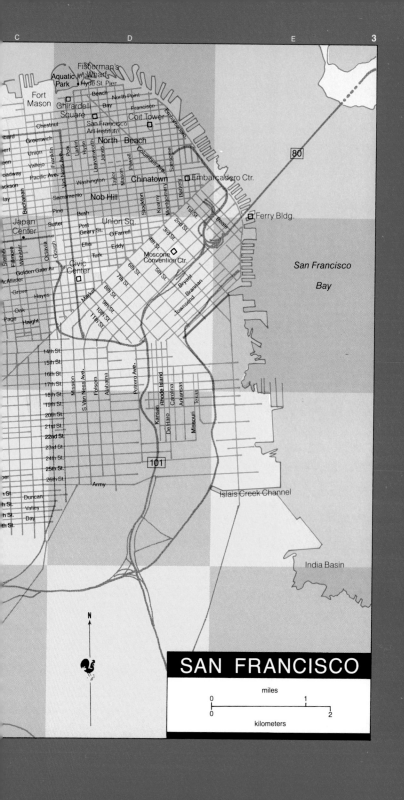

SAN FRANCISCO

miles
0 ————————————————— 1

0 ————————————————— 2
kilometers

SAN FRANCISCO
BART AND BUS MAP

miles

.5

kilometers

.5

0

0

N

San Francisco Bay

Embarcadero

Pier 39

Red & White
Fleet Ferry

Fisherman's
Wharf

Coit Tower

Telegraph Hill

North Beach

Union

Montgomery

Grant

Stockton

Powell

Mason

North Point

Ghirardelli
Square

Russian Hill

Broadway

Hyde

Polk

Fort Mason

Van Ness

Lombard

Gough

32

42

42

42

19

32

32

19

42

15

42/15

15

30

42/30

19

19

42

49

30

30/30X

42

45

30X

45

41

41

41

15

15

6X

30X

30X

32

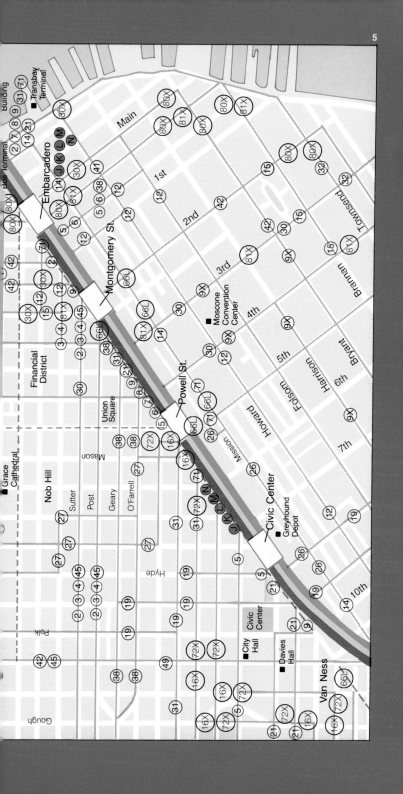

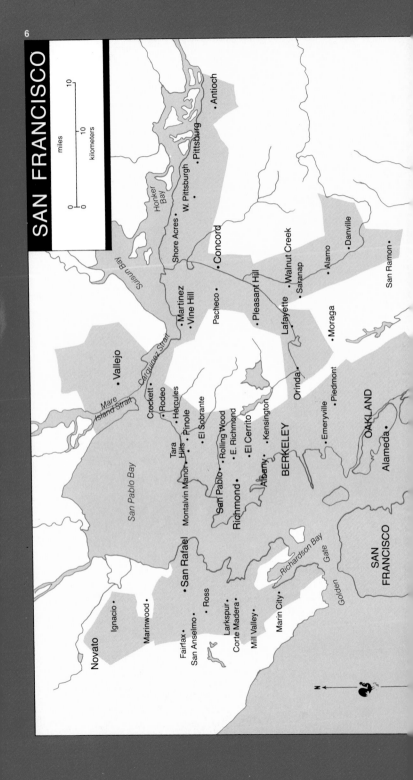

CHINATOWN

FINANCIAL DISTRICT

Chinatown Gateway

Bush St.

St. Mary's Square

Bank of America

Old St. Mary's Church

Wax Museum

Sacramento St.

California St.

Fairmont Hotel

Huntington Park

Wells Fargo Museum

Commercial St.

Clay St.

Sansome St.

Montgomery St.

Transamerican Pyramid

Portsmouth Square

Spofford Alley

Joice St.

Stockton St.

Washington St.

Cable Car Barn

Powell St.

NOB HILL

Mason St.

Taylor St.

Pine St.

Jackson St.

Pacific Ave.

Grant Ave.

Columbus Ave.

Kearny St.

Chinese Historical Society Museum

Broadway

Vallejo St.

N

miles
0 .1
0 250
meters

FISHERMAN'S WHARF

Filbert St.

Coit Tower

TELEGRAPH HILL

St. Peter & Paul

North Beach Playground

Greenwich St.

Lombard Street

Filbert St.

Lombard Street Hill

Art Institute

Russian Hill

Larkin St.

Polk St.

Van Ness Ave.

Franklin St.

Grant Ave.

Stockton St.

Powell St.

Chestnut Street

Francisco Street

Jones St.

Columbus Ave.

Leavenworth St.

Hyde St.

North Point Street

Bay Street

Mason St.

Taylor St.

Wine Museum

Ghirardelli Square

The Cannery

Aquatic Park

Fort Mason Maritime Museum

The Embarcadero

Kearny St.

Beach Street

Jefferson Street

Hyde St. Pier

Maritime State Historic Park

Pier 35

Steamship Dock

Pier 39

Pier 43

Pier 43½

Pier 45

Municipal Piers

N

miles
0 .5
0 500
meters

16

MONTEREY PENINSULA

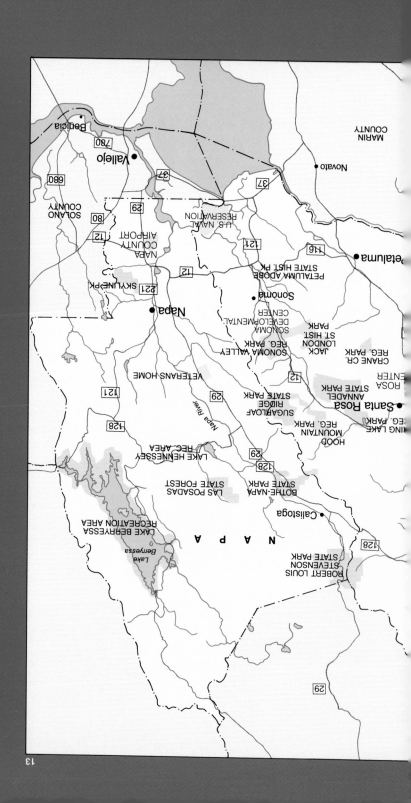

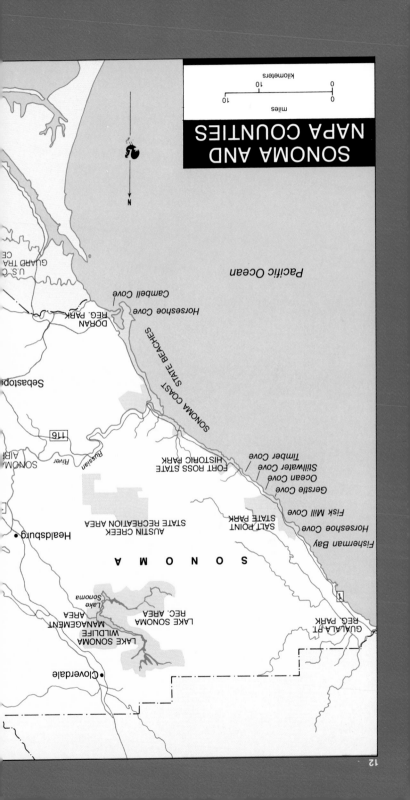

SONOMA AND NAPA COUNTIES

miles

0   10

0   10

kilometers

N

Pacific Ocean

Campbell Cove

Horseshoe Cove

DORAN
REG. PARK

U.S. C
GUARD TRA
CE

Sebastopo

116

Russian River

SONO
AIR

SONOMA COAST STATE BEACHES

Timber Cove

Stillwater Cove

Ocean Cove

Gerstle Cove

FORT ROSS STATE
HISTORIC PARK

Fisk Mill Cove

SALT POINT
STATE PARK

Horseshoe Cove

Fisherman Bay

GUALALA PT.
REG. PARK

1

AUSTIN CREEK
STATE RECREATION AREA

Healdsburg

S O N O M A

LAKE SONOMA
WILDLIFE
MANAGEMENT
AREA

Lake
Sonoma

LAKE SONOMA
REC. AREA

Cloverdale

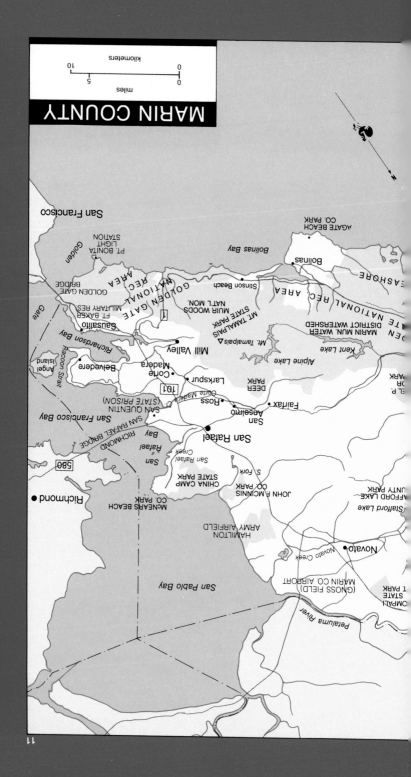

MARIN COUNTY

miles
0   5
0   10
kilometers

Richmond ●

San Pablo Bay

Petaluma River

OMPALI
STATE
T. PARK

(GNOSS FIELD)
MARIN CO. AIRPORT

Novato Creek

Novato ●

HAMILTON
ARMY AIRFIELD

Stafford Lake

AFFORD LAKE
UNTY PARK

JOHN F. MCINNIS
CO. PARK

McNEARS BEACH
CO. PARK

CHINA CAMP
STATE PARK

S. Fork

San Rafael Creek

San
Rafael
Bay

RICHMOND
BAY
BRIDGE

580

San Rafael

SAN RAFAEL BRIDGE

SAN QUENTIN
(STATE PRISON)

San Francisco Bay

Fairfax

San
Anselmo

Ross

DEER
PARK

101

Corte Madera C.

Larkspur

Corte
Madera

Alpine Lake

Kent Lake

MARIN MUN. WATER
DISTRICT WATERSHED

▲Mt. Tamalpais

MT. TAMALPAIS
STATE PARK

MUIR WOODS
NATL. MON.

Mill Valley

Belvedere

Angel
Island

Racoon Strait

Richardson Bay

Sausalito

FT. BAKER
MILITARY RES.

GOLDEN GATE
BRIDGE

Gate

Golden

GOLDEN
GATE
NATIONAL
REC.
AREA

PT. BONITA
LIGHT
STATION

San Francisco

Stinson Beach

Bolinas Bay

Bolinas

Bolinas

AGATE BEACH
CO. PARK

EASHORE

TE NATIONAL REC. AREA

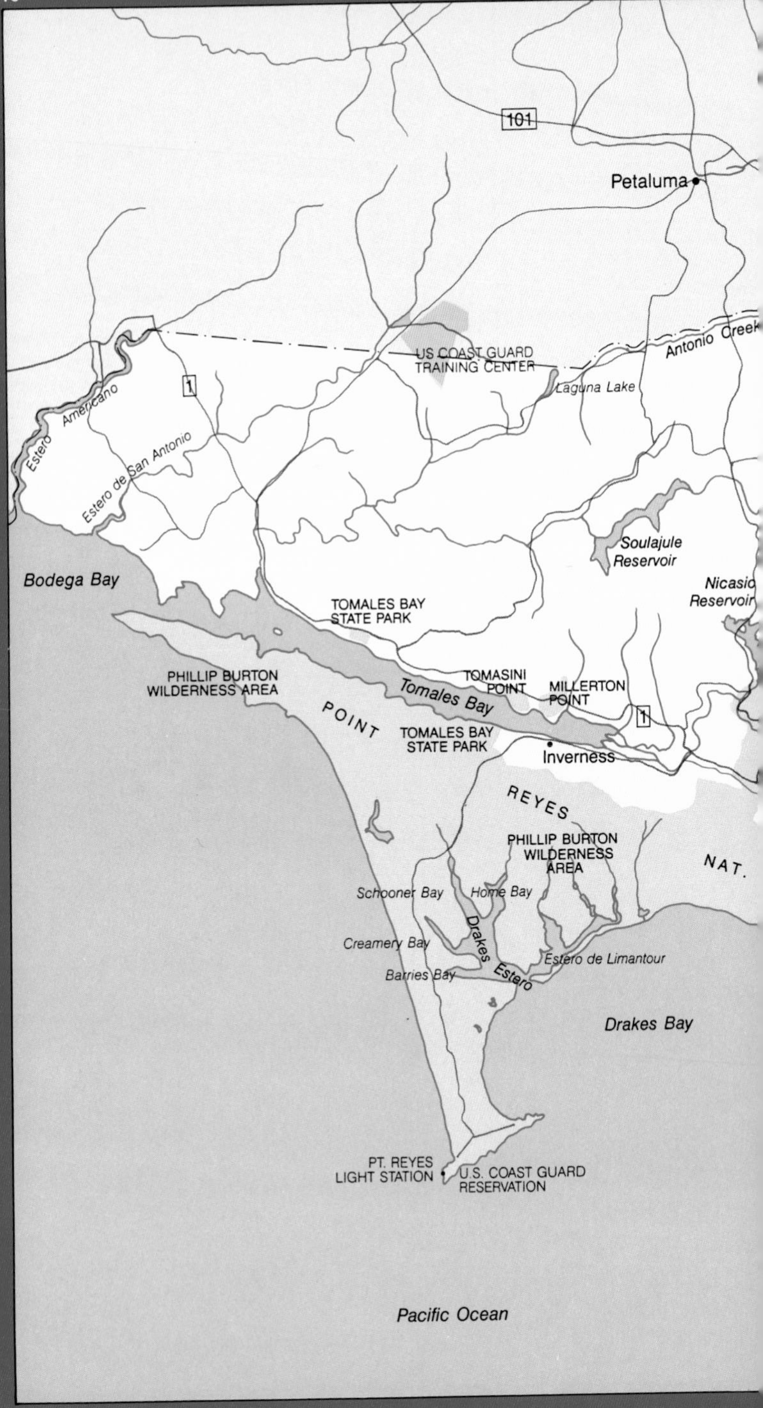
101
Petaluma
Antonio Creek
US COAST GUARD
TRAINING CENTER
Laguna Lake
1
Estero Americano
Estero de San Antonio
Soulajule
Reservoir
Nicasio
Reservoir
Bodega Bay
TOMALES BAY
STATE PARK
PHILLIP BURTON
WILDERNESS AREA
TOMASINI
POINT
MILLERTON
POINT
Tomales Bay
1
POINT
TOMALES BAY
STATE PARK
Inverness
REYES
PHILLIP BURTON
WILDERNESS
AREA
NAT.
Schooner Bay
Home Bay
Creamery Bay
Drakes
Estero
Estero de Limantour
Barries Bay
Drakes Bay
PT. REYES
LIGHT STATION
U.S. COAST GUARD
RESERVATION
Pacific Ocean

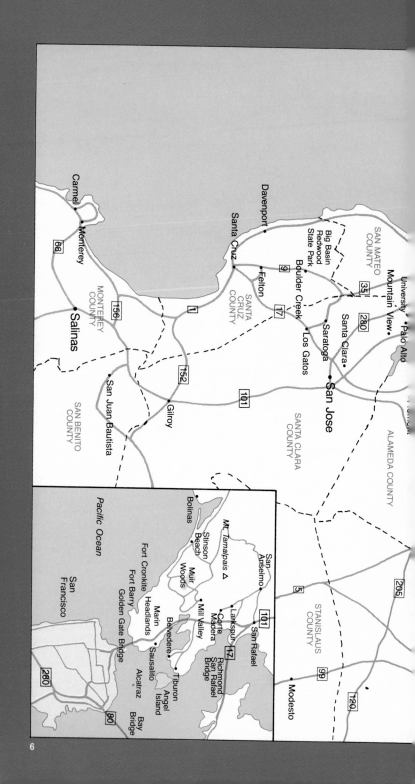

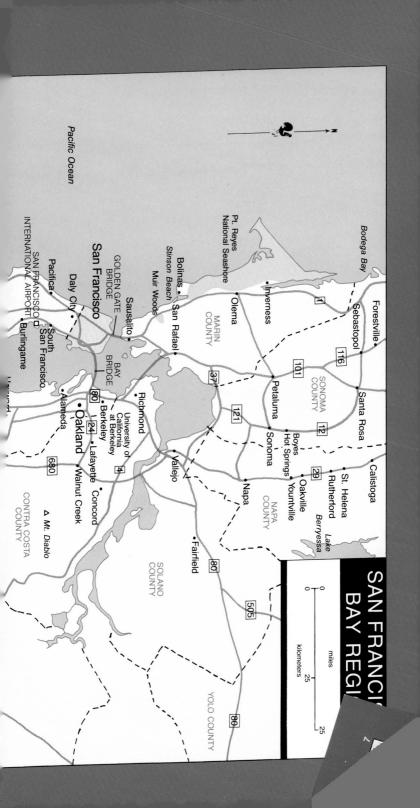

SAN FRANCISCO
BAY REGION

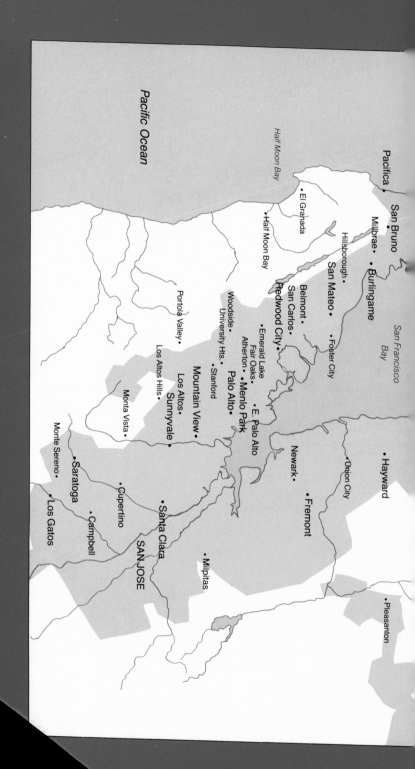